Generations

'Brilliant. Duffy has built a powerful toolkit for understanding the forces and relationships that shape the world we live in – and the one our children will inherit.'

Rafael Behr, *Guardian* columnist

'The most comprehensive, compelling and careful account for how and why the generations diverge, come together and can better connect.'

Danny Dorling, Professor of Geography, Oxford University

'A truly brilliant and engaging explanation of a new way to think about how and why we're changing. Duffy picks clever and often amusing examples to illustrate his analysis, while he also recognises the important concerns we all have about the future and our place in it.'

Dame Louise Casey, former Director General of the Department for Communities and Local Government

'This important book deserves our attention. Duffy casts new light on the endlessly fascinating issue of what links the generations and how they differ.'

Lord David Willetts, author of *The Pinch*

Bobby Duffy is Director of The Policy Institute at King's College London and Professor of Public Policy. Formerly Global Director of Ipsos Social Research Institute, he has also been seconded to the British Prime Minister's Strategy Unit and to the Centre for Analysis of Social Exclusion (CASE) at the London School of Economics. He is the author of *The Perils of Perception: Why We're Wrong About Nearly Everything.*

Generations

DOES WHEN YOU'RE BORN
SHAPE WHO YOU ARE?

Bobby Duffy

Atlantic Books
London

Published in hardback and trade paperback in Great Britain in 2021 by
Atlantic Books, an imprint of Atlantic Books Ltd.

10 9 8 7 6 5 4 3 2 1

A CIP catalogue record for this book is available from the British Library.

Hardback ISBN: 978 1 78649 972 1
Trade paperback ISBN: 978 1 83895 260 0
E-book ISBN: 978 1 78649 974 5

Design, graphs and typesetting benstudios.co.uk
Printed in Great Britain by Bell & Bain Ltd, Glasgow

Atlantic Books
An imprint of Atlantic Books Ltd
Ormond House
26–27 Boswell Street
London
WC1N 3JZ

www.atlantic-books.co.uk

For Jimmy, Birdie, Bobby, Mary, Jim, Anne, Jim,
Louise, Bridget and Martha – four generations of
my family who will see 200 years of history

Contents

Introduction

The Question of Our Generation

We are teetering on the brink of a generational war. Wherever you look, battles and betrayals across the generations are poisoning relations between old and young. Older people have stolen the future from younger generations, while the young are killing the traditions that older generations hold dear. Emerging 'social justice warriors' find themselves facing a 'war on woke'. Baby Boomers are selfish sociopaths, while Millennials are narcissistic snowflakes.

This, at least, is the endlessly repeated story. But is any of it true?

I began the research that would inspire this book with the intention of separating the myths about different generations from the reality. We seem to intuitively grasp that the concept of generations helps us understand something important about who we are and where we are headed. However, much of what passes as discussion on the topic is based on stereotype and lazy thinking, making it useless or even dangerous. My argument is that, while we can learn something very valuable about ourselves by studying generational dynamics, we will not learn anything from a mixture of fabricated battles and tiresome clichés. Instead, we need to carefully unpick the forces that shape us as individuals and societies; the generation we were born into is merely one important part of the story, alongside the extraordinary power of our lifecycles and the impact of events.

More systematic generational thinking, and the long-term perspective it encourages, will show that the real problem isn't warfare between generations but a growing separation between the young and the old. It will show us that people's resentments of other generations are more to do with the changing nature of economic, housing and health inequalities. It will explain how and why our culture is changing, particularly on key issues such as race and gender identity. And it will help us to see how support for political parties is shifting, and to understand whether democracy is really dying. It can tell us a great deal about many of the biggest issues humanity faces, from climate change to our mental health.

Ultimately, it will show that the social progress we've come to expect as an inevitable feature of new generations is actually far from inevitable. It is the product of collective intergenerational will, a dedicated desire to protect the opportunities that mean a better future for our children and grandchildren. Instead, their future looks increasingly under threat.

* *

The COVID-19 pandemic has only increased the urgency of this type of generational perspective, not least because the virus itself and the measures that have been introduced to control it have affected different generations in extraordinarily different ways.

Most obviously, the immediate health threat was hugely dependent on your age. For those born at the start of the Second World War or earlier, without vaccinations in play, there was a one in twenty chance of dying if you caught the virus. At the other end of the age spectrum, the probability of dying was vanishingly low. The risk of death doubled with every eight years of age, a generational example of the gruesome exponential curves we've learned to dread during the pandemic.[1]

At the start of the pandemic, this massive disparity led to a spate of commentary fretting that the young would flout the measures to control the virus ('A Generational War Is Brewing Over Coronavirus', claimed the *Wall Street Journal*[2]). For a brief moment, some called the virus a 'Boomer remover', but the term was distasteful to all but a tiny minority and it quickly fizzled out.[3] But what really surprised people was the level of solidarity between generations. The overall picture, across countries and age groups, was of incredible compliance with extraordinary measures imposed mainly to protect older generations.

This lack of rebellion from younger generations was despite the fact that they were the ones experiencing the greatest negative economic and educational impacts from lockdown. In the UK, for example, young people are two and a half times as likely to work in the sectors most affected by social distancing measures, such as hospitality.[4] In addition to this direct impact, economists also talk about the 'scarring' that these types of exceptional shocks leave on an economy, where progress can be lost for good, both for countries and for individuals. While we can't yet know the scale of this loss, we can be sure that the young will suffer more than the old, because they live with the scars for longer.[5] This is an incredible misfortune for younger generations, already disproportionately affected by the 2008 financial crisis – which was previously considered our era-defining economic event. This enormous global recession had already stalled or reversed economic progress for a generation of young people in very many Western countries.

A pandemic where the disease disproportionately affects the old and protective measures disproportionately affect the young seems almost designed to fracture intergenerational ties. But we are only surprised at the real outcome because we have been so conditioned to view generations as opposed factions.

Take climate change, for example. At the end of 2019, Greta Thunberg was named *Time* magazine's Person of the Year. Just 16 years old, she was the youngest ever recipient of the award. The magazine called her a 'standard bearer in a generational battle, an avatar of youth activists across the globe'. Her young peers, it suggested, looked to her example in their fights for everything from gun control in the US to democratic representation in Hong Kong and greater economic equality in Chile.

The award was clearly deserved, given Thunberg's extraordinary campaigning achievements, but is *Time*'s suggestion that she is at the frontline of a war between old and young correct? It is true that she triggers a lot of ire from a particular type of older (and mostly male) critic. There was Donald Trump, of course, with his suggestion that she needed to work on her 'anger management problem'. And the television presenter Piers Morgan, who mocked her for claiming that her childhood had been stolen even though she sailed across the Atlantic to New York on a racing yacht. But, as we'll see, the data on how people really feel about climate change doesn't suggest it is a simple age-based battle. Climate campaigning, for example, stretches from one end of the lifecycle to the other, from Thunberg and thousands of other young activists at one end, via Roger Hallam and Gail Bradbrook, the founders of Extinction Rebellion (aged 55 and 48), to the author and climate campaigner Bill McKibben (60), the former US vice president Al Gore (73) and David Attenborough (95).

Concerns about climate change, growing inequality, stalling economic progress and polarizing politics relate to how *all generations* see the future. They are fundamentally generational issues, because they are connected to our desire to see our children, and their children, do better than us. Our confidence in generational progress was already failing before the pandemic, particularly in many Western economies, and is a key reason why people of all ages are more likely to question whether our economic and political systems are working.

While no simplistic 'war' exists between age groups, this sense of stalled progress and future threat is nonetheless stronger in young people. Age has become one of the most prominent political dividing lines in a number of countries, and it seems likely that the pandemic will accelerate these trends. Throughout history, influential thinkers have asserted that tumultuous times awaken generational awareness. One of the fathers of generational thinking, the Hungarian sociologist Karl Mannheim, outlined a compelling vision of why it matters, drawing on the upheaval of his own lifetime, in the first half of the twentieth century. For Mannheim, generations are not just a group of people born at the same time; they have a social identity formed by common, and often traumatic, experiences.[6] We tend to form our value systems and behaviours during late childhood and early adulthood, so major events have a much stronger impact on people who experience them while coming of age. When generations are shaped by different contexts and have different life prospects, the connection between them becomes strained.

As Mannheim understood, periods of rapid technological and social change also increase both the importance and the difficulty of maintaining intergenerational connections. We need to be careful when assessing claims that our own times are changing more quickly than previous eras, as every generation tends to think this, but the speed of adoption and the reach of some modern technologies have been different. While it took decades for the inventions of previous industrial revolutions to be widely adopted, it took just 13 years for the near-global adoption of the central technology of modern life: the smartphone.[7] According to the German sociologist Hartmut Rosa, a 'circle of acceleration' has developed, where 'technical acceleration tends to increase the pace of social change, which in turn unavoidably increases the experienced pace of life, which then induces an ongoing demand for technical acceleration in the hopes of saving time'.[8] Whether our era is experiencing a 'Great Acceleration' or not, these technological changes contribute to a growing disconnection between age groups. Today's generations live increasingly separate lives in distinct physical and digital spaces, allowing deeper misperceptions and stereotypes to breed.

Faltering economic progress, threats that may prove existential for coming generations, and a pace of technological change that splinters the connection between young and old – each of these trends makes generational analysis vitally important in helping us to understand our futures.

A generational perspective also encourages us to take a longer-term view. The ability to envisage a distant future and work towards it is one of our defining characteristics as humans, but in evolutionary terms it is a relatively new skill. We are usually most concerned with the immediate future, vaguely worried about the medium term, and put the long term entirely out of our minds. This is a huge gamble in the face of existential threats like climate change, and means that we often miss the opportunity to actively shape a better future.

However, the generational analysis in this book is not focused solely on these huge social, economic and technological challenges. It will also help us to understand the evolution of our attitudes, beliefs and behaviours, across all aspects of life. For example, even apparently minor behaviours, such as whether a person chooses to own and use a car, have shifted significantly in recent decades. Is this because young people today have a different attitude towards fossil fuels, have less money to spend, lead a more urban lifestyle, or are less independent and growing up more slowly? Understanding why these changes are emerging helps us to plan for our likely futures.

My aim is not to prove that everything can be explained by generational differences or that they are always the most important divisions in society. Indeed, a significant part of this book is dedicated to debunking generational myths that distract us from the real trends. My goal is to find out whether and how societies are really changing, and what that might mean for the future.

Our lives in lines

Most people recognize that our current crop of adult generations runs, from youngest to oldest: Generation Z, Millennials, Generation X, Baby Boomers and, finally, the oldest living generation, Pre-War – those who were born before the end of the Second World War. Yet we don't necessarily know what these divisions actually mean. Our primary way of understanding generations is through superficial and poor-quality punditry that identifies a multitude of generational differences that don't exist. While these fake differences may, on an individual level, seem trivial and sometimes even funny, they collectively set a tone that can infect the opinions and actions of even sensible sceptics. Assertions that all Millennials are either narcissistic, materialistic or civic-minded (depending on who you listen to) don't help anyone. This multi-million-dollar 'generation industry' encourages researchers to reduce vast swathes of the population to a handful of characteristics and behaviours.

Another equally unhelpful strand of generational thinking regards generations as repeated waves of predictable archetypes that each react to the previous one. Developed by US authors William Strauss and Neil Howe in the 1990s, this long-term view suggests that every generation falls into one of four types – Idealist, Reactive, Civic or Adaptive – defined by common characteristics. They claim that these generations have appeared in the same order throughout US history, in an 80-year cycle of crisis and renewal, and that this in turn has driven the dominant social conditions of each era. Their account is fascinating and compelling, but it reinforces our assumptions that generations are irreconcilably different from one to the next, and it represents a dubious reading of history that is closer to astrology than academic study. Their analysis has been embraced by the likes of Al Gore and the Republican strategist Steve Bannon (although to very different political ends) and can feel prophetic now – not least because they predicted that an era of crisis would engulf the mid-2000s to the mid-2020s. It would be foolhardy to bet that the COVID-19 era we are living through will not later be regarded as a historically recognizable crisis. But the fact that the pandemic was instigated by a novel coronavirus that originated in the Wuhan district of China only highlights the absurdity of claiming that this crisis is the result of a particular constellation of generational types and the four-generation cycle of catastrophe that Strauss and Howe claim to have identified.

We have simultaneously gone in two bad directions. One strand of thinking, inspired by Strauss and Howe, zooms out by a million miles and assures us that generations fall into a repeating cycle of types before offering something that resembles a horoscope. The other approach claims that frothy, exaggerated differences in generational characteristics are in fact real, shifting tides.

In contrast, true generational thinking can be a powerful tool that helps us to understand the changes and challenges of our day. It starts with recognizing an underappreciated fact: there are just *three* explanations for how *all* attitudes, beliefs and behaviours change over time:

- period effects;
- lifecycle effects; and
- cohort effects.

By studying how these three effects individually and collectively shape us, we can develop a powerful new understanding of how and why societies are changing, and a much greater ability to predict what comes next regarding the biggest issues of our times.

Period effects: The attitudes, beliefs and behaviours of a society can change in a consistent way across all age groups. These period effects often occur in response to a major event that affects everyone, whether directly or indirectly, such as a pandemic, war or economic crisis. When charted on graphs, they often make the pattern we see in Figure 0.1. This example measures concern about terrorism in France. Few people in any generation were worried about terrorism before 2015 and 2016, when there was a severe spike of concern following a series of attacks in

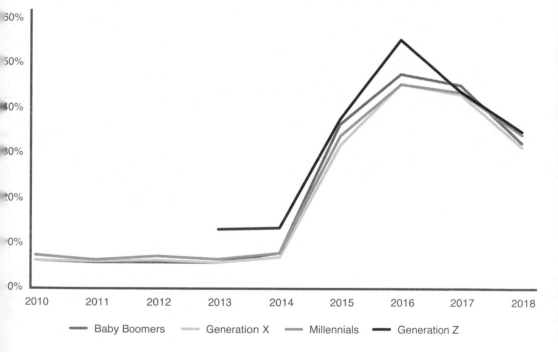

Figure 0.1: Percentage of adults in France who say terrorism is one of the most worrying issues in their country[9]

which over 200 people were killed. Every generation of adults surveyed responded to this series of tragic events in the same way.

Lifecycle effects: People also change as they age, or as a result of major life events, such as leaving home, having children or retiring. Figure 0.2 tracks the proportion of each generation of adults in England who are classified as being a 'healthy weight' as they get older. You can follow your own generational line and see that, on average, people get fatter as they get older (as I'm all too aware). Each generation slowly drifts downwards, the result of too many calories and not enough exercise for their falling metabolism, until, in middle age, only around a quarter of people are still a healthy weight.

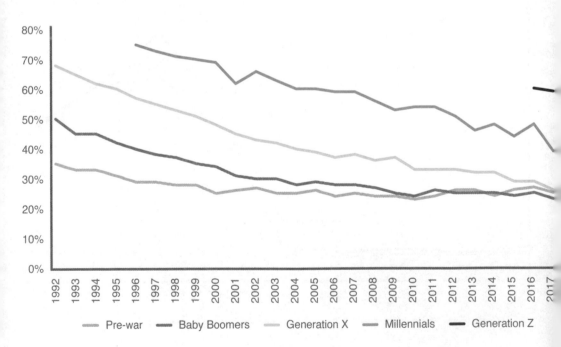

Figure 0.2: Percentage of adults in England with a healthy weight (defined as BMI score between 18.5 and 24.9)[10]

Cohort effects: A generation can also have different attitudes, beliefs and behaviours because they were socialized in different conditions from other generations, and thus will remain distinct from other cohorts even as they age. Figure 0.3 shows the proportion of US adults who say they attend a religious service at least weekly. The oldest generation are much more likely to attend regular religious services, with clear steps down, until we reach what looks like rock bottom with Millennials and Gen Z. And this pattern of generational gaps has not changed much, all the way back to 1975, showing how important when you were born is in shaping your relationship with religion.

Every change in societal attitudes, beliefs and behaviours can be

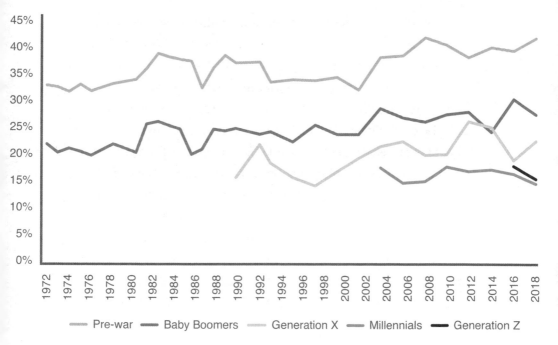

Figure 0.3: Percentage of adults in US attending religious services at least weekly[11]

explained by one – or, more often, a combination – of these three effects. This, therefore, highlights the basic problem with the generational 'analysis' in most commentary: assuming that when a person is born explains all their attitudes and behaviours relies solely on identifying cohort effects – and misses out on two-thirds of the power of this fuller understanding of societal change. This is a far more compelling and useful approach to generational thinking than the sensationalist claims that often pass for it. Once you realize that *all* societal change is explained by a combination of these three effects, you have a framework for a deeper understanding of where we are now and what is likely to come next. You may find yourself asking 'Is this a cohort, period or lifecycle effect?' about a societal change – and that simple question will help you identify what's really important.

Throughout the book, we'll unpick similar trends by looking at charts like these. It has a fancy sounding name – 'synthetic cohort analysis' – but it is entirely intuitive. All we do is define groups according to when they were born and track their average progress as they get older. Of course, most of the patterns are not as clear-cut as in the examples above, and it is not possible to entirely unpick the three effects (cohort, lifestyle, period) in any case.[12] They nearly always interact, but understanding that interaction is incredibly valuable.

In order to examine how we are changing, I have analysed some of the biggest surveys conducted in the world over the past 50 years. I've assembled a dataset of over 3 million interviews from these surveys, linked together to help separate the myths of generational difference from the reality. This allows us to get closer to the underlying changes occurring in societies around the world. I've also drawn on a series of new survey questions that were specially commissioned for this book through the global research firm Ipsos.

Before we dig in, we must first recognize some of the common misconceptions that get in the way of identifying actual change. In particular, we are often fed analysis that confuses age with generation, and which stereotypes both the old and the young.

Our generational delusions

Older people have always had a problem with the young. According to the early twentieth-century Cambridge scholar Kenneth John Freeman, the ancient philosopher Socrates indicted young people for a whole host of things, including their:

> ... luxury, bad manners, contempt for authority, disrespect for elders and a love for chatter in place of exercise ... Children began to be the tyrants, not the slaves of their households. They no longer rose from their seats when an elder entered the room; they contradicted their parents, chattered before company, gobbled up the dainties at table and committed various offences against Hellenic tastes, such as crossing their legs.[13]

Bizarre complaints about the young didn't start or stop in ancient Greece. In 1624, Thomas Barnes, a minister at a London church, complained that 'the youth were never so sawcie, yea never more savagely sawcie'. In 1771, nearly 250 years before 'snowflake' became an attack on the young, a reader's letter to *Town and Country* magazine moaned that youth were 'a race of effeminate, self-admiring, emaciated fribbles'. And in 1843, the 7th Earl of Shaftesbury lamented in the House of Commons that 'young ladies' in the market town of Bilston had taken to 'drive coal-carts, ride astride upon horses, drink, swear, fight, smoke, whistle, sing, and care for nobody'.[14] Nineteenth-century Bilston sounds like an amazing place for a night out.

Young people have also always been seen as being susceptible to the latest fads and fashions, willing to discard traditional values in favour of dangerous new entertainments and technologies. In 1906 – nearly a century before violent video games – the *Dawson Daily News* in Yukon, north-west Canada roared: 'BOYS ARE RUINED. Dime Novels Cause Lads to Murder.'[15] Going back a little further to 1859, an article in *Scientific American* warned that the new craze for *chess* caused 'pernicious excitement' among children of a 'very inferior temperament'.[16]

These repeated waves of moral panic provide a historical context to today's apocryphal stories about Millennials supposedly 'killing' everything from wine corks to wedding rings and the Olympics to serendipity.[17] In just a few short years, Millennial-bashing became an established cliché to be mocked in satirical social media posts; @NewCallieAnn tweeted, 'I cut my finger slicing open an avocado and now I can't fix my topknot.'[18]

Our relentless criticism of Millennials, and increasingly Gen Z too, is the result of a set of human biases that have nothing to do with the essential character of these generations. People tend to think the past was better than it really was because they forget the bad bits – in these cases, the dodgy behaviour of young people in their own youth. We call this bias 'rosy retrospection'. We also struggle to keep pace with changing social norms over time, and older people look at the young through the frame of the values that held sway when they were young themselves. Societal values, beliefs and attitudes shift over time but our individual ideas of what is right or acceptable are 'sticky' – they stay with us – which makes emerging attitudes and behaviours seem strange and unsettling.

Older generations fare no better than younger ones in the public imagination. Psychologists have found that many Western cultures categorize older people into seven basic stereotypes, more than half of which are negative: 'curmudgeon/shrew', 'severely impaired', 'despondent', 'recluse', 'perfect grandparent', 'golden ager' and 'John Wayne conservative'.[19] When they are shown in entertainment or advertisements, older people are almost always depicted as one of those seven stereotypes, whether they are skydiving silver foxes or frail, frightened grannies holding on tightly to their stairlifts as they slowly head to bed at 8 p.m. And that's when they appear at all – people over 60 are generally hugely underrepresented in the media, relative to their large share of the world's population and their even greater share of its wealth.

You would think that smart ad executives would have caught on to the shifting demographics a long time ago, given the number of news analysis pieces that have been written on the subject. In fact, one *Time* magazine cover story noted that some ad agencies were setting up special units to study and reflect older adults as a growing consumer force. 'There was a time when advertisers behaved as though no one past middle age ever bought anything more durable than panty hose. No more,' the article reported.[20] That story ran in 1988 – 33 years ago – yet surprisingly little has changed since then. The former CEO of a major retailer recently confessed that his company had 12 customer segments for people under 55 years old, but lumped everyone aged 55 or over into one segment.[21]

The main generation of older people today, the Baby Boomers, are also subject to attacks. 'OK, Boomer,' Gen Z's sarcastic collective eye roll, has taken a firm hold and was even used by one young MP to dismiss a heckler during a debate about climate change in the New Zealand parliament.[22] Boomers may not get quite as many scathing reviews for their behaviour as Millennials, but the ones they do receive are weighty. Forget the examples of products and traditions that Millennials have supposedly killed off, there are frequent claims that Baby Boomers have ruined *everything*.[23] When you try that contemporary test of how society views something – typing it into

Google to see what the autocomplete comes back with – Boomers
don't do so well. They are 'the problem', 'selfish', 'self-centred' and
'the worst generation'.

Between today's young and old generations is Generation X. This
is where I fit in – and yes, I recognize the irony that my obsession
with generations is in stark contrast with the scant attention my own
generation receives these days. As one fellow Gen Xer tweeted, 'I
am neither a millennial nor a boomer. I come from a generation so
irrelevant that people can't even be bothered to hate us.'[24]

It all started so well. My generation got its name from Douglas
Coupland's hip 1991 novel *Generation X*, which followed the supposed
'slacker' lifestyle of the twenty-somethings of the day. Coupland took
his title from a 1990 book on the American class system by the cultural
critic Paul Fussell. As he dissects layer after layer of class – from 'top
out-of-sight' to 'mid-proletarian' to 'bottom out-of-sight' – Fussell
describes how some young people were trying to free themselves
entirely from this rigid system: 'Impelled by insolence, intelligence,
irony and spirit, X people have escaped out the back doors of those
theaters of class which enclose others.'[25] Insolent, intelligent, ironic
and spirited – my generation is definitely the coolest.

However, Generation X has received virtually no attention
since those heady days. As one writer puts it, they're the 'smaller
"middle child" generation', squashed between Baby Boomers and
Millennials, the two demographic and cultural heavyweights.[26] The
lack of limelight for Gen X has led to a sub-genre of generational
commentary that resembles photobombing a family get-together you
haven't been invited to. Some of it claims that Gen X can save the
world (or 'keep everything from sucking'[27]), while other elements of
it tip into embarrassing youth-bashing: 'The Millennials have taken
a reputational beating in the last few years, some of it gratuitous,
most of it justified. They are needy nellies who can't take a joke.'[28]

This seems somewhat beneath a generation that takes its name from a novel in which the narrator observes, 'The car was the color of butter and bore a bumper sticker saying WE'RE SPENDING OUR CHILDREN'S INHERITANCE, a message that I suppose irked Dag, who was bored and cranky after eight hours working his McJob.' The forgotten middle child has forgotten what it felt like to be young.

Where do you fit in this generational procession? Table 0.1 outlines the most widely accepted definitions. In the US, the Pre-War generation is sometimes split into the 'Greatest Generation' (those born prior to 1928), and the 'Silent Generation' (those born between 1928 and 1945). I have grouped these together in this book, partly because the labels are generally not used outside the US, but mostly because the Greatest Generation now makes up a very small percentage of the population.

Table 0.1: Generational birth years

Pre-War	Baby Boomers	Generation X	Millennials	Generation Z
Born before 1945	Born 1945–65	Born 1966–79	Born 1980–95	Various definitions: Born 1996–2010 Born after 1997 Born after 2000
In 2021				
Age 77+	Age 56 to 76	Age 42 to 55	Age 26 to 41	Age c.11 to 25

There isn't complete agreement on where one generation ends and another starts, particularly around Millennials and Generation Z, where the boundaries are only just emerging. Where you place the cut-offs is, in any case, arbitrary to some degree. Those at the edges of each group will tend to share characteristics common to their birth-year neighbours, because social change tends to be gradual rather than sudden. But this doesn't devalue generational thinking – as we will see, there *are* distinctive characteristics that we can identify using these classifications. And many other social classifications – like class and ethnicity – also simplify the underlying realities, yet still tell us useful things about the make up of and attitudes within society.

Some researchers are already imposing an end point on Generation Z, and starting to call the group that will come next 'Generation Alpha'. We won't be looking at the very youngest generation in this book – because it's ludicrous to do so when the oldest are around ten and the youngest haven't even been born.

This desperate attempt to label a generation that consists of young children and those who have yet to be conceived demonstrates our obsession with coining the name for a generation. The US Census Bureau almost certainly came up with the term 'Baby Boomers', while Douglas Coupland undoubtedly invented and popularized 'Generation X'. William Strauss and Neil Howe are credited with coining the term 'Millennials', while 'Generation Z' follows on from the first name given to the Millennials, 'Generation Y'. But this summary hides countless failed attempts at naming generations. 'Generation Me', 'Generation We', 'the Net Generation', 'Next Boomers', 'Centennials', 'iGen', and even 'Generation K' (after Katniss Everdeen, the protagonist of 'The Hunger Games' series of novels and films), have all been tried out at one point or another.

As we may have expected, the 'COVID Generation' is already being used in media analysis about the predicted impact of the pandemic on the younger generation. Whether it takes hold will only become clear in the coming years, but it certainly has a more powerful claim than names based on characters from movies. I have no particular interest in the naming of generations – the real value is not the label but what the trends show us about the experiences of different groups in the past, and what they suggest about our future.

We *can* see the future

The generational analysis in this book is inevitably future-focused, but it does not require any spurious leaps from exaggerated differences or astrological thinking. It is built on three of the few – maybe the only – incontrovertible facts about humans: they are born, they age and they die. This is seen in each cohort's share of the adult population over time, in Figure 0.4. In 1972, around 80 per cent of the adults in the UK were born before the end of the Second World War; now they make up just 12 per cent. It won't be long until they are all but gone, while Gen Z makes its way into adulthood and 'replaces' them. There is no way to understand how society as a whole will

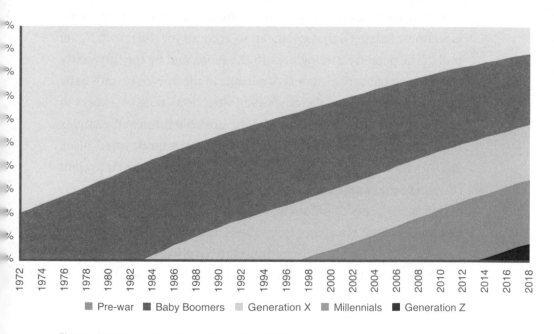

Figure 0.4: Generational profile of the UK[29]

change in the future without understanding what is really different between the generations.

Some people might take issue with the idea that we can use past generational changes to predict the future. In *The Black Swan*, Nassim Nicholas Taleb writes, 'History and societies do not crawl. They make jumps.' He argues that we largely do not see these jumps coming. Change is instead driven by 'black swan' events, such as the 2008 global financial crisis, which was the focus for Taleb's analysis, and now, even more powerfully, the COVID-19 pandemic. These events are rare, have extreme impacts and only seem predictable in retrospect, despite our tendency to believe subsequently that we knew they were coming.[30]

To illustrate the deep unpredictability of future outcomes, Taleb cites an example given by the mathematician Michael Berry, who looked at the challenge of predicting the movement of billiard balls on a table. It starts easily enough, but by the ninth impact, the outcome is so finely balanced that you need to account for the gravitational pull of the person standing next to the table, and by the fifty-sixth, the position of every elementary particle in the universe needs to be factored into your calculations. Given that, how could we expect to have an accurate understanding of the possible futures of complex human systems, particularly when we experience unexpected 'black swan' events, such as the 2008 crisis or a pandemic – the equivalent of someone coming along and upending the table?

My many years of following generational lines has left me less pessimistic about our ability to see the future. Of course, it is possible that we will suddenly stop getting more overweight as we age or that the whole of Generation Z will embrace Christianity en masse, but such things seem unlikely. Taleb recognizes that there are 'long quiet stretches' where sudden shocks don't happen, and we will see plenty of those in our charts. But generational analysis also helps in understanding the impact of the unexpected: we will vividly see the different economic life courses created for younger generations by the 2008 financial crisis, for example.

Crucially, of course, understanding how period effect shocks, like the financial crisis and the pandemic, affect people is greatly enhanced by having a clear view of the slower trajectories we are already travelling along. The impact of any crisis is shaped by the context it lands in.

A generational frame helps us to understand the impact of major demographic trends too, such as our greater life expectancy and increasingly ageing societies. This is one of the most significant changes we've seen, and it has huge implications for how we should understand the future. In Japan, the median age (the age of the middle person, if you lined up the whole population, from young to old) was 46 in 2015, and by 2050 it will have increased to 53. This increase of seven years may not seem like a big shift, but it reflects an incredibly aged society; 33 per cent of Japan's current population is over 60, but by 2050, 42 per cent will be.

Japan is often held up as the exemplar of the 'greying society', but there are even more dramatic changes coming in other countries. For example, the median age in Brazil was just 31 in 2015 but will have increased to 45 by 2050. The proportion of people in Brazil who are over 60 will rocket from just 13 per cent in 2015 to 30 per cent by 2050. The shifting age balance in our populations is not just due to increasing longevity but also the steeply falling birth rates seen around the world. A generational perspective shows that this is not a sudden change but the end of a long trend that will be incredibly difficult to shift.

I examine these trends across countries rather than focusing on a single one, because a global view is becoming increasingly important. Early twentieth-century thinkers like Mannheim tended to see generations as nationally bounded, because of the importance of shared experience in forming meaningful cohorts. But with the globalization of so many aspects of life, sociologists have recognized that generations could also be globalizing. Businesses and consumer products are now multinational by default, and new communications technologies provide many more ways to share experiences across national boundaries. Even before COVID-19, traumatic events and threats, such as the climate emergency, economic crises and the 'war on terror', had a more global perspective. The pandemic has again accelerated this trend, emphasizing our incredible global interconnections. At the time of writing, 213 countries or territories had reported cases of the virus, but also countries are much more closely tied together in their responses and the economic implications of their measures than in any previous pandemic.[31]

This is not to say that differences between countries are unimportant. 'Country before cohort' will still be a regular message in this book: even now, *where* you are born often remains more important than *when*. The true value of an international study of generations isn't in proving that there are global generational groups, but in enabling us to understand when and why generational difference is important.

Even before the pandemic, the assumption that our children will enjoy a better future had evaporated in several developed nations. For example, more than a decade after the 2008 financial crisis, only 13 per cent of people in France expected a better life for young people, while 60 per cent thought the future would be worse. The contrast with lower-income nations, such as China, Indonesia and India, is stark: at least two-thirds of people in these countries were confident of a better future for their young people. We know this is important to people: in the same study, 77 per cent of people agreed that every generation *should* have a better standard of living than the one that came before it, with only 15 per cent disagreeing.[32] However, if people in Western countries – of every generation – maintain this increasingly pessimistic view, it will have profound repercussions. Not only will we risk losing the optimism and dynamism of youth, but when people think progress has stopped, they start to question the value of the whole system.

As far as we can tell, such pessimism about the future for coming generations is a new trend in more developed economies, as these dramatic statistics from both the UK and the US show: the proportion of Brits who think the future will be better for their children halved between 2003 and 2019, and the proportion of Americans who think it's unlikely their kids will have a better future has nearly doubled.[33]

When we see how incomes and wealth have stagnated for recent generations of young people, we can start to understand why.

Chapter 1

Stagnation Generation

'The Baby Boomers – Can They Ever Live as Well as Their Parents?' This was the anxious question posed by *Money* magazine in March 1983.[1] The implied threat to the generation's financial security was seriously undermined by the accompanying photo shoot of a real-life couple, which contained glimpses of a luxurious and tastefully decorated (for the 1980s) home. The cover line offered a more direct spoiler: the couple were 'Not yet 30' but had 'two strong careers and a prospering business on the side'. It's clear that they were hardly the 1980s equivalent of minimum-wage employees toiling in an Amazon warehouse on zero-hour contracts, supplementing their meagre earnings by trading on eBay and waiting for their jobs to be taken by drones.

Of course, *Money* magazine had a particular target market – well-off middle managers who were interested in tables of mortgages and tax-efficient saving schemes. That makes the uncertainty implied in the question all the more striking now, when we know how things turned out. The question 'Can they ever live as well as their parents?' reflects the fundamental belief that animates the 'social contract' between generations. As individuals, we have a deep desire for our children to do better than us, and we've become accustomed to guaranteed generation-on-generation progress across society as a whole.

It's easy to forget that progress was not always a given for Baby Boomers. Several serious economists raised doubts about their financial future. In his 1980 book *Birth and Fortune*, Professor Richard Easterlin argues that being part of a big cohort like the Baby Boomers is bad for your economic success, given the competition for education, resources and jobs. Being a member of a smaller cohort, like the inter-war generation, marks you out as part of the 'lucky few', where wages would rise as demand for workers outstripped supply. That seemed a perfectly reasonable assumption to many then, but, as David Willetts outlines in his 2010 book *The Pinch*, globalization entirely changed the calculation.

After countries with lower labour costs like China opened up to world trade in the 1990s, the generations following the Boomers had to compete with many more people, which kept wages down. As Willetts puts it: 'The Boomers gain in two ways. When it comes to political power and all the decisions taken by national governments, they are a big cohort. But when it came to the post-war global labour market they were part of a small cohort: they were a scarce resource that could get away with charging a higher price for their labour.'[2]

Downward trends in financial progress in many Western countries came after the Baby Boomers were well established in their careers and more able to weather the storm. And then came the 2008 financial crisis. Before the COVID-19 pandemic, this was *the* generation-defining economic event and the cause of a largely lost decade that hit younger generations particularly hard. There were tentative signs of a recovery in generational progress in the late 2010s, which has made the timing of this latest generation-defining shock even more cruel.

The net effect has been that income growth for younger generations in many countries has ground to a halt or reversed, while the vast majority of gains in wealth that we have seen in the last decade or so have gone to older generations. A generational perspective, separating period, cohort and lifecycle effects, is vital if we are to understand how these shifting economic conditions have utterly changed the life course of whole cohorts. Not only have your chances of economic success been affected by the accident of when you were born, but they are also affected by your parents' assets – to an increasing degree.

Poorer longer

The UK-based think tank the Resolution Foundation has analysed personal incomes across the US, the UK, Spain, Italy, Norway, Finland and Denmark, using data that stretches all the way back to 1969, when the oldest Baby Boomer was 24 years old. The study compares average disposable real incomes – that is, adjusted to take inflation into account and after subtracting housing costs – for three five-year slices of cohorts, to compare generations when they were the same age: in their thirties (Millennials vs Gen X, Gen X vs Baby Boomers), forties (Gen X vs Baby Boomers, Baby Boomers vs Pre-War) and sixties (Baby Boomers vs Pre-War).[3] It shows a cascade of ever-decreasing gains for each new generation.

Baby Boomers enjoyed significantly improved incomes in middle age compared with the Pre-War generation, up 26 per cent aged 45 to 49. At the same age, Gen X started off well compared with Boomers, but their incomes stalled as they ran into the aftershocks of the 2008 recession, which hit when the oldest were in their early forties, and ended up only 3 per cent ahead of Boomers. Most strikingly, Millennials' real disposable income was actually 4 per cent down on Gen X when they were each in their early thirties. Progress didn't just stall, it *reversed* – driven by the financial crisis.[4]

These averages hide significant variation across countries. One of the best places to be a Millennial is Norway. There, Millennials aged 30 to 34 earned 13 per cent *more* than Gen Xers at the same age. Not too bad, you might say (while researching Norwegian work visa requirements). But this still represents a slowing down in economic progress: at the same age, Gen Xers earned 35 per cent more than Baby Boomers.

More typical is the pattern in the US. Gen Xers had 5 per cent lower real incomes than Boomers at 45 to 49, while Millennials earned 5 per cent less than Gen Xers at 30 to 34.

As demoralizing as things are in the US, they're nothing compared with elsewhere. In Italy, Gen Xers had 11 per cent less income than Baby Boomers at 45 to 49, while Millennials had 17 per cent less income than Gen Xers at 30 to 34. This is not so much a ratcheting down as a freefall.

The trends in the UK have not been as dire, but they still represent a shuddering halt to progress, particularly with Millennials. Data from 2018 shows that Gen Xers were slightly ahead of where Baby Boomers were when they were in their mid-forties, but Millennials were slightly behind where Gen Xers were when they were in their early thirties.[5]

These economic realities are powerfully reflected in how the different generations in Britain *feel*. This is a key question, because if groups feel hard done by, they're more likely to question the entire social contract. Since 1983, the British Social Attitudes survey has asked people what income group they identify themselves as being in: high, middle or low. And when we look at the proportions of each generation placing themselves in the 'low income' group over the past three and a half decades, in Figure 1.1, we can see huge life stories being played out in five simple lines.

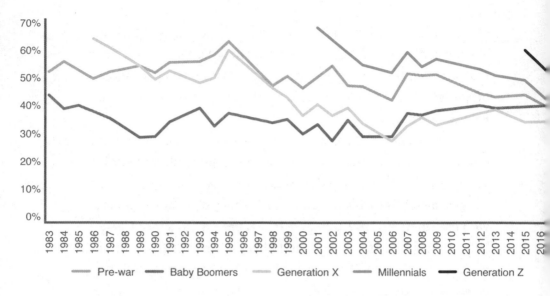

Figure 1.1: Percentage of adults in Britain saying they have a 'low income' when asked, 'Among which group would you place yourself: high income, middle income or low income?'[6]

One sad story stands out. Look at the gap between Millennials and all other generations for the years between 2008 and 2015. It is not normal for this many people in their early to mid-career (the oldest Millennial was 35 in 2015) to feel poorer than the rest of the population, including retired generations, for so long.

A large part of the explanation for the relative experience of Millennials is the remarkable fall in the proportion of people in the oldest living cohort, the Pre-War generation, who count themselves as having a low income over the last couple of decades. The trend is especially unusual given the changing labour market position of this group during this period. In 1983, only 26 per cent of the Pre-War generation had retired – but by 2017, when the youngest was 72, nearly all had retired.

While this may partly be due to decreased expectations (people generally expect to have less money in retirement), it also reflects the much stronger pension position for many in this generation compared with the generation before them, and compared with working-age people today. The UK's Office for National Statistics estimates that the average pensioner's disposable real income increased by 16 per cent between 2008 and 2018, while it increased by only 3 per cent for working households.[7] By 2016, net incomes after housing costs were actually £20 per week *higher* for the retired than they were for working-age people, having been £70 per week *lower* in 2001. That's a huge switch. More than this, the pattern extends down into the poorest ends of each group. The poorest fifth of working-age households are getting by on £2,000 less per year than the poorest fifth of pensioners.[8]

The end of the chart appears to promise a hopeful future for younger generations, with a steep drop in the proportion of Millennials who said that they had a low income, and Generation Z having entered adulthood much closer to the overall average than Millennials did. These are still the two generations that are most likely to feel poor, but the difference is less than in the recent past. It is too early to assess the lasting impact of the COVID-19 pandemic on incomes, but the signs are that these faint glimmers of optimism will be snuffed out. Analysis across China, South Korea, Japan, Italy, the US and the UK shows that everywhere except South Korea, the young are much more likely than others to have already experienced a drop in income, with the UK seeing one of the biggest relative declines.[9]

Blaming the victim

These major shifts in income make the 'advice' that is regularly targeted at these younger generations particularly maddening. 'Small "Swaprifices" Could Save Millennials Up to £10.5bn a Year'[10] was one especially toe-curling example of this trend, in a press release from Barclays Bank in 2019. Not only does it confirm that awful attempts at catchy portmanteau words should be a sackable offence, it also typifies the victim-blaming of young people for their tough financial circumstances.

The thrust of the 'analysis' was a breakdown of how young people spend £3,300 per year on daily treats, going out and fashion, followed by some finger-wagging about how this group could save a 'whopping' amount by making 'minor changes to their spending habits'.[11] Of course, £3,300 is not a huge amount to cover all those different types of spending in a year, especially when they include things like 'food' and 'clothing'. Even the frivolous-sounding 'daily treats', for example, totalled just £441 a year, or about £1.10 per day.

This is typical of the curious double whammy experienced by younger cohorts today. Not only have they had a much tougher time financially, but they are also criticized for the reduced spending they do manage. It's also a case of us missing the real shift in circumstances. In the UK, for example, over-fifties account for around one-third of the population but 47 per cent of consumer spending, which has increased by eight percentage points since 2003.[12] In the US, over-fifties already account for more than 50 per cent of spending, and they've been responsible for more spending growth in recent years than any other cohort.[13] The figures are staggering: the American Association of Retired Persons (AARP) estimates that, in the US, the over-fifties spend nearly $8 trillion each year – more than the combined GDP of France and Germany.[14]

A new consumption gap has opened up between younger and older households in many countries. In 1989, 25 to 34 year olds and 55 to 64 year olds in the UK both spent about £260 per week on non-housing consumer goods, such as clothing, entertainment, travel and eating out. By 2014, 55 to 64 year olds were spending, on average, £50 a week – nearly 20 per cent – *more* than 25 to 34 year olds.

Although this narrative of profligate youth massively misses the point, it remains pervasive. In a global survey of 20,000 people, the second most popular adjective picked out to describe Millennials was 'materialistic'. The stereotype sticks partly because it is endlessly repeated, for both Millennials and Gen Z. As the author of *Generation Me*, Jean Twenge, puts it: '[Millennials'] brand of self-importance also shows up in materialism.'[15] In her later book on Gen Z, *iGen*, Twenge draws on a long series of surveys of US high-school students to conclude: '[Gen Z] are very interested in becoming well-off and less focused on meaning than previous generations.'[16]

Those are some sweeping generalizations that you'd need cast-iron data to support. Yet, on each survey measure that is held up as evidence of materialism – whether it's wanting to earn more than your parents, believing it's important to be financially well off, or thinking there's nothing wrong with advertising that encourages people to buy products they don't need – the major shift actually happened between Baby Boomers and Generation X, and there is nothing particularly new in Millennial and Gen Z attitudes. And there are also plenty of counter-trends – for example, recent generations care half as much about what their friends and family have.[17]

These figures don't suggest some emergent trend in materialism, newly presenting in Millennials and Gen Z as a distinctive characteristic. Instead, Gen Xers blazed the trail and younger cohorts have stuck to it. It might be that American Gen Xers were raised in a period of increased consumerism and exposure to advertising that hasn't changed all that much over the past 40 years, despite new technologies. Or it could be that these generations came of age during a shaky financial period and carry the scars of that experience. In the US, in fact, income stagnation set in earlier, with Gen Xers rather than Millennials.

It makes sense that money becomes more of a focus when your financial prospects are diminished. Indeed, we see this tendency in behavioural science studies of poverty, which show that a lack of resources induces a 'scarcity mindset',[18] where immediate goals take precedence over peripheral goals: 'scarcity orientates the mind automatically and powerfully toward unfulfilled needs'.[19] For the young people in the US high-school surveys cited by Twenge, the data reflects the undeniable fact that financial progress was less certain when they were coming into adulthood.

These blunt characterizations reflect a tendency to pick on younger generations for traits that are created by their context. This faulty interpretation of cause and effect is related to another common bias, which social psychologists call the 'fundamental attribution error', a term coined by the Stanford University professor Lee Ross. This is the tendency for people to overemphasize personality-based explanations and underemphasize situational explanations for behaviours that we observe in others. For example, a driver who cuts us up in traffic is a jerk – but when we do the same thing it's because we're late for a vital appointment. This is often why we blame the victim for their own misfortune.

The surveys of high-school students cited above are a powerful resource, but they cannot unpick what is truly generational about the behaviour because they track the same age group over time. We don't know how each successive wave of high-school kids behaved or changed as they aged, and that is why it is also useful to check these trends with generational analysis.

Consider the example in Figure 1.2 from Germany. At just about any point from 2003 to 2012, this data could be summed up with a headline: 'Materialistic Millennials are twice as likely to say it's important to be rich than their wiser elders'. But that headline could also have been repeated between 2014 and 2016 for Gen Z. It's clear that focusing on getting rich is primarily a lifecycle effect, a feature of youth that we tend to grow out of.

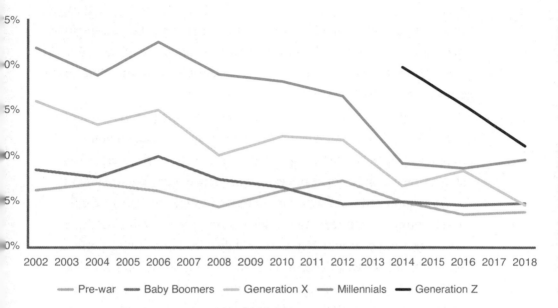

Figure 1.2: Percentage of adults in Germany who say that 'It is important to be rich' is true of themselves[20]

The wealth of generations

Actually achieving these childhood dreams of becoming rich is increasingly about the wealth you have, rather than the income you earn. The main economic change of the last few decades, across numerous countries, is how much more quickly wealth has grown than income, largely driven by a housing boom. And because wealth is more unequally distributed than income, including by age, this has resulted in greater concentrations of wealth among older groups. In fact, since 2007, *all* of the extra wealth created in the UK went to people over 45, with two-thirds going to those over 65.[21] This feels less fair than income differences, because the amounts are so large and wealth is not as clearly linked in our minds to merit or hard work.

The UK is far from alone in this trend. Credit Suisse, the international investment bank, produces an annual global wealth

report, which I always look forward to, in order to ogle the ultra-high-net-worth individuals. Their 2017 report included less pleasurable reading for younger generations, however, with a whole chapter dedicated to 'The Unlucky Millennials'.[22]

The report describes how the 2008 recession, and subsequent higher levels of unemployment and lower wage growth, hit younger people's savings potential, especially in richer countries. As well as stagnating incomes, house prices also remained high, as government action supported existing homeowners through interest rate cuts and by pumping money into the system. In several countries, these factors were coupled with rising student debt loads, creating a 'perfect storm' for stifling wealth accumulation. In contrast, according to the authors, Baby Boomers' 'wealth was boosted by a range of factors including large windfalls due to property, pension and share price increases'.

Separate analysis in Australia illustrates this increasingly unbalanced distribution of wealth. More than two-thirds of the A$2.3 trillion of household wealth generated in Australia in the first half of the 2010s went to those aged 55 or older. Those aged 65 to 74 were, on average and in real terms, A$480,000 wealthier in 2015–16 than those in the same age group 12 years earlier. In contrast, households headed by 35 to 44 year olds were, on average, only A$120,000 wealthier, and for 25 to 34 year olds, the figure was a measly A$40,000.[23] Figure 1.3 shows this incredible wealth curve, where only older cohorts are benefiting significantly.

These gains are not due to the frugal habits of older people, yet that is the view encouraged by a stream of articles on how the young could learn a thing or two about finances from their elders. A *Forbes* piece on '5 Money Tips Millennials Can Learn from Their Grandparents' includes this timeless piece of wisdom from one grandfather: 'Eat at a reasonably priced restaurant ... It all comes

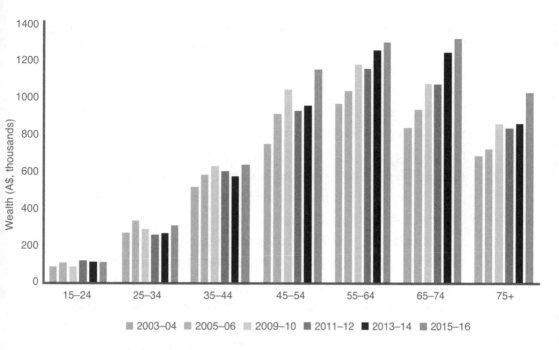

Figure 1.3: Gains in wealth among Australian households, 2003–16[24]

out the same the next day.'[25] As the Credit Suisse report suggests, older generations' greater wealth hasn't come from following such nauseating advice, but is rather the result of unexpected financial windfalls.[26]

Economists distinguish between 'passive' asset gains – where we benefit from the overall performance of the market – and 'active' gains, where our investment decisions influence outcomes. The vast majority of gains across most Western countries are a result of people just sitting back and benefiting from repeated waves of property booms and stock market rises.[27]

You might be thinking that the young should suck it up for now and wait for their own 'passive gains' of inheritance from their loaded parents. Surely all those assets gathering at the top of the generational hierarchy will soon be flowing down to the youngsters? There is, after all, a lot more wealth out there: the value of estates passed down has more than doubled in the UK in the past 20 years, and it will double again in the next 15.[28]

Unfortunately, that will not help hard-pressed middle-aged groups through tough times. Firstly, inheritance is shifting to later in life. In the UK, the average predicted age for today's 20 to 35 year olds to inherit is 61 years.[29] That's a long wait for cash-strapped Millennials and Gen Zers, and it is increasingly likely to be eaten up by the cost of caring for their longer-living parents.[30]

It is, of course, possible to bring forward some of this transfer in wealth through gifts or loans, and many do – through an increased reliance on the 'Bank of Mum and Dad' (BOMAD). In its early days, BOMAD, as typified by a 2004 BBC TV series, was the generational equivalent of an intervention with an alcoholic,[31] as parents and experts were drafted in to teach feckless youngsters the value of money. Today, it is a much bigger business. For example, nearly two-thirds of US Millennials say that their parents helped them out 'a lot' or 'some' when they were just starting out, compared with 36 per cent of their parents who received this level of financial help at the same life stage.[32] A study by academics at the London School of Economics (LSE) shows that, in 2017, some 34 per cent of first-time home buyers in England received money from their parents to put towards their deposits. The amount contributed is substantial: in 2018, the BOMAD gave enough money to be ranked tenth among UK mortgage lenders.[33]

But BOMAD isn't a real bank, of course, not least because almost all transfers of wealth are gifts rather than loans. As one of the parents surveyed by the LSE, a 67 year old, said: 'I think that young people today have it far tougher than my husband and I did. Our son and daughter-in-law have the triple whammy of student debt, horrendously high rents and rocketing house prices. I am just so pleased that we are able to help.' Another, a 75 year old, noted: 'Aren't we lucky that we were able to help our children like this? And aren't they?'

They are, indeed, lucky to have parents who can help, because the average growth in wealth among older generations hides huge variations. Plenty of older people have acquired very little or nothing. My own inheritance so far has been a Seiko watch and a love of whisky, both from my dad – and, although they mean a lot to me, they aren't going to help me pay off my mortgage. This disparity is one of the big challenges for the future. If younger cohorts and those following them have to depend on inheritance to accumulate wealth, it will reinforce inequality, increasing the gaps between the top and bottom.[34]

Of course, the rich have been passing on their wealth to their children throughout history. In one study, the economists Gregory Clark and Neil Cummins created a database of 634 rare surnames (including wonderful examples like 'Bigge', 'Angerstein' and 'Nottidge') so that they could track inheritance across five generations in English and Welsh probate records between 1858 and 2012. They tagged each person who died in the first generation as either rich or poor, based on the value of their estate, and watched the wealth flow down to the present day. Even after high inheritance taxes were introduced between the wars, the children of the rich remained rich – to quite a remarkable extent. As Clark and Cummins conclude, 'to those who have, more is given'.[35]

While the pattern may be old, the increased scale and generational concentration of wealth is new. In the UK, for example, in 2016, Baby Boomers at the top (75th percentile) each have around £600,000 in total wealth, while those at the bottom (25th percentile) hover around £100,000 each. The increases in wealth for Boomers overall over the last ten years largely come down to acceleration in growth at the top: the 75th percentile gained around £100,000–200,000 each between 2006 and 2016, while the 25th percentile barely gained at all.[36] The same pattern was seen in the US. In 2004, the top 5 per cent of American Baby Boomers owned 52 per cent of all financial assets within their cohort, a figure that increased to 60 per cent in 2016. By contrast, the bottom 50 per cent saw their tiny share of wealth decrease, from 3 to 2 per cent.[37]

The huge growth and uneven concentration of wealth bakes in the generational transfer of inequality, and this involves much more than just pure cash, as the sociologist Robert D. Putnam powerfully argues in his book *Our Kids*. Advantages have piled up for the kids born to the right parents, all but guaranteeing their own success in life – in stark contrast to those struggling at the bottom. Putnam presents dozens of 'scissors graphs' showing the top pulling away from the bottom on all sorts of factors, including obesity, maternal employment, single parenthood, financial stress, college graduation and friendship networks. This increasingly has a geographical dimension, with economic sorting seen at the neighbourhood level, and social sorting within schools, churches and community groups. Putnam writes: 'Whether we are rich or poor, our kids are increasingly growing up with kids like them who have parents like us.' This represents, he warns, 'a kind of incipient class apartheid'.[38]

These increasing gaps between rich and poor have consequences not just for the individuals left behind but for how people see the system as a whole. One of the questions in the World Values Survey – the biggest social survey in the world, covering 100 countries – asks people whether they think wealth can grow so that there is enough for everyone, or whether people get rich at the expense of others. In a number of advanced economies, younger generations are the most suspicious about whether increased wealth at the top really does trickle down. In Germany, for example, nearly two-thirds of the Pre-War generation agreed that 'wealth can grow so there is enough for everyone' in 1997. By the mid-2010s, only around half of this oldest generation still believed that to be the case, and only one-third of Millennials thought the same thing. There are both cohort and period effects at work here, with everybody having a gloomier outlook than people born before the end of the war, and a general decline in faith across each generation.

These perceptions are based on economic reality. Through much of the post-war period, 'a rising economic tide lifted all boats', according to the sociologist Douglas Massey.[39] And, as Putnam puts it, in the early decades of this period, 'the dinghies actually rose slightly faster than the yachts'.[40] In fact, incomes for the bottom fifth of society in the US grew a bit more each year, compared with incomes for the top fifth. However, in the 1980s, the tide started to change: first, income gains stalled and then, after the 2008 financial crisis, they reversed in many cases.

As the sentiments seen in Germany show, a majority of the oldest generation are holding onto the view that the system works *because it used to*, but this belief is fading with them.

So why have we let this happen? A large part of the reason is the continuing rise in individualism across countries, which is a very powerful cultural tide that informs many of the trends we'll see throughout this book. For decades, Ronald Inglehart, director of the World Values Survey and professor emeritus at the University of Michigan, and his colleagues have tracked the shift from 'security values' (such as the importance of economic growth and maintaining order) to 'self-expression values' (such as valuing freedom of speech and gender equality) across dozens of countries.[41] Others, such as Geert Hofstede and Shalom H. Schwartz, have measured similar factors using different models.[42] Each of these thinkers have brought distinct angles to this research, but they all find a similar trend – of a slow, evolutionary and generational shift towards the individualist end of the spectrum in each measure across many countries.

Long-term trends in our politics have also pushed us along the path to individualism. Margaret Thatcher's 1975 Conservative Party conference speech is an excellent example of this political worldview: 'We believe [people] should be individuals. We are all unequal. No one, thank heavens, is like anyone else, however much the Socialists may pretend otherwise.'[43] Ronald Reagan was a fellow staunch supporter of 'rugged individualism'. In his famous 'A Time for Choosing' speech in 1964, he described his resentment at the tendency in some quarters to refer to the people as 'the masses' and asserted that individual freedom was still the best approach to solving the complex problems of the twentieth century.[44] Younger generations today are at the end of this long shift, and have a particularly strong sense of personal responsibility for how life turns out. They tend to blame themselves.

The end of the social contract?

I ran a survey on generational differences with *The Guardian* newspaper several years ago.[45] It was one of the first to unpick the decline in people's belief, in the world's richer countries, that young people would experience a better future. I wasn't the only one concerned. So, too, was Ángel Gurría, Secretary-General of the Organisation for Economic Cooperation and Development (OECD). 'What would be tragic is if the very trait that we count on the young to infuse into our societies – optimism – were to somehow become permanently scarred,' he said in response to the survey. 'We can't afford that.'[46] There is a reason why leaders of global economic organizations are alarmed by generation-on-generation declines in the belief in a better future. If things aren't going to get better, what's to stop people from attempting to overturn the system altogether? Our long drift to individualism and increased sense of personal responsibility has decreased the likelihood of that outcome – but even that has a breaking point. And even if we're not heading towards revolution, this stalled generational progress is behind a lot of the explosive tension in contemporary societies.

So what should we do? There is a lot of analysis that suggests it's simple: take from the old to give to the young. The tone is set by countless stories in the media about how 'selfish' Baby Boomers have looted the economy and the environment in lives of happy abandonment, leaving future generations to fend for themselves. A number of books with titles like *The Theft of a Decade: How the Baby Boomers Stole the Millennials' Economic Future* have been published in recent years. Some of them are well-reasoned analyses that point out the coincidence of many converging sets of fortuitous circumstances and political decisions that have caused today's generational divergence. However, such polemical framing suggests that a whole generation is to blame for a trend that they simply happened to benefit from. One book, *A Generation of Sociopaths: How the Baby Boomers Betrayed America*, scores this cohort against indicators of sociopathy.

In fact, a number of generational analysts have been predicting a breakdown in the intergenerational contract for some time. For example, in 1992, David Thomson, an academic from New Zealand, asked: 'Why should the young adults of the 1990s and beyond feel bound to pay for the welfare state of their predecessors? What bonds, what obligations, what contract requires this of them? Why would they not argue that there now is no contract between generations, because it has been voided by the behaviour of their elders?'[47]

This may seem a compelling argument, but it underplays some clear 'bonds' and 'obligations' within families, and overplays the generational drivers of our motivations. In fact, the vast majority of people don't want to act on grudges against older generations. For example, a question in the US General Social Survey asks whether the government should be responsible for providing a decent standard of living for the old: in 1984, around nine in ten people agreed, with no difference between the generations – and in 2016 the position was *exactly* the same. Indeed, American Millennials and Gen Xers are slightly *more* likely to say that more money should be spent on retirement benefits.[48] This pattern is mirrored in other countries: for example, a majority of each generation in the UK consistently selects benefits for the retired as a priority for any extra government spending.[49]

There are *no* countries where there is strong agreement among any age groups that older people get more than their fair share. For example, in a UK study on how younger people might achieve a better quality of life, all the most popular answers are actions that could benefit everyone: making jobs more secure, supporting economic growth, increased housing and improved healthcare. Only tiny minorities select shifting the balance of taxation to the old or reducing welfare benefits for the retired.[50]

Whichever way you look at the evidence, there is little sign of a coming 'generational war' based on economic resentment – and there are a number of very good reasons for this. Most obvious are our family connections, which are driven by both practical and emotional factors: we don't want our parents and grandparents to be penalized, partly because we love them and partly because it might cost us time or money. More generally, we have a strong belief that those who have contributed should receive support – and that older people, having been around longer, have contributed the most.[51]

This lack of generational tension is also related to the fact that we inevitably pass through each age range ourselves. Unlike gender, race, ethnicity, or even social class or income, we *cannot avoid* switching categories ourselves (except by dying). As a result, we see our own futures in the older people ahead of us, and that includes the level and nature of support we'll get from government. Contrary to common misconceptions, the main outcome of taxation and welfare is *lifetime* redistribution – the transfer of money between different periods in someone's life – rather than the redistribution of money between different income groups.[52] And when you see the system in those terms, the idea that younger generations would want to tear up the intergenerational contract makes much less sense. If a generation shifts the balance away from the old, they will very likely lose out themselves at a later life stage. Overall, it's no surprise that young people are not ready to go to war with their grandparents.

We cannot dismiss concerns that current young generations will have a poorer economic future than their parents. The social contract between generations is under real strain. However, this is more the result of increasing economic precarity for large proportions of the population, with wealth increasingly concentrated among the few. It is this growing imbalance and the consequent baked-in inequality that is the real issue. And this is where we need to focus in order to regain a sense of optimism for future generations.

Chapter 2

Home Affront

In the late 1960s, four well-dressed Englishmen are reminiscing about their tough upbringing over a fine bottle of Château de Chasselas. They've done well for themselves, having each grown up very poor. You might say they got lucky, entering the workforce during the post-war boom, but they also had that famous Yorkshire grit to draw upon. The state of their childhood housing, for example, was shocking:

- We used to live in a tiny, tumble-down old house, with great holes in t' roof.
- House? You were lucky to have a house! We used to live in one room, twenty-six of us, all there, no furniture, 'alf the floor was missing, and we were all 'uddled in one corner for fear of falling.
- Room? You were lucky to have a room! We used to have to live in t' corridor!
- Corridor? Ah, we used to dream of livin' in a corridor! That would ha' been a palace to us. We used to live in a water tank on a rubbish tip. Ah, every morning we'd be woke up by having a load of rotting fish dumped on us! House? Huh.
- Well, when I said 'house', I mean, 'twere only a hole in t' ground covered by a couple of foot of torn canvas, but it 'twere house to us.

- Well, we were evicted from our 'ole in the ground; we 'ad to go and live in the lake.
- Hey, you were lucky to have a lake! There were over a hundred and fifty of us living in a small shoebox in t' middle o' t' road.
- Cardboard box?
- Aye.
- You were lucky.[1]

The Yorkshiremen conclude that, if they had tried telling this to the coddled young people of their day – the Baby Boomer generation – 'They wouldn't believe you.'

I can hear Michael Palin's broad Yorkshire accent from this Monty Python sketch every time I read the responses to articles about how rough the housing situation is for young people today. For every tale of Millennials and Gen Zers being victim-blamed by landlords for mould in apartments caused by them 'breathing at night', or for rat infestations because they're 'keeping food in cupboards',[2] there's also a stream of responses from older generations recounting their own miserable housing stories: 'Renting has always been shit. Why do you think you lot are so special?'[3]

The keyboard warriors have a point, of course. The reality is that housing was much worse in the relatively recent past, not just because of unscrupulous landlords but also in terms of basic amenities. In 1967, around one in seven American and British households still had no flushing inside toilet,[4] and 22 per cent of Brits didn't have running hot water.[5] In 1970, only one-third of British homes had central heating, which typically meant that – in two-thirds of homes – only one room was heated.[6] These living conditions were the childhood experiences of many Baby Boomers, including my parents.

It's not outlandish to expect improvements in living conditions over decades, but headlines like '"Slugs came through the floorboards": What It's Like to Be a Millennial Renting in Britain' miss the story.[7] The real problem is that a combination of skyrocketing housing costs, stricter mortgage lending rules, stagnating incomes, rising debt and faltering economic growth following both the 2008 financial crisis and the COVID-19 pandemic are delaying the point when young people leave their parents' homes, swallowing up more of their income on housing, and diminishing their prospects of buying their own home. These major shifts in circumstances are having knock-on effects on young people's lives: on their potential to generate wealth, the nature of their family relationships, their feelings of independence, and the timing of their transitions into long-term relationships and parenthood. When you were born really does shape your housing prospects and outcomes in many countries – it's a crucial aspect of an apparent trend towards 'delayed adulthood' and a slower life course.

Even without these long-term effects, this unsettled situation has changed how many young people experience their youth, as the housing horror story of Lindi, a 63-year-old Baby Boomer, shows.[8] In the 1970s, Lindi lived in what she and her partner called 'Maison Crap', on the top floor of a London block where pigeons were the only other tenants on the derelict floors below. But Lindi, rather than moaning that 'kids today don't know they're born', recognizes the huge increase in housing costs faced by current younger generations. When she was in her twenties, she spent around a quarter of her salary on rent, while the average young private renter in London these days spends around half their income on accommodation.[9] 'It pains me to see people in their twenties not enjoying life as we were,' she says. 'A lot of people of my generation were lucky enough to be carefree.'[10]

The story of housing, as we will see, has little to do with the feebleness or fecklessness of the young and everything to do with increasing financial barriers to property ownership over recent decades. The financial crisis and its aftermath have transformed the housing lifecycle of younger generations, illustrating how powerful unmet aspirations can be when we're deflected from what we see as the natural path to progress – and how difficult it will be to meet or manage those expectations.

Locked out?

The gaps in wealth accumulation between generations that we saw in Chapter 1 are, to a large degree, explained by the enormous boom in house prices over the past few decades. There is now an unimaginable amount of money stored in people's homes – about US$200 trillion, or three times as much as all publicly traded shares globally.[11]

In some countries, house prices have more than tripled between the 1970s and 2019, after taking inflation into account. For instance, prices have increased in real terms by 256 per cent in Ireland, 227 per cent in the UK, 212 per cent in Australia and 197 per cent in Canada. The figures are not as dramatic in the US, but an increase of 69 per cent in real terms has still pushed homeownership beyond affordability for many, particularly in the context of income stagnation. In 1975, it would have taken someone on the median wage nine years to save up a 20 per cent deposit for the median home in the US; today, it would take 14 years in the US as a whole, and up to 40 years in expensive cities like San Francisco and Los Angeles.[12] It is even worse in Britain: it would have taken an average family headed by a 27 to 30 year old just three years to save for an average-sized deposit in the 1980s; by 2016, this had ballooned to 19 years, partly the result of increased house prices but also stricter lending rules.[13]

It's no surprise then that younger generations are increasingly locked out of homeownership. This is especially evident in Britain (see Figure 2.1). Back in 1984, when the average Baby Boomer was in their late twenties, two-thirds of their generation already owned their own home. When Generation Xers were the same average age, in 2001, a slightly lower 59 per cent were homeowners. But by 2016, when the average Millennial was in their late twenties, only 37 per cent of them owned their own home. This is a precipitous fall in homeownership in the space of two generations.

We can see all three types of societal change – period, lifecycle and cohort effects – playing out in the diverging generational lines in this chart. The cohort effect is obvious for Millennials, who started

Figure 2.1: Percentage of adults in Britain living independently from their parents who own their own home or have bought with a mortgage[14]

out and have remained at a much lower level of ownership than older generations. But we can also see how ownership lifecycles have been utterly reshaped. There had been a clear pattern of ownership rates increasing as we aged, as shown by Gen Xers until the mid-2000s, when they looked set to end up at a similar level of ownership to the Baby Boomers and the Pre-War generation. But then the house price boom and subsequent credit crunch changed their course entirely. The flatlining in homeownership for Gen Xers since 2008 shows the life-changing impact of that huge period effect.

So it's not just Millennials who've had the housing ladder kicked away from them. Many more people in this middle-aged cohort are now facing very different living arrangements from those they could have expected, if they'd been born just a handful of years earlier. For example, the number of flat-shares among Britons aged between 35 and 44 nearly doubled between 2009 and 2014, and tripled for those aged between 45 and 54.[15] The comedian and actor David Mitchell, who starred in the long-running British sitcom *Peep Show*, called it a day after nine series, when he was 41, saying: 'Two middle-aged men sharing a flat like that, that's too sad. It's got to stop, because we've got older.'[16] Tragically, he would have been more on trend to keep it going: its depiction of a maddeningly claustrophobic domestic lifestyle and the despair that comes from surviving on a tight budget ('Butter the toast, eat the toast, shit the toast. God, life's relentless') is becoming an increasingly familiar portrait of middle age.

Apart from awkward flat-sharing, the inevitable consequence of decreased homeownership among younger generations has been a huge increase in renting. And in a country with constrained social housing such as Britain, renters end up in the more expensive and less regulated private rental market. Just 11 per cent of British Baby Boomers were renting privately in 1984, when they were, on average, in their late twenties. This had nearly doubled for Generation Xers in 1999, at roughly the same average age. And within a generation it has doubled once again, with 44 per cent of Millennials renting privately in 2016, again in their late twenties on average – and there is no sign of this declining.

The financial implications of this are truly life-changing. Across all types of tenures, housing costs have been increasing for decades. In the UK, only 9 per cent of the average Pre-War generation's income was spent on housing when they were in their late twenties. That figure is 24 per cent for Millennials. But it's worse for private renters, who now spend over a third of their income on rent, with no prospect of this enormous slice of their earnings generating any wealth. Instead, they are boosting the wealth of (mainly older) landlords.[17]

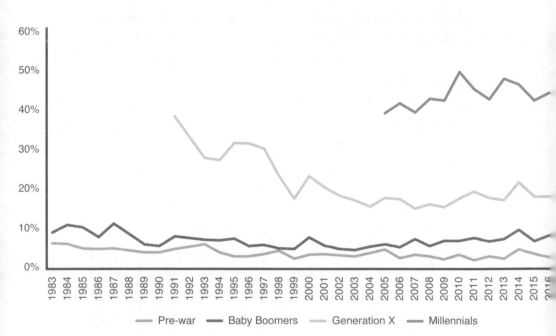

Figure 2.2: Percentage of adults in Britain living independently from their parents who are private renters[18]

The pattern of homeownership in the US, shown in Figure 2.3, is eerily similar to Britain's. In 2004, for example, 54 per cent of Gen Xers owned their own home when they were, on average, in their early thirties, a figure that was slightly ahead of Baby Boomers when they were the same age, in 1986. Homeownership for Gen X continued to rise steeply right up to the 2008 financial crisis and looked set to meet Baby Boomer levels, which had levelled off at around 80 per cent. But, as in Britain, Gen X homeownership then decreased and stagnated: now in their forties and fifties, they are well behind Baby Boomers when they were the same age. The housing and financial crisis occurred when Millennials were at an early stage in their potential homeowning years, and in 2018 they reached an

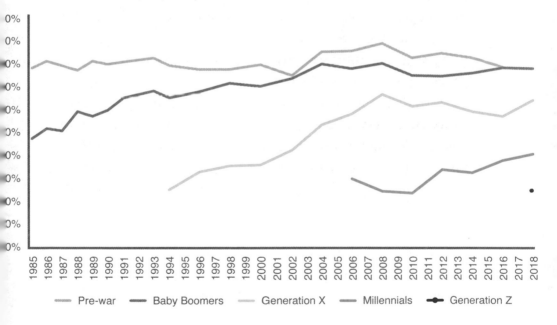

Figure 2.3: Percentage of adults in US living independently from their parents who own their own home or have bought with a mortgage[19]

average age of early thirties with just 41 per cent owning their home, significantly below Gen X at the same age.

Even countries that have a very different housing market are starting to show the signs of generational pressures on homeownership. In Germany, for example, rates of homeownership have traditionally been significantly lower than most other countries, and owning a home there has tended to come later in life. German Baby Boomers only reached peak homeownership (66 per cent) in 2012, when they were an average age of 57. The explanations for these differences flow from a long series of choices, going back to the rebuilding of the housing stock following the Second World War, including more sensitive regulation of and support for the private rented sector, stricter financing of mortgages and an absence of the government tax incentives that pushed people towards homeownership elsewhere.[20] German society chose to favour renting over owning to a much greater extent than many other countries, and ownership rates and house prices have been more stable as a result.

Up until recently, each successive German generation seemed to follow a very similar path, with Millennials tracking the homeownership trend line of Gen X. But new analysis shows that this is changing: just 12 per cent of 25 to 34 year olds now own their home, compared with 23 per cent of the same age group at the end of the 1990s.[21]

A broken market and broken dreams

The fact that homeownership among the young is even declining in Germany, where house price rises have been less extreme than elsewhere, suggests that the trend is about more than the market value of homes. Instead, decades of policy decisions helped older generations to buy homes – and then, when the property bubble burst, there was a push to introduce stricter regulation. For example, older generations in the US benefited from less restrictive planning regulations and tax relief on mortgage payments, while British Baby Boomers in the 1980s and 1990s were given the 'Right to Buy' council homes at a discount of up to 50 per cent of market value and with a 100 per cent mortgage guarantee.[22] Although the Right to Buy scheme continues, its terms are far less attractive and accessible. In the wake of the 2008 financial crisis, governments helped existing owners to avoid repossessions and then tightened lending rules for newcomers to the market. This happened in other countries, too.[23] Greater difficulty in getting a mortgage and larger deposit requirements are two of the main reasons cited for lower homeownership among the young in Germany, for instance.[24]

Ultimately, it is the interaction between these policies and changing economic circumstances that drives homeownership levels – although the generation-shaping breakpoint was caused by the 2008 crisis, pressures had been building for some time. These included the income stagnation we saw in Chapter 1, in addition to other financial burdens that fell more heavily on recent generations. For example, researchers from the Federal Reserve Bank of New York have found that the increase in education debt explains up to 35 per cent of the decline in homeownership for American 28 to 30 year olds between 2007 and 2015.[25] Nearly half of US Millennials borrowed money to pay for their education – ten percentage points higher than Gen Xers and more than 25 percentage points higher than Baby Boomers – and they also borrowed much larger amounts.[26]

Again, it is the *interaction* between when you were born and other inequalities that affects your chances of owning property. For example, in the US, the gap in homeownership rates between those who are more and less educated has tripled between 1990 and

2015.[27] A quarter of all Millennial homeowners in the US have had parental help with both their college tuition fees and the deposit on their home – although homeowners constitute just 3 per cent of the overall Millennial population.[28] This illustrates how a cumulation of advantages has flowed down a 'funnel of privilege' that only the luckiest enter.[29]

The consequence is more people renting into middle age[30] – and because the likelihood of buying for the first time decreases once we get through our forties, more people will rent into retirement, which has widespread implications. The Australian academic Alan Morris has charted the impact of private renting versus homeownership on older people. The higher housing costs cut into their pension, which results in them having less money for socializing and therefore feeling greater isolation and loneliness.[31] The idea that all older people are lonely is one of the laziest generational stereotypes, but it *is* true for some groups, and especially where resources are scarce or living arrangements are unstable. Morris's analysis identifies trends among a relatively small proportion of older people, but if generational changes in homeownership hold, they will become much more common in the next few decades.

There are many reasons why people prefer to own their own home – which can be expressed in terms of a home's *use value* (the value you get from using it), its *exchange value* (its stored wealth) and its *symbolic value* (including feelings of achievement, status and belonging).[32] There are also a number of specific behavioural benefits, including the fact that mortgages are a form of 'forced saving'.[33] Some of these benefits apply wherever you live, while others depend on national economics and culture. In countries such as Germany, many of the motivations for ownership are relatively weak; in the UK, the US and Australia, the motivations make homeownership a near-universal aspiration.

This wasn't always the case. It's true that for the past 20 years, roughly 80 per cent or more of people in every generation in Britain have said they'd prefer to own rather than rent their home, but before that there was much less of a consensus. In the early 1990s, only half of the Pre-War generation said they'd ideally like to buy. We have been socialized into thinking of buying as the clear best choice, and this began when prices started to take off.

Nevertheless, there is a real societal threat in the gap between aspiration and reality among younger age groups, and in the bleak future for the growing numbers of people who are locked out of the system. The geographer Joel Kotkin sees these recent trends as part of a return to something akin to a feudal system, where 'This generational gap between aspiration and disappointment could define our demographic, political, and social future.'[34]

The aftermath of the COVID-19 pandemic will most likely bring further disruption. In the early stages of the crisis, the focus in the UK was on the extent to which house prices were holding up or even increasing, bolstered by huge government stimulus packages that supported businesses and incomes, and direct support for the housing market, such as the stamp duty holiday. Analysts' predictions are for significant falls in property prices as the longer-term economic impact of the pandemic plays out,[35] but this may, once again, underestimate government desires to prop up house prices. We shouldn't count on there being a price correction to make housing more affordable for younger generations.

This is a cause for concern, because the financial pressures faced by renting pensioners will make them more dependent on state support: according to one calculation, it would increase the cost of pensioner housing benefits by over £3 billion per year in the UK.[36] This future additional cost should provide the impetus to improve the housing situation now.

Stuck in the nest

While owning your own place remains the clear aspiration in many countries, an increasing number of young people are not even making it out of their childhood bedrooms. The vision may be of a swish downtown apartment or a cosy suburban house, but the reality for increasing numbers of young adults is sleeping in their old single bed, surrounded by tatty posters of pop bands from their teens. As one 28 year old who had recently moved back in with her parents says: 'It's hard to feel like an adult when you're living with the people who used to brush your teeth.'[37]

Of course, living at home into adulthood is not uncommon in many countries. In fact, what stands out in the global data is the incredible variety of circumstances across the world. For example, around half of Italians aged 25 to 34 still live with their parents, compared with around 5 per cent in Norway and Sweden; the UK and the US fall between these two extremes.[38] For such a key influence on formative experiences, that's a huge range.

It is, however, a new reality that increasing numbers of families in many countries are having to come to terms with. As Figure 2.4 shows, around 18 per cent of American Gen Xers were living at home in 1999, when they were an average age of around 27, but this had increased to 31 per cent for Millennials of the same age in 2014. Millennials are finally moving out now that their average age is over 30, with only 16 per cent still living at home in 2017. But this is not the end of the trend: it looks as though Gen Zers are even more likely to be stuck at home than previous generations.

In the UK, the pattern is almost identical. Only 20 per cent of Generation Xers were still living at home in their late twenties, but this had increased to 31 per cent for Millennials by 2014. As in the US, British Millennials have started to move out as more of them have edged into their thirties, and by 2016 the percentage was down to

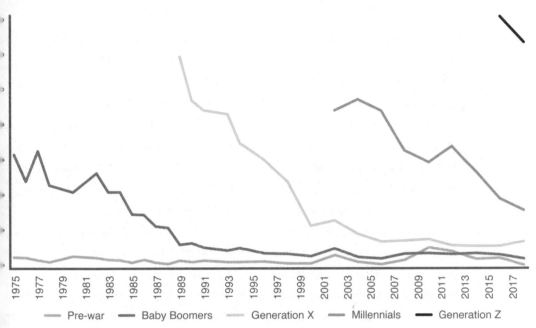

Figure 2.4: Percentage of adults in US living in parents' home[39]

19 per cent – but again, the trend is continuing with Gen Z. In total, *over 1 million* more young adults were living at home in the UK in 2019 than in 1999, which is an extraordinary change in how we live.[40]

We can even see a similar story in Germany. According to the World Values Survey, 40 per cent of German Millennials said that they were living with their parents in 2013, compared with 26 per cent of Gen Xers in 1999. The historical base level of young adults living at home in Germany may be higher, but the direction of travel is the same.

Sons are more likely to be living at home in adulthood than daughters, for all sorts of reasons: women tend to form relationships with men who are older than them, and men tend to have less access to housing benefits because they are less likely to be caring for children on their own.[41] But, contrary to how it is often portrayed, this trend isn't simply the result of increasing numbers of hairy, 34-year-old manboys living happily in their parents' basement playing video games. The big changes have been concentrated at the younger end of the age range, with significant leaps in the proportion of 25 to 27 year olds living with their parents over the last 20 years, now up to a third. In contrast, only 6 per cent of British 33 to 34 year olds were still at home in 2018, a figure that had barely changed since 1996. For the vast majority of individuals, this is more of a short-term coping strategy than a permanent lifestyle choice.

However, it does seem to be a lasting shift in how we live. Some even consider it a new life stage – 'emerging adulthood', as coined by Jeffrey Jensen Arnett, a psychologist at Clark University.[42] Arnett sees this as a distinct phase between adolescence and full adulthood, a time of identity exploration 'in love, work and worldviews' between the ages of 18 and 29. The theory has attracted some criticism from developmental psychologists, partly because it suggests it is an active choice rather than the result of a person's financial circumstances.[43] As one US study shows, individuals in households that had incomes in the bottom half of the distribution were less likely to move out before the age of 27 than those in the top half, and those who had homeowning parents were more likely to move out than those who didn't.[44] 'Delayed adulthood' is a better description than 'emerging'.

The reaction to this shift, particularly in countries where it's increasingly common, has not been very understanding. The subtitle to an infamous 2013 *Time* magazine cover story branding Millennials the 'Me Me Me Generation' was 'Millennials are lazy, entitled narcissists who still live with their parents'.[45] The term 'boomerang generation' implies that, no matter how hard their parents try, they can't get their kids to stay away. And a Pew Research Center survey from 2019 suggests that many people are not getting used to this shift, with 64 per cent of the American public thinking you should be financially independent from your parents by the age of 22 – when only 24 per cent actually are.[46]

Drifting apart

The fact that young people are living at home for longer in countries like the US and the UK, and the parallel increase in the number of multi-generational households over the last decade or so, should not been seen as all bad. It is a sensible strategy in tougher economic times, and in some circumstances it helps to bolster connections between generations.

However, this increased intergenerational contact is dwarfed by larger forces that are pushing the young and the old apart. Over the last century, the US has gone from being one of the most age-integrated societies in the world to one of the most age-segregated,[47] so much so that in many parts of the country, age segregation is as stark as ethnic segregation.[48] In one study, Americans over the age of 60 said that only a quarter of the people they had discussed 'important matters' with during a six-month period were 35 or younger; if they didn't count relatives, the number dropped to just 6 per cent.[49]

The separation of ages came from the gradual introduction of all sorts of reforms: formal education became finer-grained, from a single schoolroom to distinct stages; the workforce became specialized through industrial methods; young people moved to cities while older people separated into their own communities, as they went into senior centres, care homes and then retirement communities. As the author Marc Freedman, the architect of a number of intergenerational programmes, says, we began to 'warehouse' older people, who were 'viewed increasingly as useless drains on the economy, families and our collective resources'.[50]

This separation seemed to meet a latent demand. When the real estate developer Del Webb opened Sun City, America's first large-scale self-contained retirement community, in the Arizona desert in 1960, it promised 'greying as playing', free from the annoyance of younger generations. It was a way to forestall thoughts of mortality – as Freedman suggests, a nostalgic 'trip back to summer camp'. It might even have felt like a 'low-tech attempt at the fountain of youth' – after all, 'if everyone is old, no one is old'.[51] On its opening weekend, 100,000 people flocked to the new town, producing the largest traffic jam in state history.

This trend has become so widespread that it's easy to forget it is a relatively new phenomenon, in contrast with centuries during which generations lived in close proximity. As the Cornell professor Karl Pillemer says, 'We're in the midst of a dangerous experiment. This is the most age-segregated society that's ever been.'[52]

The US is far from alone in this. A study in the UK shows that, in 2001, just 15 local council areas out of 343 had an average age that was 10 per cent higher than the national average, while 17 had an average age that was 10 per cent lower. But by 2018, these figures had more than doubled.[53] As the authors of the report pointed out, we tend to characterize countries as either 'young' or 'old', but to do so hides the extent of variation within countries. For example, in 2015 there were 60 local authorities in the UK – mainly rural and coastal areas like North Norfolk – that had a higher average age than the oldest country in the world, Japan (at 46 years of age). At the other end of the scale, there were 23 local authority areas – including university cities like Oxford – with an average age lower than Chile (at 34 years of age), one of the youngest OECD countries.

Longer-running analysis stretching back to 1981 by the Centre for Towns, a British think tank, illustrates how new a phenomenon this is. Figure 2.5 shows the old age dependency ratio, which measures the number of people who are aged over 65 as a percentage of those of working age. There was little change until 1991, but since then

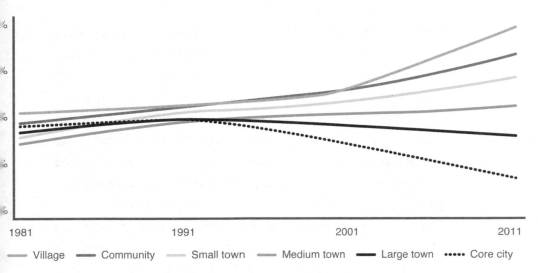

Figure 2.5: Old age dependency ratios in different types of locations in UK[54]

different sorts of areas have gone in different directions, with villages getting older and cities getting younger.[55]

What is causing this rapid separation of young and old? The average age of an area can only really be affected by a few factors: the rate of births, deaths, and immigration and emigration, either from other countries or within a country. And the analysis suggests that a combination of these effects is responsible, depending on which direction the area is going. Speedily ageing areas are particularly affected by a lack of immigration and the lower birth rates that result from fewer people being of childbearing age, while an influx of younger migrants from other parts of the UK and abroad are the key causes of cities becoming younger. This is also driven by the increasing concentration of economic opportunities in cities, along with their growing student populations.[56]

The physical separation of generations is affecting our ability to develop positive relationships with each other. The US social psychologist Gordon Allport pioneered 'intergroup contact theory', which is the idea that well-managed contact between different groups – if they have equal status in the interaction and common goals – can reduce stereotyping, prejudice and discrimination.[57] Time and again, and in different contexts, experiments have shown that this type of contact works: familiarity breeds positive feelings, not contempt. This approach has mostly been used across racial and religious divides, with much less focus on bridging the gaps between age groups. But the same principles apply, and the growing physical separation of age groups makes action increasingly necessary.

There are significant benefits to contact between different age groups, across all ages. Large numbers of studies have shown that seniors in retirement homes benefit from spending time reading to children and playing with them, while young people gain the chance to absorb wisdom and life experience.[58] These mutual needs of old and young are the basis of a number of excellent initiatives that bring different age groups together. For example, there is a trend for retirement communities in America being built near college campuses, allowing seniors to attend events alongside students, and some retirement communities are being built with schools incorporated. A 2018 study by Ohio State University and Generations United, a non-profit organization promoting intergenerational contact, established 105 shared-site programmes in the US.[59]

The evidence of the impact of these various initiatives is clear, but their scale is tiny relative to the magnitude of the trends pushing us apart. While these social entrepreneurs should be applauded, it's depressing that there hasn't been more systematic support from government, particularly since we've known about the problems for so long. In the UK, a 1949 report by the National Old People's Welfare Council said: 'It is essential that old people should not be segregated from the rest of the community, but that dwellings should be included as part of the general housing. This will prevent the feeling of loneliness and isolation from which the aged tend to suffer.' The problem has crept up on us because we have failed to pay attention.

Unmet expectations

Our collective memory plays tricks on us. This isn't just the blatant reimagining that some, like Monty Python's Four Yorkshiremen, indulge in to promote a heroic image of their own past. Instead, we misunderstand what is truly different now compared with the past, and we have a false sense that things were always destined to turn out how they have.

Our susceptibility to this 'hindsight bias' was brought to prominence in a seminal paper by Amos Tversky and Daniel Kahneman in the early 1970s.[60] It has since been shown to exist in all sorts of areas, from the financial sector to the judiciary and medicine. It's even been found in Wikipedia, where articles written before disasters barely mention the vulnerability of, for example, the Fukushima nuclear reactor to a tsunami, but articles written afterwards point out the inevitability of the outcome.[61] The same tendencies have emerged with governments' responses to the COVID-19 pandemic – all missteps look absurdly incompetent in retrospect, regardless of how justifiable they may have seemed at the time.

This hindsight bias infects our view of how and where we live. The increasing separation of old and young into different communities feels natural, when it is in fact an entirely new way of life. The good fortune of older generations, with their high rates of homeownership and the wealth this has brought them, now seems inevitable. The reality is that they neither had it entirely easy nor knew how uniquely lucky they were destined to be, relative to what would follow. The housing pressures when they were young led to some extreme measures that would draw a lot of attention today. For example, the BBC tells the story of young couples camping out in muddy fields for four days in 1964, in a bid to be first in the queue for a new housing development being built in Sunbury-on-Thames, near Heathrow Airport.[62]

There was no indication then that they were going to strike it rich, despite how it looks today. Indeed, there were times when homeownership looked more like a burden than a wise investment – for example, nearly 400,000 homes in the UK were repossessed between 1990 and 1996, after interest rates spiked to 15 per cent.[63] However, once something has happened, we are much more likely to believe that we 'knew it all along'. Our resentment at the apparent inevitability of Baby Boomers' good fortune is partly a trick of our minds.

Nevertheless, our generational lines demonstrate the massive scale of the deflections from the paths of previous cohorts. Expectations of independent living and homeownership have been raised far beyond any attainable reality, and this promises a lifetime of unmet aspirations. Given the importance of housing to our lives, this regression is a key factor that undermines our belief that we are making progress. Our own path is increasingly related to the resources we can draw on from our families. In fact, it is hard to see how governments can revitalize the social contract between generations without finding a solution to the homeownership problem.

Although the approach required will vary from country to country, it boils down to a choice between meeting current aspirations for homeownership and changing them. If we view the good fortune of older homeowning generations as a decades-long aberration that we can't sustain, then we are in for a difficult period of readjustment. Furthermore, given the higher cost of renting and the wealth gaps that would continue to grow between owners and others, we will be baking further intergenerational inequality into the system. Instead, our post-COVID recovery schemes should have housing at their heart if we are to 'Build Back Better'. This will not, however, be achieved simply through the supply of more homes to buy but will require a comprehensive range of measures. We need to support those struggling to get out of their childhood homes through an increased supply of social housing and a better regulated private rental sector, and we should help those trying to get a foothold on the ownership ladder by providing more direct support to those first-time buyers who can't rely on the Bank of Mum and Dad.

Chapter 3

Reaching Higher, Falling Flat

'There is ... a disconnect between young people, their hopes, goals and expectations, and what companies think young people want. I see my role as a translator.' This is the view of a self-ascribed 'generational consultant', who advises large corporations on how to better engage with younger members of their workforce. 'Generational consulting' has become its own mini-industry: in 2015, US companies spent up to $70 million on it, with some experts making as much as $20,000 an hour, and over 400 LinkedIn users describing themselves solely as a 'Millennial expert' or 'Millennial consultant'.[1] Of course, you may also call it, as a contributor to a *Wall Street Journal* article on the phenomenon suggested, 'a racket' built on 'pseudo-expertise, playing to bureaucrats' anxiety that they don't have their fingers on the pulse'.

It's easy to understand this sentiment when you see the insight being peddled by some of the consultants – and eagerly bought by major companies. The US retail chain Target gave managers a single sheet of paper with a guide to each generation's work style, view of authority figures and attitude towards balancing work and family. For example, managers were told that Pre-War generation workers liked to get 'personal acknowledgement ... for work well done', compared with the 'public praise' preferred by Millennials. Baby Boomers were deemed to be greedy in terms of salary expectations compared with

Gen Xers, who were said to be happy to trade money for time off. As a reporter who got hold of a copy of the guidelines said: 'Coaching tips for every single generation: patronise everyone in their own way.'[2]

In some respects, there is nothing unusual or especially egregious about this particular branch of consulting. Consultancy often involves giving advice a sheen of rigour using frameworks that may not be completely correct or based on particularly rigorous research. But this generational stereotyping has a destructive force. The money companies are prepared to pay provides a clear incentive for the exaggeration of generational difference, which is not just wasteful but harmful. The distracting 'insights' from this generational consulting also crowd out discussion of some of the biggest shifts between generations in modern times. We get clichés about today's young workers being particularly lazy and disloyal, which immediately collapse under scrutiny, but still divert us from real and dramatic changes in the worlds of education and work.

There are more important dilemmas than whether to give praise by email or in a group. And by carefully separating lifecycle, cohort and period effects on our experience of work and education, we can gain insight into important questions of social progress – whether higher education still pays, how increasingly precarious employment affects both young and old, and how AI and automation are set to transform the nature of work.

The most educated generation

When you ask people in Britain what areas of life they expect will be better for young people than for their parents, education is one of only four areas where more people still expect improvements than a decline. The only areas where the outlook is more positive are the freedom of self-expression, the ability to travel abroad, and access to information and entertainment.[3]

This relative optimism is based on incredible rises in education levels around the world over the past few generations, particularly in emerging economies. For the older generations in these countries, access to secondary – let alone tertiary education – was limited. China provides a particularly vivid example. Secondary school enrolment leapt from 64 per cent in 2006 to 94 per cent in 2016, and the increasing numbers of students completing secondary school has had knock-on effects. In 1999, just 6.4 per cent of China's young people were studying at a tertiary level. This number had more than tripled, to 21 per cent, by 2006, and nearly doubled again, to 39 per cent, by 2014.[4] The raw figures are staggering: 8 million Chinese students graduated from university in 2017 – ten times more than in 1997.[5] Until 1998, there were twice as many US students enrolling in higher education each year than Chinese students, but just ten years later, the situation had reversed. The expansion was far from an accident. Starting in 1999, the Communist government rolled out a series of reforms to increase both the rate of enrolment (at home and abroad) and the quality of secondary and higher education in China – it clearly worked.

Other countries have also experienced huge growth in higher education, even without this level of centralized planning.[6] Figure 3.1 shows the proportion of birth-year cohorts with a tertiary-level qualification when they were aged 25 to 34. The top bars are roughly representative of the older half of Gen X, the middle bars of the younger half of Gen X and the oldest Millennials, and the bottom bars of a large proportion of Millennials.

The pattern is the same in every country: each cohort has a higher level of education than the previous one, and there are some remarkable shifts. For example, in South Korea, 37 per cent of those born between 1966 and 1975 had a tertiary qualification in their late twenties or early thirties; a generation later, nearly 70 per cent did.

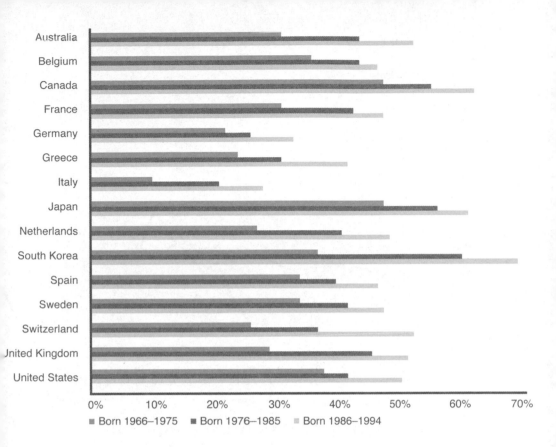

Figure 3.1: Percentage of 25 to 34 year olds with tertiary-level educational qualifications, OECD countries[7]

A similar near-doubling of graduate numbers can be seen in the UK. When that first half of people in Generation X were in their late twenties or early thirties, around one quarter had university degrees. At that time, Britain lagged way behind most countries, particularly Canada and Japan, where over 40 per cent of young people had degrees at the same age. But by the time the first wave of UK Millennials made it through to their late twenties and early thirties, the proportion with higher education qualifications had shot up to 50 per cent. Australia and Switzerland have followed a similar trajectory.

These trends can be seen in Figure 3.2, tracking what proportion of different generations reached degree level in Britain. Millennials

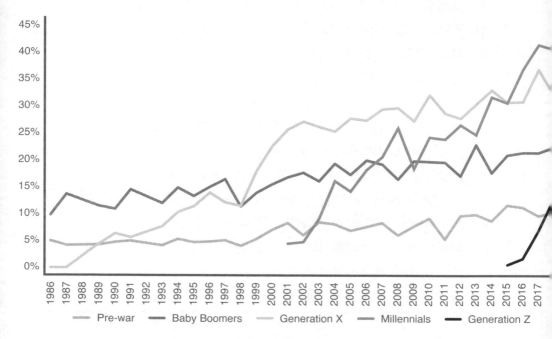

Figure 3.2: Percentage of adults in Britain with a university degree[8]

have already overtaken Gen X, and the gap will continue to grow in the next few years, as some in the Millennial cohort are still making their way through the education system. This is easier to see when you compare each generation at the same average age: for example, 40 per cent of British Millennials had a degree in 2018 when they were on average about 30, while only 26 per cent of Gen X had one at the same average age in 2002.

There is a similar pattern of expansion in the US, with only a few variations. There was a much later boom in university education in the UK, with bigger gaps between the Pre-War, Baby Boomer and Gen X groups than in the US. Older generations of Americans had much greater access to university than their British peers, and US Baby Boomers are on a par with Gen Xers in their educational qualifications. Some of this difference between the countries is due to America's GI Bill, passed in 1944 to help soldiers returning from the

Second World War to gain a university degree. More than 2 million members of the US Pre-War generation – nearly half of those who served in the Second World War and about 43 per cent of those who served in Korea – had taken advantage of the opportunity by 1956, confirming a tertiary degree as part of the American Dream. After Vietnam, nearly 80 per cent of veterans enjoyed the education benefits.[9] In contrast, the later surge in higher education in the UK is clearly visible in the Gen X line from the late 1990s onwards, following the commitment of Tony Blair's Labour government to get half of young people to university.

Another feature stands out: the slow but steady rise in the proportion of older generations with degrees. For example, in 1986, when the youngest of the Pre-War generation was 42 years old, just 5 per cent had a degree; by 2018, this was 10 per cent. This may look like a minor revolution in continuing education, but that would be a misleading interpretation. Rather, it is down to differences in education-related life expectancy – a more significant explanation. For example, men with a tertiary education can expect to live an average of seven years longer than those who didn't finish high school, due to a series of factors that drive unequal health outcomes for different social and economic groups.[10] Older cohorts are, on average, gradually becoming more educated – but, sadly, this is mostly because the less well educated die younger.

Despite these very long-term advantages, there are growing questions over whether the return on our increased investment in higher education pays off, both for individuals and for nations. A plethora of articles have asked whether it is still 'worth it', following the huge expansion in the number of people going through higher education and the equally significant increase in cost. In the US, for example, registration at a state university in the 1940s and 1950s cost around $300, and a year's tuition cost around $600[11], or around

$6,000 in today's money. Today, the average annual cost of tuition alone is around $20,000. The Federal Reserve Bank of New York calculates that the average student debt for a 25 year old more than doubled between 2003 and 2015,[12] with the total figure owed by US graduates a staggering $1.5 trillion. The class of 2017 owes an average of $28,650 each.[13]

Even with these frightening costs and the reduced rarity of a degree, on the face of it, university still pays. People with a degree earn significantly more, on average, than their non-graduate peers: in the UK, male graduates can expect to earn an extra £130,000 over their lifetime, factoring in taxes and tuition repayment, while the figure for women is £100,000.[14] The pattern is the same in the US. The 'average rate of return' for a university degree in the US has come down slightly in recent years, but it was still 14 per cent in 2018 – nearly double the rate of return for the same level of degree in 1980.[15] While university students often forego three to four years of full-time work to pursue their degree, their extra earnings pay off the costs in relatively little time, compared with the length of working life. In the US, the costs of higher education are paid off, on average, by the time graduates are 33,[16] a pattern also seen in other countries.[17]

These calculations are not the full picture, however. Firstly, this graduate dividend may reflect the pre-existing abilities or resources of graduates: they may have done just as well without their degree, due to their own skills or support from their typically wealthier families. There is some evidence that this does explain quite a lot of the difference. For example, the Institute for Fiscal Studies (IFS) in the UK calculates that the graduate dividend for men, once these factors are taken into account, is only 8 per cent.[18]

Secondly, there are huge variations depending on where and what you studied. Another IFS report has identified twelve institutions in the UK where graduates have earned *less* by the time they get to 29 than those who didn't go to university at all, and subject areas such as creative arts where the relative return is negative, regardless of which university you go to. In stark contrast, men who study medicine or economics can expect to earn an additional £500,000 over their lifetime.[19] Overall, while 80 per cent of graduates see a net return, 20 per cent don't. This variety of outcome is mirrored in the US, and helps to explain the varied view of graduates when they are asked whether it was worth it: a quarter each say 'definitely yes', 'probably yes', 'probably no' and 'definitely no'.[20]

Finally, there is the question of whether a degree adds value or skills, or is instead an expensive vetting process for employers, who use it as a signal of desirable underlying characteristics. The latter is what economist Bryan Caplan argues in his book *The Case Against Education*. When access to higher education expands, some seek other distinguishing characteristics – degrees at higher levels or from particular institutions – and others end up working in non-graduate jobs. Caplan draws an analogy with a concert. If a few audience members stand up, they will be better able to see the performance, but when those around them start standing too, the result is that everybody is less comfortable and nobody has a better view. The challenge is that it becomes very difficult to convince people to sit down, particularly (to stretch the analogy) new generations who are arriving at the back of the audience.

It's no surprise then that, despite the huge expansion of higher education, there is still significant appetite for it, particularly among the young. Levels of support have fallen away among Baby Boomers in Britain, for example, but around half of Gen Xers, Millennials and Gen Zers say they would like access to higher education to be increased. Few in any generation – at most around 16 per cent of each of the Baby Boomers and Pre-War generations – say they would like to see it *reduced*.

We continue to prioritize university education, in part because of the value we put on the broader experience, not just the economic payoff. At an individual level, higher education provides exposure to new ideas and people beyond lectures and tutorials, and the space to explore new interests, find new talents and develop broader skills. The benefits from this are hard to quantify, but some have attempted to measure the 'cognitive' benefits of attending university. Based on 30 years of research, the psychologists Ernest Pascarella and Patrick Terenzini show that those who attend university demonstrate greater development in critical thinking skills than predicted simply by their pre-university level and family characteristics. And it's not just what happens in the classroom that matters: out-of-classroom experiences contribute about half of the increase in critical thinking skills.[21]

This doesn't mean that returns aren't falling, or that better systems would not provide even greater benefits. In countries like the UK and US, we have become so focused on higher education that we have neglected support for non-academic education and training. As David Goodhart argues in *Head, Hand, Heart*, 'Isn't it better to widen the sources of achievement and to try to raise the status of "not university" rather than send as many people as possible to university, and in the process raise expectations of professional success that in many cases are likely to be disappointed, while starving the economy of the middling technical skills it needs?'[22] The rapid rise in young people with degrees is a success that should be celebrated, but it is difficult to make such a fundamental change without knock-on effects. Key among these effects seems to have been a neglect of those not following this route, and this partly explains why education levels have become such a key social divide.

Real change and lazy myths at work

The labour market has transformed in just a few generations. One of the clearest examples can be seen in the extraordinary increases in women's employment levels across just three or four generations, in nearly all countries.[23] For example, in 1941, only 22 per cent of Canadian women aged 15 or over were economically active, but by 2016 this had shot up to 61 per cent.

Immediately prior to the COVID-19 pandemic, the UK was at record levels of employment among the working-age population, at 75 per cent,[24] and this had been largely driven by increased employment among women. Each generation of women has made gains, particularly in their mid-twenties to mid-thirties, largely due to higher rates of employment during child-rearing years. For example, nearly 70 per cent of women Baby Boomers were employed when they were around 20 years old – but this then dropped down to 56 per cent by their late twenties. Employment rates for Gen X and Millennial women hit 70 per cent when they were slightly older, because of their increased participation in higher education, but didn't dip at all as they moved into childrearing years.

In terms of supporting higher female employment, the importance of shifting social norms on gender roles, reduced birth rates, better maternal health and increased childcare is clear from the fact that nearly all the generational increases in female employment are concentrated among married women. For example, the participation of married women in the American labour market went from around 30 per cent in the 1950s to around 60 per cent by the 1990s, explaining the vast majority of the overall change in women's employment rates.

The other major shift in recent employment patterns is the extraordinary rise of older workers. The US has seen a huge increase in the total number of people employed in the last couple of decades, up 22 million since 1998. But, as Lynda Gratton and Andrew Scott, authors of *The 100-Year Life*, point out, this has relatively little to do with the dynamism of Silicon Valley or the (largely invented) entrepreneurial obsession of today's young people.[25] In fact, 90 per cent of the increase is due to higher employment levels in workers aged 55 and over. And this isn't just because there are more old people – the biggest element of the change is the greater proportion of older individuals who are staying in or entering workplaces.

The employment rate for this 55-plus age group has doubled in the UK and tripled in Germany. Across Germany, Japan, the UK and the US, some 29 million jobs, from the 33 million created, have gone to these older workers. The change is particularly striking among older women: the number of working women aged 55 to 64 in Germany has increased from around one in four to two in three.

However, while employment has become more evenly spread by age and gender, work has become less secure – and younger generations are more often the victims of this trend. Youth unemployment is always higher than overall unemployment, but the young were hit particularly badly in the recession that followed the 2008 financial crisis. At the lowest point of the downturn, across 35 countries, over 20 per cent of young people were unemployed, while total unemployment remained at around 8 per cent. And some countries saw incredibly dramatic swings – for example, youth unemployment in Italy surged to over 40 per cent, while overall unemployment was around 12 per cent. The same pattern is playing out with the COVID-19 crisis. An incredible 25 per cent of young people lost their jobs in the first three months of the crisis in the US, twice the level of other age groups.[26]

Younger workers also tend to be affected first by structural changes in the nature of work, because they can't afford to be choosy when they're starting out in their careers. Millennials are, for example, more likely than older generations to be working in 'non-standard' or 'insecure' employment. One in 30 people in the UK workforce are on so-called 'zero-hour' contracts – a form of employment on demand that does not guarantee the number of working hours – but among people under 25, the figure is around one in ten.[27] These changes help to explain why overall earnings are often flat for younger generations, despite all those years of extra education. In some countries, such as Spain, Italy, France and the US, earnings are rising for most cohorts, but not nearly as much as they did in the past. And in other countries, such as Greece and the UK, real earnings have been falling for most cohorts, and each successive generation is doing worse than the last one at the same age.[28]

With this increased precarity of work and tighter finances, it's no surprise that young people who have permanent jobs are holding on to them as tightly as ever – in stark contrast to their image as disloyal job-hoppers. *Forbes* declared in a 2017 piece on 'Millennials and the death of loyalty'[29] that 'Millennials are coming to have no faith in the concept of loyalty. Instead, they're playing games of leap frog, going from here to there and staying on the move, thinking that when you stand still, you get crushed.' However, while it is true that young Americans spend less time with each employer – on average three years when they are in the 25 to 34 age group – than older employees, that has been true since at least 1983, when the young people were Baby Boomers.[30]

In fact, it's older workers who have become more mobile, with particularly big declines in long-term job tenures for those aged 55 to 64.[31] These figures are for all job moves, so some may have been forced rather than voluntary, but similar analysis in the UK looking only at voluntary moves suggests that redundancy is not the key factor. Millennials are 20 to 25 per cent less likely to move jobs voluntarily than Gen Xers were at the same age, and Gen Xers moved less than Baby Boomers.[32] Far from flightiness, successive generations are staying put longer – largely because secure jobs are harder to come by, and so people hold on to what they have.

This generational myth is even worse than the usual one of young people being blamed for changes in their situation – not only is it not true but changing jobs infrequently actually reduces your income. Being loyal is typically not good for pay progression – you need to move out to move up, especially in the early stages of a career. In 2016, the average pay rise for someone who stayed in their job was just 1.7 per cent, but a switcher received an average hike of 7.8 per cent.[33]

When younger generations aren't being wrongly accused of disloyalty, they are being called lazy. Laziness was cited on the *Time* magazine 'Me Me Me' cover, and is also one of the top adjectives associated with younger cohorts in our global survey of the public. These themes are frequently tied to the workplace, in headlines like 'Millennials work far fewer hours than our parents – so why are we much more stressed?'. However, they are based on a partial reading of the data that mixes up period and cohort effects.[34]

The reality is that the number of hours worked per week has fallen significantly for all age groups in the long term, reflecting shifting types of employment and increases in productivity. For example, the average working week in France in 1870 was 66 hours; by 2000 it was 37.5 hours.[35] In the UK, the normal working week during the Industrial Revolution was six days – the common usage of the word 'weekend' to refer to two days, rather than a single day of rest, did not appear until 1878, according to the *Oxford English Dictionary*.[36] The government didn't restrict the working day to ten hours until 1847, and that was only for women and children. These historical trends have continued into modern times; for example, the average weekly hours worked in Germany have fallen from 41.5 in 1984 to 39 in 2017. As Figure 3.3 shows, *all* generations are working fewer hours – this isn't about lazier younger

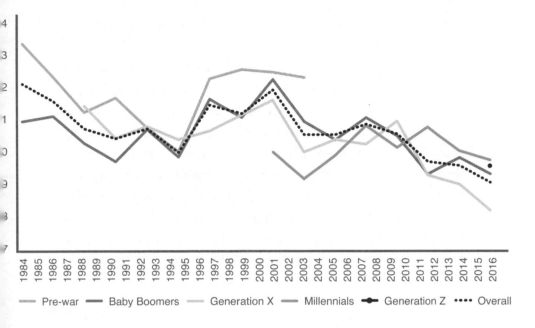

Figure 3.3: Average number of hours worked per week, including overtime, by adults in Germany[37]

people dragging down their more assiduous elders. And similar patterns are seen in other countries, including the UK.[38]

Indeed, younger people say they'd like to work *more* rather than less – if it means that they can earn more. Norway offers a typical example: each generation is more likely to be keen to work longer hours when they're younger, and this then declines as they age.[39] This seems to contradict trends that Twenge outlines among senior-year high-school students in the US, where there has been an increase in the proportions of those who say they 'don't want to work hard', from around 25 per cent in 1976 to around 40 per cent in 2015.[40] But the US data for the question on 'working longer to earn more' shows the same pattern as elsewhere, with the youngest adults keenest on the idea. It's easy for high-school kids to *say* they'd like to work less, but when they need to earn a living, they're at least as motivated as previous generations.

This doesn't mean that younger generations are driven purely by the financial reward that work offers. In fact, they are much less likely to agree that 'a job is just a way of earning money', as the example of Japan in Figure 3.4 shows. This also seems to contradict a trend that Twenge identified in the US, where there were big increases in the proportion of final-year high-school students who agreed that work is 'nothing more than making a living' between 1976 (Baby Boomers) and 2015 (Gen Z). But again, when they get to adulthood, the pattern in the US is the same as elsewhere: Gen Zers are the least likely to agree that work is just about the money.[41] This demonstrates the power of lifecycle effects that change the views of each generation as they go through various

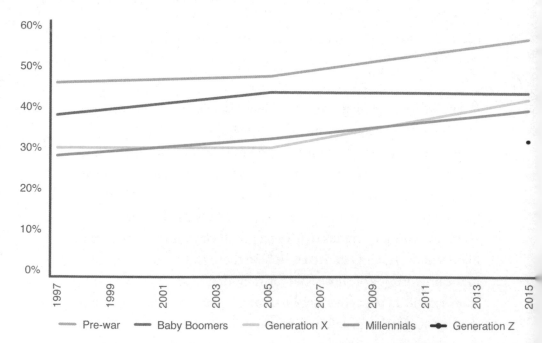

Figure 3.4: Percentage of adults in Japan saying that a job is just a way of earning money[42]

life stages – and the dangers of generalizing about what a generation of adults will be like from their views when they were kids.

The end of work?

The bigger question of what work is *for* increasingly occupies academics and policy-makers, as we face the prospect of a world in which there is a lot less for coming generations of humans to do, due to the acceleration of automation and AI. The list of affected occupations no longer includes only those we'd previously have viewed as 'routine' or easy to automate, but highly specialized roles we'd expect to require judgement and even intuition, such as medical diagnoses. For example, whereas a highly skilled dermatologist can draw on their hard-won skills developed over many years to determine whether a mole is cancerous, a programme can search through hundreds of thousands of cases and come to a more accurate diagnosis.[43]

Of course, we've been here before: many times in the past, people have been anxious about technological changes that, in the end, resulted in huge progress and continued work for humans. In Germany, when Anton Möller invented the labour-saving ribbon loom in 1586, Danzig city council didn't just turn down his request for a patent, they apparently issued an order that he should be strangled! More recently, great leaders and thinkers, from John F. Kennedy to Albert Einstein, have warned that automation will be the cause of a dislocation that may overwhelm their creators. But at each turn, so far, the growth created has far outstripped the direct loss of jobs.

But there are reasons to think it could be different in the future. In *A World Without Work*, the economist Daniel Susskind outlines how the impact of automation on the number and nature of jobs has always been a balance between the 'substitution' effect, where the machines take the work away from humans, and 'complementing' forces.[44] The latter lead to increased productivity, which makes goods or services cheaper, creating growth and wealth. As Susskind puts it, these innovations make a 'bigger pie', so there is more for humans even if the robots take some of it. These advances can also free up humans to provide goods and services that we can't conceive of at the moment.

However, Susskind believes that we will inevitably reach a tipping point in the balance between these substitution and complementing effects, because there seems to be no limit on the progress of technology. This won't come as a big bang, but a withering away. The end of work is likely to happen in spurts, where particular sectors are affected greatly, but overall it will be gradual, if relentless. A study by McKinsey & Company examined the trends in around 50 countries and across 800 occupations, and estimates that 400 million, or 15 per cent of all jobs, could be displaced by 2030.[45] And as with so much else, COVID-19 is likely to accelerate this existing trend, as businesses look to make their operations 'pandemic-proof'. Long-term social distancing measures, as well as the fear of future novel viruses, will make investment in robots a more attractive proposition.

The advice for us now is uncertain, because so much is unknown. Saying that one profession is safe while another is doomed fails to recognize how wrong such projections have been in the past. As Susskind points out, it's often not whole jobs that are automated, but tasks within them. We, therefore, need to be suspicious of the simple lists and league tables of 'zombie jobs' that the media and commentators love to focus on. However, we still need to prepare ourselves for a huge realignment, learning lessons from a careful understanding of the past. While the overall impact of progress in the Industrial Revolution was incredible, the short-term effects on individuals were often catastrophic – wages stagnated for decades, infant mortality rose and life expectancy fell. Even those who have an optimistic view of the future recognize that there will be what economists call 'frictions'. People's existing skills, their connection to their current occupation and their physical location mean they can't instantly pick up new opportunities.

On the surface, it might seem as though automation will have a genuinely generational impact, in the sense that it will hit particular cohorts much more than others. This could be dramatic, if it came about as a singularity moment, where the machines either launch a hostile take-over or free us from the burden of work. We could then be talking about a 'Golden Generation', with life full of meaningful leisure time, or a 'Terminator Generation' if things don't turn out so well. But given the more likely gradual nature of the shift, the impact will be spread over generations. And as with all major shifts in how we live, its impact will depend on where you are in your life and career. Older groups may struggle to adapt and retrain, while younger generations are likely to see those routine task-based early-career roles – which they depend on to get started – dry up.

The shocking scam of generational workplace research

With such transformational change in the pipeline, it's hard to believe that the focus of discussion about generations and work is so often on nonsense about how different each wave of new workers is. This is pushed by those generational consultants who have helped to popularize unfounded stereotypes through seminars called things like 'Dude, What's My Job? Managing Millennials in Today's Workforce'.[46]

Their advice usually starts with some big generalizations:

- 'Generation X are cynical and independent. Millennials are optimistic and focused on themselves. Gen Z are open-minded, caring, with a sense of integrity and tenacity.'[47] (These descriptors work just as well for star signs – incredibly, Taurus, Aries and Sagittarius respectively have exactly the same attributes. Maybe. I just guessed.)

They then move on to similarly sweeping workplace implications that flow from these character insights:

- 'Millennials like a collaborative workplace and might not be excited about Gen Z's desire to work independently. Millennials' group lunches, pod workspaces and collaborative projects may not be what many in Gen Z prefer.'[48] (Why can't Gen Zers hang out with the also independent-minded Gen Xers, and leave Millennials to their team-building exercises?)
- 'Praise is the name of the game. When it comes to Millennials, we're talking about a generation where everybody got a trophy, everybody got praised, and everybody got rewarded for showing up.'[49] (I also like praise.)
- 'The national surveys proved that Gen Z was not at all like the Millennials. In fact, they were quite different. One thing was for sure: Gen Z is ready and eager to kick some serious butt at work.'[50] (The surveys did not prove this, whatever it means.)
- 'Dream big with them. Dreams are a big part of a Millennial's life. They were encouraged to dream ever since they were children, and they keep doing it on a daily basis ... If they see that your dreams are not as big as theirs, it can be demotivating for them.'[51] (Generational consultants focus a lot on hopes and dreams.)
- 'The average attention span of a millennial is a whopping 12 seconds – and for Gen Zers, that number is an even more disappointing 8 seconds.'[52]

This last claim is an undying zombie of generational myths, which has been doing the rounds for many years now. First applied to Millennials and since bequeathed to Gen Z, there appears to be absolutely no reliable evidence to back it up. The most frequently cited source is a report in 2015 by Microsoft Canada's Consumer

Insights team, which in turn points to the Statistic Brain website, which provides no actual data on generational attention spans.[53] In practice, 'attention spans' are complex concepts. The tests by which they are usually measured aren't straightforward, and cannot give you one simple average in seconds for each generation.[54] In the end, there is no trend data that allows us to accurately compare the average human attention span in the way claimed.

Each of these stereotypes is risky and damaging as they colour our view of whole generations. As the American professors of organizational psychology David Costanza and Lisa Finkelstein have pointed out, 'generational membership' is not a protected category. While most people would feel uncomfortable saying that older people can't concentrate, that black people are cynical or that women are addicted to praise, it's acceptable to brand entire generations with the same attributes.[55]

So what truly generational differences do exist in the workplace? Virtually none. As a meta-analysis of twenty studies that focused on differences in job satisfaction, organizational commitment and intended job moves concludes: 'The pattern of results indicates that the relationships between generational membership and work-related outcomes are moderate to small, essentially zero in many cases.'[56] As Jennifer Deal, author of *Retiring the Generation Gap*, concludes in a *Harvard Business Review* podcast: 'Fundamentally, Millennials want what older generations have always wanted: an interesting job that pays well, where they work with people they like and trust, have access to development and the opportunity to advance, are shown appreciation on a regular basis, and don't have to leave.'

Not everything is generational

The separation of cohort, lifecycle and period effects is the best guard we have against falling for generational myths. Some of the clichés peddled as generational insight, such as those that focus on how different cohorts behave and respond in the workplace, are so gratuitous that they're easy to bust. Of course, people at different stages of their career are looking for different things, but there is no conclusive evidence that these lifecycle effects have shifted greatly over recent decades.

The danger of workplace myths is not just wasted time and money; they also allow companies to blame whole cohorts for employers' own failings. If companies have a problem with the motivation and retention of younger or older people, they should look to themselves rather than to magic answers based on astrological thinking. It seems bizarre that the workplace has been the context for the frothiest claims – it's almost as if there's money to be made in fabricating and then troubleshooting generational challenges.

Lifecycle effects, particularly at key transition points in our lives such as the start of our careers, pull us into line as we pass through them. This is important because a lot of the myths about each generation's attitude to work start early, drawing on findings from when they were still teenagers. Unsurprisingly, these differences are flattened out when people grow up – people change with experience in these formative years, and this often blows away unreliable signals from our teens. Mark Twain may not actually have said the following, but whoever did had a point: 'When I was a boy of fourteen, my father was so ignorant I could hardly stand to have the old man around. But when I got to be twenty-one, I was astonished at how much he had learned in seven years.'

The shame of these myths is that they distract us from the extraordinary recent changes in education and work, many of which have been truly generational. Women born just a few decades apart have had hugely different experiences of the labour market; older people today are staying in the workforce far longer than their parents did and younger workers face new forms of employment precarity. The incredible gradients in the generational lines for graduates should be a cause for celebration, but such a rapid change is bound to create tensions and raise questions. Most importantly, it has distracted us from supporting alternative routes in education and training. In future years, we need to see a similar growth path for young people completing high-quality apprenticeships and other types of technical education, to avoid a further widening of the divide in life chances.

Chapter 4

Happy Now

I t seems blindingly obvious that happiness should be a core aim of life. Even governments now see it as part of their role. Following the lead of Bhutan, France and the UK attempted to make 'Gross National Happiness' a national priority, alongside Gross Domestic Product (GDP). In 2019, the New Zealand government developed their first 'well-being budget'.[1] The United Arab Emirates now has a minister solely dedicated to implementing their 'National Program for Happiness and Well-being', and the UK has appointed a 'Minister for Loneliness'.

These latest interventions may seem like a logical response to a deep and constant human ambition to be happy – but the active pursuit of happiness is actually a relatively recent development. Looking way back, the Ancients thought that suffering was a natural condition. The Greek historian Herodotus grimly captured this idea in the fifth century BC: 'There is not a man in the world, either here or elsewhere, who is so happy that he does not wish – again and again – to be dead rather than alive.'[2] That's my next inspirational Facebook post sorted.

Historians generally agree that the notion that happiness is an attainable emotional state, rather than an earned outcome of a virtuous life, can be traced back to the Enlightenment. These changes accelerated in the twentieth century, with improvements in the basics of life, allowing space for greater emotional focus and a growing sense of individual entitlement to happiness. In the 1920s, a spate of books started appearing in America, with titles like *Happiness Is a Choice*, and *A Thousand Paths to Happiness*.[3] In later decades, happiness was tied to growing consumerism and formalized as a method of selling more stuff. Major corporations jumped on the bandwagon, such as Disney with its mission statement to 'Make People Happy', and Coca-Cola urging people to 'Have a Coke and a Smile'. Happiness also became a new aim of parenting. Work and obedience had previously been the focus, but parenting manuals began to include the well-meaning, if plainly wrong, advice that happiness is 'as essential as food'.[4]

These shifts reflect the acceleration of human progress in the past couple of centuries, as we have left behind millennia of subsistence and moved from 'survival' towards 'self-expression'. This comes with downsides, of course – the pressure to be happy can produce frustration when expectations aren't matched. The shuddering halt in generational progress has had far-reaching implications, including a loss of hope for the future among whole sections of society and even resulting in the tragedy of suicide.

We have developed our understanding of life satisfaction since the 1970s and 1980s, when psychologists suggested humans are stuck on a 'hedonic treadmill',[5] where nothing that befalls us, neither lottery wins nor losing a limb, will shift our individual happiness levels significantly in the long term. This now seems less clear-cut and, while there may well be a fixed component to our happiness, a baseline level that each individual will tend to hover around, it can move as a result of what happens to us. However, happiness remains a complex and mysterious subject, and a lot around it is still contested and unexplained. We are constantly looking for new and simple answers, but they often lead us astray.

This confusion is not helped by abounding casual myths and stereotypes around generations. We caricature whole decades as having different relationships with happiness, from the swinging 1960s, to the dour 1970s, the greedy 1980s and the hedonistic 1990s. We overlay these eras with cohort characterizations, from the stoic Pre-War generation, carefree Baby Boomers and morose Gen Xers, through to the emotionally damaged 'snowflakes' of today's younger generations. We hold exaggerated ideas of how our relationship with happiness changes through our life course, spurred on by sensationalist headlines on the anxiety of youth, the misery of middle age and the loneliness of the elderly.

There is often an element of truth in these different images of periods, cohorts and life stages, but we are poor at separating them out and understanding what is really important. As we will see, claimed 'epidemics' of suicide among the young, or loneliness among the old, give a greater sense of threat and change than the actual trends warrant. When we more carefully separate the different effects, it's often a less frightening picture than we're led to believe – but these myths can also obscure important, often tragic, realities.

One of these hidden truths is that a lot of the most important stories around happiness are not about the young or old, but those in the middle.

Midlife misery?

'This is the worst day of my life,' Bart Simpson groans. He'd earlier been goaded by Homer into skateboarding to Krusty Burger and back while 'fourth-base naked'. Bart was initially reluctant ('girls might see my doodle'), but had no choice when Homer threatened to declare him 'chicken for life'. It was going surprisingly well, until the police stopped him 'in the name of American squeamishness', and cuffed him to a lamp-post while they went for a burger. Homer, of course, arrived to rescue his son, bringing a T-shirt and socks, but, crucially, no pants or shorts. But while Homer had failed in every practical way, he did bring his usual reassuring wisdom, as he corrected Bart: 'The worst day of your life so far.'

And Homer is correct – the likelihood is that things will go downhill for Bart. This is not just because of the bad individual life choices or unfortunate paths awaiting grown-up Bart, where he's nearly always still mooching off his family or working through a fraught divorce. Beyond a cartoon character's imagined futures, there is significant evidence from a number of studies that younger people tend to be happiest.

The best-known model is the 'U-shaped happiness curve', where we begin adult life happy, bottom out at a low in our late forties or early fifties and then gradually get happier again.[6] Two of the key analysts of life satisfaction, Andrew Oswald, a UK academic, and David Blanchflower, a former Bank of England policy-maker, have examined this relationship for decades, across a huge range of countries and surveys. In his latest study,[7] Blanchflower covered 145 countries, and concludes: 'No ifs, no buts, well-being is U-shaped in age.'

Blanchflower finds that, in the dozens of richer countries included in his study, the absolute low point of happiness is at 47.2 years. I should confess that this is my exact age as I'm writing this chapter. It may help to explain my dark mood about the book-writing process – but looking on the bright side, by the time you're reading this, I'll be on the upward curve. I can recognize a lot of the features often held up as explanations for unhappiness in middle age. It's a life stage often defined by pressure, when we tend to be caught between responsibilities to kids, parents and careers, which puts a strain on time for ourselves and our personal relationships. We may also begin to reassess our lives; more is behind us than in front, and the reality doesn't always live up to what we dreamed of in our youth. The Irish comedian Dylan Moran boiled down Shakespeare's seven ages of man to just four, and perfectly captured the ennui in the middle: 'Child, failure, old, dead.'[8]

The relative consistency of Blanchflower's U-shaped pattern across many countries raises the intriguing possibility that this is a pure age effect that exists due to our biology. This explanation was reinforced in a study by Oswald and four other scholars, in which zookeepers and other animal caretakers rated chimpanzees' and orangutans' state of mind over time, in Australia, Canada, Japan, Singapore and the US. The apes' well-being bottomed out at ages that were comparable to between 45 and 50 in humans. As the authors conclude: 'Our results imply that human well-being's curved shape is not uniquely human and that, although it may be partly explained by aspects of human life and society, its origins may lie partly in the biology we share with closely related great apes.'[9]

The U-shaped happiness curve attracts significant controversy. Other studies find relatively flat lines, a U-shape with happiness trailing off again for the oldest group, or even *inverted* U-shapes.[10] These different results sometimes occur because studies are looking at different measures of well-being or are conducted in different countries: the U-shaped pattern is associated with more developed Western nations, while other parts of the world see variable patterns. But even in Western countries, it is hotly disputed. An exhaustive review of published research across economics, psychology and gerontology concludes that it is not possible to say with any certainty whether the happiness relationship is really U-shaped, because it depends on how you approach the analysis.[11]

There are three points that help us get to grips with the real changes in happiness as we age. Firstly, these analyses are not always a simple presentation of survey results. Most analyses, including

Blanchflower's study that led to the identification of 47.2 years as the height of misery, control for other factors that relate to life satisfaction, to try and identify the pure impact of our age on our happiness.

For example, we know that there is a relationship between happiness and characteristics like employment, wealth, health and relationship status. We also know that your place within each of these categories depends to a large degree on your age. Some analysts, therefore, take the view that, if we want to understand how *just our age* relates to our happiness, we should strip the effect of these other factors out of the data. This typically increases older people's 'adjusted' happiness, because they tend to have worse health and are more likely to be widowed and live alone. For example, Figure 4.1 shows one chart from Blanchflower's study that uses Eurobarometer data from 35 European countries, and you can see that the U-shape is more pronounced after these controls are included; without them, there is a much less dramatic bounceback in later years.

Some regard these controls as 'fiddling with the data', as it means the results don't reflect the actual life satisfaction levels of different age groups. Richard Easterlin, another prominent analyst of happiness, writes: 'If one wants to know whether a person is likely to be happier in his or her golden years than when forming families, one would not want to set aside the fact that older people are likely to have lower income, and be less healthy and are more likely to be living alone.'[12] This is true, but understanding the pure age effect is also useful. As Blanchflower points out, when we look at the risks to our health from smoking, we control for other factors that relate to both smoking and illness, such as income, in order to gain a true idea of the impact of smoking alone. The real problem is how the findings are reported, and the fact that they are simplified into those 'middle-age misery' headlines.[13]

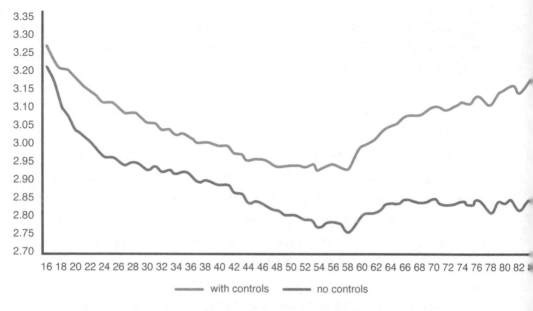

Figure 4.1: Life satisfaction (out of four) by age in Europe[14]

The second important point we need to understand is how big the midlife dip in our happiness actually is. The differences are statistically significant – partly because the surveys are so huge – but we also need to know what statisticians call the 'effect size'.[15] If you look back at Figure 4.1, you can see that, through the vast majority of our lives, we tend to score between 2.8 and 3.1 out of a possible 4. These small changes are not to be dismissed: from peak to trough, they may represent the average impact of becoming unemployed, for example. But we shouldn't interpret the dip as guaranteed midlife despair – it is simply a dip. Happiness doesn't vary hugely between most people, and our own individual happiness is pretty well established, regardless of circumstances, and we tend to be able to adapt when things do change.

The final point is that part of the reason for the conflicting results is that there are an awful lot of things that impact on our happiness levels. The focus is overwhelmingly on age effects, but other studies find a relationship between our happiness and when we were born (cohort effects) and what was happening in our countries at the time (period effects). The evidence for cohort effects is messy and inconsistent across countries, mostly because when you were born tends to have a fairly small impact.[16] One study stands out as an exception: Blanchflower and Oswald find that life satisfaction among US men decreased with each successive decade of birth during the twentieth century. We'll return to this pattern later, when we examine the growth of 'despair' in the US.[17]

There is more consistent evidence that particular periods of time are either happy or unhappy for entire populations of countries. Not surprisingly, the onset of the COVID-19 crisis had a particularly dramatic impact on happiness levels; for example, the proportion of people in the UK giving themselves the lowest score increased to 21 per cent as the lockdown started, compared with just 8 per cent at the end of 2019.[18] However, these scores also started to recover within a few weeks. Our happiness is resilient, even in extreme circumstances.

However, this is unlikely to be the end of the pandemic's impact on happiness. It is clear that there is a link between how the economy is doing and our life satisfaction, and that economic busts make us much sadder than booms make us happy. In a study of over 150 countries, the economists Jan-Emmanuel De Neve and Michael Norton show that recession years are significantly associated with losses in well-being, but that there is a much weaker relationship between positive growth years and increased well-being.[19] For example, when they draw on the same Eurobarometer study as Blanchflower, they find that our subjective well-being is around six times more sensitive to the negative effects of recessions than the positive impacts of booms. Greece provides an extreme example: life satisfaction there barely shifted from the 1980s through much of the

2000s, despite the economy growing by over 50 per cent. But well-being then plummeted to historic lows following the 2008 recession.

This asymmetry can partly be explained by the trends we've seen in earlier chapters: ordinary people have not benefited significantly from economic growth in recent decades, as wage growth has stalled, and downturns have continued to hit them hard. But it is also partly related to our strong 'loss aversion': we feel losses keenly, while we tend to bank gradual gains without really noticing them.[20] We also have a 'complaint bias' – when things are going well, we keep pretty quiet about it, in the hope that it continues or even increases. But when things go wrong, it makes sense to make our feelings known, in order to encourage change.[21]

You get a much clearer image of the relative importance of these competing age, period and cohort effects when you plot our happiness in generational lines. For consistency with Blanchflower's analyses, I used the same Eurobarometer data – and what stands out across countries is not a large midlife dip in life satisfaction, but rather how much it undulates for all age groups over time, with relatively small gaps between generations. There is only one clear and repeated exception: each generation of young people tends to start out notably happier than older generations.

Spain is typical of these patterns, as shown in Figure 4.2. You can see the rollercoaster of period effects among all Spanish generations, with significant falls around recessions in the early 1990s and in 2008, and then a gradual recovery from 2012. There is no clear sign of a cohort effect, where generations are different and stay different over time. There also doesn't seem to be much of a midlife trough; for example, Gen X don't become notably more miserable than other generations in recent years as they reach their late forties.

The one age-based pattern that does stand out is that as each new generation comes into the data, they start off as the happiest

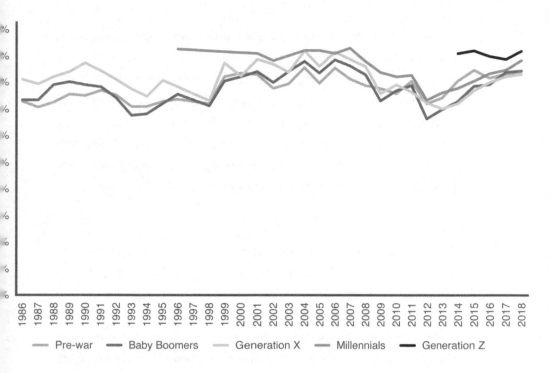

Figure 4.2: Percentage of adults in Spain who are very satisfied or fairly satisfied with the life they lead[22]

of all cohorts – before being dragged down into the pack. Gen X arrived relatively bright-eyed in the late 1980s, as did the Millennials in the early 2000s and Gen Z in the last few years – but these repeated waves of positivity soon dissipate. We see the same sort of pattern in the Netherlands, Italy and the UK, among other countries.

So, overall, the middle-aged can stake a decent claim to being the most miserable, but not by as much as some media reports imply. Because most of the models correctly assume that worse is to come as we age – in terms of our health and relationships – and control for this, this contributes significantly to our relative unhappiness. The data highlights significant truths about middle-aged angst and the resilience of older age, but the generational lines show how much is going on, both between groups and across time. Reassuringly, there is not much evidence of big differences between cohorts; instead, it's the repeated relative happiness of youth that stands out, regardless of when you are born. Despite all the difficult circumstances facing young people, there is no sign of a wholesale decline in happiness among our current generation of young people compared with previous ones, in the large majority of countries.

Are the kids alright?

This relatively rosy picture may seem at odds with concern for the mental health of younger generations. Headlines abound on how first Millennials and now Gen Z are the 'most mentally ill generation'[23] or 'so anxious and unhappy'.[24]

But this apparent mismatch between our data on happiness and the narrative that is presented in the media is not a straightforward generational myth. While happiness and mental health are clearly related, they are distinct dimensions of human experience.[25] For example, those with a severe mental illness can still have a high level of well-being, if their condition is managed well. And even where mental health conditions do reduce an individual's happiness, they still affect only a relatively small proportion of the population, and these trends may not move the average happiness level for young people as a whole.

This seems to be what's happening in the US. A 2019 study by Jean Twenge and colleagues[26] shows that the proportion of US adolescents reporting symptoms consistent with major depression in the last 12 months increased from 8.7 per cent to 13.2 per cent between 2005 and 2017. Young adults saw an almost identical trend, in both major depressive symptoms and serious psychological distress. There were no corresponding increases among other age groups over this period – it looks like a pattern that's emerged among the current generation of young, rather than a more general period effect.

These are large proportional increases in severe mental health conditions, but as they only affect relatively small proportions of the young, they don't mean that young people are, on average, less happy than older groups. Indeed, Twenge shows in her book on Gen Z that overall happiness levels have remained relatively high among young people.[27]

The picture for young people in England is starting to show worrying parallels with the US. Figure 4.3 traces our generational lines from 1991 to 2016 on a measure called the General Health Questionnaire-12 (GHQ-12), part of the Health Survey for England. This widely used measure covers twelve items on general levels of depression, anxiety, sleep disturbance and self-confidence; Figure 4.3 charts people with a total score indicating a high likelihood of a common mental health disorder.[28]

For the most part, different generations hover around the same level throughout the period, and there are few significant changes (with a notable blip in 2009, following the global financial crisis). There is, however, an indication that something may be different with Gen Z. Over a fifth of this latest generation of young people (22 per cent) are starting out adult life with signs of a common mental health disorder, compared with 15 per cent of Millennials back in 1998, when they were the same average age.

This is just a single data point that uses a simple, non-clinical survey measure of possible mental health disorders, so we should be cautious about placing too much emphasis on its results. However, it is reinforced by other British studies, which also suggest that, underneath this overall trend, there is a particularly worrying pattern for recent generations of young women and girls. For example, the Mental Health of Children and Young People survey uses a detailed

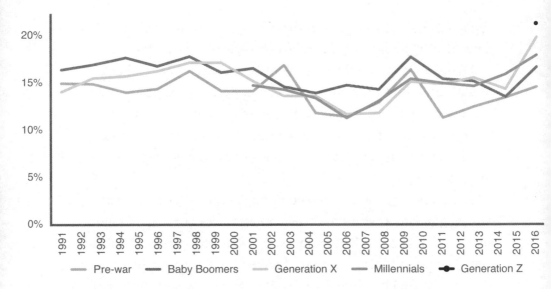

Figure 4.3: Percentage of young people in England with a score of 4 or higher on the GHQ-12 measure of common mental health disorder[29]

diagnostic tool for mental disorders, and all cases are reviewed by clinically trained professionals. Again, on first glance, it is not that worrying. Emotional disorders, such as anxiety and depression, did increase among children aged between 5 and 15, from around 4 per cent in both 1999 and 2004, to around 6 per cent in 2017. But there are some startling differences between age groups and genders, with 22 per cent of girls and young women aged 17 to 19 classified as having an emotional disorder.[30]

Other studies in England suggest that this is an emergent trend, such as the Adult Psychiatric Morbidity Survey, which includes people aged 16 to 24. As Figure 4.4 shows, there has been a stark increase in girls and young women classed as having severe anxiety or depression, from under 10 per cent in 1993 and 2000 to around 15 per cent by 2014, while the figures for boys and young men have barely changed. The study also highlights the extraordinary rise in

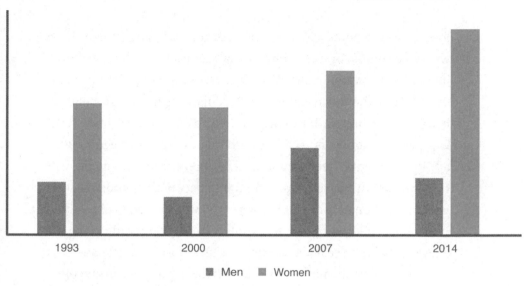

Figure 4.4: Percentage of people in England aged 16 to 24 with severe anxiety and depression[31]

reports of self-harming over the same period, from around 6 per cent of girls and young women to nearly 20 per cent, with the figure for boys and young men also increasing but to a much lower level of around 8 per cent.[32]

These gender-specific findings are eerily similar to results in the US, where the prevalence of major depressive episodes shot up for teenage girls, from around 12 per cent in 2011 to around 19 per cent by 2015, with boys remaining quite stable at around 5–6 per cent.[33] The overall trends in Britain are maybe less marked, but it seems to be following a worryingly similar path. And nor is this just a UK and US phenomenon: the World Health Organization has flagged its concern about the 'increasing rate of mental health and behavioural problems' in adolescents and young people across Europe.[34]

Early reviews of the mental health impact of the COVID-19 pandemic suggest that the direct effects of social isolation and the longer-term repercussions on the economy will accentuate these worrying trends. In fact, a number of studies have already shown increases in mental health disorders across the population.[35] The president of the Royal College of Psychiatrists in the UK believes it will be the 'biggest hit to mental health since the second world war', with as many as 10 million people thought to need new or additional mental health support as a direct result of the crisis.[36] However, as with so much around the impact of the pandemic, this is disproportionately affecting those who were already vulnerable[37] – including children and young people. One tracking study in the UK shows that 18 to 24 year olds are twice as likely to feel 'hopelessness' as a result of the pandemic, compared with the population as a whole.[38] How these huge shocks impact on people is largely determined by much slower, longer-term shifts.

One culprit in particular is often blamed for this shift among the current young generation: the advent of the smartphone and social media. Jean Twenge believes this is the 'worm at the core of the apple', and she's not alone. In the UK in 2019, the Health Secretary Matt Hancock proposed a new law banning under-13s from using social media, citing the impact on their mental health. And the head of the NHS, Simon Stevens, was unequivocal in pointing the finger at technology companies and social media platforms for leaving 'the National Health Service to pick up the pieces – for an epidemic of mental health challenge for our young people'.[39]

On the surface, the evidence seems clear-cut. For example, my own analysis of British data shows that children who spend three or more hours on social networking sites on a weekday are over twice as likely to have mental disorder symptoms than those who spend no time on them (27 per cent compared with 12 per cent).[40] Other studies show even larger effects for high-level users. For example, one study of over 10,000 14 year olds shows that 12 per cent of light social media users and 38 per cent of heavy social media users had depressive symptoms.[41] This explanation is particularly tempting because it also provides a logical rationale for the growing gap between girls and boys: 40 per cent of girls use social media for three or more hours a day, compared with only 20 per cent of boys.

It seems like a closed case – but it's not.

In the first place, these associations don't account for other factors that could cause both higher social media use *and* mental health issues. When researchers include a wider range of factors in their models, the impact of social media and technology becomes much less dramatic. In one major study covering over 350,000 interviews in the UK and the US, smoking marijuana and bullying, for example, have much larger negative associations with adolescent well-being than technology use.[42] And simple activities, such as getting enough sleep and regularly eating breakfast, have much more positive associations with well-being than the average impact of reduced technology use.

In fact, the association between well-being and regularly *eating potatoes* was nearly as negative as the association with technology use – but it's much harder to find articles bemoaning how potato consumption is 'destroying a generation'.[43]

A separate UK government study, focusing specifically on the impact of social media, also shows its use was only marginally related to psychological health when the researchers controlled for other factors.[44] The positive effect of getting enough sleep and seeing friends was about three times larger, and the negative effect of being bullied, whether online or offline, was about eight times larger. When the researchers accounted for these other factors, social media use had a minimal unique association with psychological health.[45]

In the end, the best conclusion is that social media use has a relatively small association with well-being for children and young people overall. While there may be stronger links between social media and mental health among specific groups, such as teenage girls, there is evidence that it is the wider effects associated with high use that are more important. For example, time spent on social media is associated with more sedentary behaviour, which is related to a range of poor health outcomes. Social media may also expose young people to more opportunities for bullying and it might also interfere with sleep hygiene, both of which are associated with mental health problems, including depression. You might think that limiting social media use is a good idea if it improves sleep and activity levels and reduces bullying. However, the crucial point is that social media use is not even a particularly good predictor of these mediating factors, when you compare it with other effects relating to a young person's family and social life, their financial, social class and educational situation, their genetics, and so on.

It is vitally important that we get this right, as there are significant risks in being wrong. There is little in the current evidence to suggest that encouraging parents to take away mobile phones, or legislators to bring in laws on the use of social media platforms, will significantly reduce the problem. Our tendency to accept a simple answer that seems right is a strong human trait, but these are complex issues where there is hardly ever a single solution. Even with all the details we know about young people across these studies, we can only explain around 30–40 per cent of the variation in happiness levels. There is a lot that we just don't know.

We need to be particularly suspicious of simple answers to big questions when they relate to an emergent technology. 'Moral panics' ensuing from all sorts of innovations have been repeated throughout history – everything from the mass translation and printing of the bible to novels, bicycles, electricity and violent video games have been seen as threats to the established social order. At its root, this is a deeply generational phenomenon. New generations are more proficient at adapting to innovation, which can create a perception among older generations that they are losing control of the culture they helped shape.[46]

I was surprised by the certainty of senior politicians and officials in their calls for legislative action on social media, given the paucity of evidence, but it's a repeated pattern. In 2005, Hillary Clinton attempted to introduce a bill to strengthen the regulations on violent video games, citing evidence that they 'increase aggressive behavior as much as lead exposure decreases children's IQ scores'.[47] But the Supreme Court ruled that the evidence did not support the action. Clinton was far from the first to call attention to a threat from video games. In 1983, the US Surgeon General suggested that games like Asteroids, Space Invaders and Centipede were a leading cause of family violence.[48] The reason that older examples of these panics sound more ridiculous to us than the latest ones is *not* that the world is getting worse – it's just that we're getting old.

Only the lonely

It's understandable why the head of the NHS in the UK would talk about a 'mental health epidemic' among young people – even prior to the COVID-19 pandemic, which seems set to accelerate the trend. The increase in prevalence that we'd already seen, although just a few percentage points, represents hundreds of thousands of additional young people accessing support, which places an enormous strain on already stretched services.

However, the hundreds of media articles over the last few years that claim we have been experiencing a 'loneliness epidemic' are more misleading. Sometimes the epidemic was focused on young people[49] and sometimes the old[50] – both versions are becoming increasingly accepted truisms across many countries. This is strange, because the evidence is almost entirely absent. I would love to present a compelling generational chart of a loneliness measure, but I have been unable to find data for the general public in any country over a long period of time.

The trend data that does exist tends to be for specific sections of the population and suggests that there has been little change over the long term. For example, a study by a group of US psychologists and social scientists examined whether loneliness is greater among Baby Boomers relative to a Pre-War cohort; they find no evidence that loneliness is substantially higher among the Baby Boomers, or that it has increased over the past decade.[51] Studies of other rich countries have yielded similar results. In Sweden, repeated cross-sectional surveys with adults aged 85, 90 and 95 years have found no increase in loneliness over a ten-year period.[52] Using data from the Berlin Aging Study, researchers find that loneliness levels are substantially *lower* among 75 year olds in more recent birth cohorts, while another study finds lower rates of loneliness in more recent Finnish cohorts of 70 year olds compared with earlier ones.[53]

At the other end of the age spectrum, a team of psychologists analysed long-term trends among teenagers in the US and have found no signs of increasing loneliness between 1976 and the 2010s. In fact, they found a statistically significant *decline* in loneliness among high-school students, but the size of the effect was small.[54]

Loneliness does vary between age groups, but these patterns seem to be constant over time. Perhaps surprisingly, given the focus in recent years on loneliness among the old, it is clear that younger adults are more likely to feel lonely, as studies in the UK, US, New Zealand and Japan confirm.[55] You can see this from generational lines from a study in England, in Figure 4.5. This is too short a run of data to tell us anything about generational change, but you can see why a casual reading gives rise to headlines about rising loneliness among

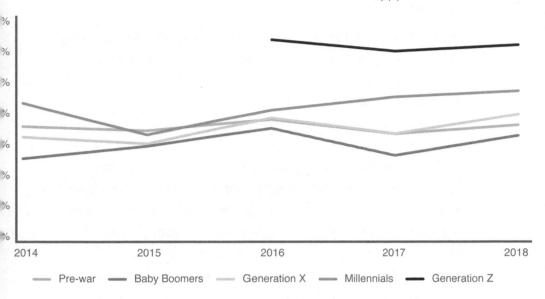

Figure 4.5: Percentage of adults in England who say they 'sometimes' or 'often' feel lonely[56]

young people: Gen Zers are around twice as likely to say they feel lonely than older age groups. However, the scant evidence available suggests that this is the norm for young people.

At a personal level, it's easy to recall feelings from our own youth that suggest why the young feel loneliness the most – it's a time in life when socializing is very important to us and social isolation hurts greatly. Loneliness, properly defined, is the subjective discrepancy between our actual and our desired level of social connection: it depends on our expectations.

Even with this more precise definition, it may seem surprising that there is not at least some evidence of a long-term increase in loneliness, given the huge changes in how we live. As the sociologist Eric Klinenberg puts it, 'our species has embarked on a remarkable social experiment'. Humans are now living apart more than at any time in our history.[57] For example, 2018 estimates from the US Census Bureau show that 28 per cent of all US households are made up of a single person, compared with just 9 per cent in 1950.[58] And this is a common pattern across countries. My own analysis of Eurobarometer data from over 30 countries shows an increase in single-person households from 11 per cent in 1971 to 24 per cent in 2019.

Solitary living is not an entirely recent phenomenon then, and has caused waves of similar concern over many decades. As Julianne Holt-Lunstad, a US psychologist who has focused on the impact of loneliness, explains: 'We have worried about loneliness since the rise of industrial society. Since we started moving away from the village and we agglomerated into towns where we didn't know as many of our neighbours, we worried about loneliness ... We worried about the loneliness of apartment dwellers, of people driving in cars, of people who went to movies, of people who got the telephone instead of going into social life.'[59]

Drawing on a similarly long-term perspective in *A Biography of Loneliness: The History of an Emotion*, the British historian Fay Bound Alberti suggests that loneliness is a product of our industrialized society, noting that the term hardly ever appeared before 1800.[60] Modern loneliness, in Alberti's view, is the product of capitalism and secularism, and is caused by the divisions between 'the self and the world' that have developed since the eighteenth century. Living alone and feeling alone have been driven by the politics and economics of individualism. As with so many of the other patterns we've seen, the most important trends are the result of long-term cultural evolutions rather than overnight epidemics.

This is not to say that the effects of loneliness are unimportant. The American psychologist John Cacioppo has produced some of the most important work in understanding its mechanisms and impact, and he likens it to a biological drive that is similar to hunger or thirst.

Loneliness plays a useful role in motivating us to seek out others, because throughout our history, being around others has been a form of protection and a more effective use of effort. The feeling of loneliness can also increase our sense of threat, which can in turn lead to biological responses, like higher blood pressure.

Beyond these direct biological impacts, some researchers see loneliness as being behind other destructive behaviours. As Vivek Murthy, the former US Surgeon General and one of the people raising the profile of the impact of loneliness, explains: 'When I began my time as Surgeon General, I started to recognize that many of the stories that I was hearing from people in small towns and big cities all across America were stories about addiction, about violence, about depression and anxiety. But behind them were threads of loneliness.'[61]

There have been some eye-catching studies that seem to confirm these dire consequences of loneliness – including one suggesting that loneliness is as likely to kill you as smoking 15 cigarettes a day. The claim has been used by many people making the case for the importance of loneliness, including Murthy. The source of the claim is a meta-analysis of 148 studies across North America, Europe, Japan, China and Australia.[62] The study finds that people who were more socially connected had a 50 per cent increased chance of survival over time than those who had low social connections, a figure that is indeed comparable to quitting smoking. Crucially, however, the researchers were measuring the impact of *all* social connections rather than loneliness specifically. This included a wide range of measures – for example, whether subjects received practical support from others, and their perceptions of how supported they were, as well as whether they were married, the size and depth of their network of friends and whether they lived alone. We also need to remember that these studies can only prove an association rather than a causal relationship. The comparison with smoking is eye-catching, but it's difficult to be as sure about the causal link.[63]

However, given its prevalence and likely importance, paying more attention to loneliness is ultimately a good thing, even if the epidemic rhetoric is sometimes overblown. Raising the profile of a relatively hidden issue may be a benefit in itself, and the impact of COVID-19 may actually help, in bringing the discussion to the fore. Tracey Crouch, the first 'Minister for Loneliness' in the UK, says: 'I think we are in loneliness where we were with mental health a decade ago. People didn't talk about poor mental health, whereas now we are removing the stigma.' We need to use this increased focus to take action that builds practical and emotional connections between people. This includes supporting places where people can meet and interact, and finding new ways to reach the right people. For example, a significant proportion of visits to doctors have their root cause in loneliness; as Crouch suggests, 'social prescribing', where people can be connected to local organizations that can provide support networks, might be more effective than pills.

Killing ourselves slowly

I have much less sympathy with claims that we are facing yet another 'epidemic' – of suicide among young people. For example, a *Sunday Times* headline in 2019 called Gen Z a 'Suicidal Generation', citing a doubling in the death toll among teenagers in the UK over the previous eight years. However, as the journalist Tom Chivers succinctly puts it, this reading of the data and the broader claims of an epidemic are 'absolute bollocks from top to bottom'.[64]

The first point to bear in mind is that suicide is incredibly rare. Fewer than seven in 100,000 young people kill themselves each year in the UK, a lower rate than for just about any other age group. In contrast, for example, around 18 in 100,000 of those aged 45 to 49 killed themselves in 2018. The common misconception that suicide is more of an issue among young people is partly because it *is* one of the top killers among the young – after cancer, it's the most common cause of death in teenagers across many countries, including the UK, Canada, the US and Australia – but this is mostly because young people don't die very often.

Of course, the focus on youth suicide is in some ways understandable because of its rarity, and because each case is a particular tragedy, given how much life each victim had ahead of them. It would be a real concern if the rate really was consistently doubling, but examination of the data shows this to be a gross misdirection. The *Sunday Times* article picked the lowest available point to compare the latest figures against, in order to show the largest possible short-term increase. When you look at the actual trends, as in Figure 4.6, the real pattern has been a long-term decline in suicide among younger people, from a high in the late 1980s and 1990s.[65]

The danger of this sort of sloppy reporting is that it distracts us from the real pattern in the data. This is much clearer in striking analysis by the UK's Office for National Statistics (ONS), which plots suicide by age over the long term.[66] In the early 1980s, suicide was spread across all age groups in the England and Wales population and, if anything, affected those in their sixties and seventies more. But from around 1986, a wave of higher suicide rates started to make its way through the age ranges, starting with a peak for people in their early twenties, exactly when those born at the start of Gen X would have reached this age. By 1998, the peak shows up when people are in their late thirties, and in 2018 it straddled those in their forties and fifties. Each of these points mark a perfect trail of Gen X making their way through life. I've been trying to identify cohort effects for over a decade, and this was an awful one to find. Gen X, sadly, can be much more accurately described as 'the suicidal generation'.

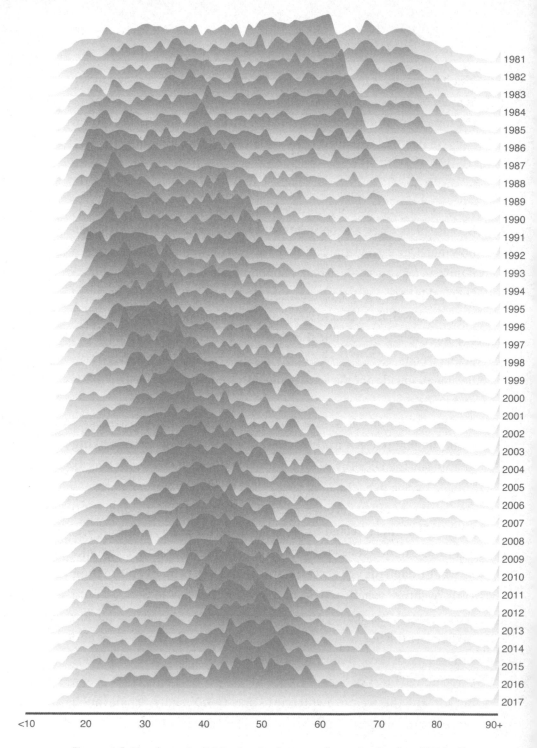

1981
1982
1983
1984
1985
1986
1987
1988
1989
1990
1991
1992
1993
1994
1995
1996
1997
1998
1999
2000
2001
2002
2003
2004
2005
2006
2007
2008
2009
2010
2011
2012
2013
2014
2015
2016
2017

<10   20   30   40   50   60   70   80   90+

Figure 4.6: Number of suicides by single year of age, England and Wales[67]

Of course, this is still a grossly overblown epithet; even among this cohort, suicide is still extremely rare, and it varies hugely between men and women and rich and poor. For example, in the latest figures for 45 to 49 year olds, men make up three-quarters of all cases. Suicide rates are also over twice as high in the most deprived areas of the UK than in the least deprived.[68] It seems that being born a man, in a poor area of Britain and as part of Gen X is a particularly toxic combination.[69]

As for why there might be such a strong cohort connection between Gen X and suicide, one theory relates to the 'middle child' position of Gen X: they straddle two distinctive cultural and economic periods, and some have ended up getting the bad from both. They've borne more of the brunt of economic stagnation and austerity than older UK cohorts, but are more reticent in seeking help when they're struggling than younger cohorts.[70]

Another sad element of the Gen X story is shown in further analysis by ONS, tracking deaths from drug poisoning. These trace the same horrible path, following Gen X over time – the peak of drug deaths moves from people in their early twenties in 1992, to those in their mid-forties by 2017.

This might be explained by the greater availability of opioid drugs, particularly heroin, from the 1980s in the UK, just when Gen Xers were coming into their teenage years. Heroin was responsible for over half the deaths from drug poisoning in 2017.[71] A further lifecycle element makes this increasingly tragic over time. Deaths from drug poisoning in each year cohort within Gen X have tripled, from around 50 in the early 1990s to around 150 now. The ONS report speculates this could partly be a lifecycle effect: the older bodies of drug users from this generation are less able to cope with the effects of long-term use.

Economists Anne Case and Angus Deaton have shown that these apparently separate phenomena of suicides and drug poisonings are connected in the US. They suggest that the relationship between them is blurred, given the difficulty of identifying motives in deaths caused by drugs and the reticence to classify any death as suicide. Their suggestion is that, along with deaths related to alcoholism, they should be considered 'deaths of despair', which are increasing hugely in the US.[72] These self-destructive trends are having an extraordinary impact on sections of US society, and are even affecting overall levels of life expectancy, which, after decades of consistent improvement, have started to *fall* in the US. Their analysis shows that, rather than being a population-wide phenomenon, the reversal was concentrated almost entirely among less-educated white people.

Case and Deaton show that 'deaths of despair' among white men and women aged 45 to 54 without a bachelor's degree tripled between 1990 and 2017, while there was little change for middle-aged white American graduates. They focus their analysis on middle age, but the cohort effect in the US is quite different from the one I've just described in the UK: each cohort is doing progressively worse than the one preceding it. For example, at 45 years old, white Americans without a bachelor's degree from the cohort born in 1960 faced a 50 per cent higher risk of dying from suicide, drugs and alcohol than those from the 1950 birth cohort, while the 1970 cohort faced a risk that was more than twice as high again. This is a true generational tragedy: when less educated white Americans were born really has shaped who they are.

There is no single accepted explanation as to why this is happening. Case and Deaton's main argument is that deaths of despair reflect a long-term loss of a way of life for the white working class. This is not solely about poverty, inequality or the 2008 financial crisis, although each have played a role. For example, they echo Robert D. Putnam in suggesting that, after the great recession, 'Capitalism began to look more like a racket for redistributing upward than an engine for general prosperity.'

Case and Deaton's analysis is deeply generational, and not just in the sense of the relentless decline in life chances for successive cohorts. They also highlight how embedded the expectation of generational progress had become, and how, when it failed to appear, this contributed to the despair. As they outline: 'Progress in health and living standards in the twentieth century was prolonged enough that, by the century's end, people could reasonably expect it to continue and to bless their children's lives just as it had blessed theirs ... Not only that, but the rate of improvement since the end of the Second World War had been so steady and so prolonged that it seemed obvious that future generations would do better still.' Alongside the immediate tragedy of so many lives cut short, the sense of betrayal from this shocking reversal has threatened society's faith in the system.

Whether this is a peculiarly American phenomenon is a key question. Perhaps the problem is really one of contemporary capitalism, and the US is setting a trail that other countries will soon follow. But either way, there are certainly contributing factors that are particular to the US: Case and Deaton suggest that the history of racial tension and prejudice, lower levels of social protection and a very particular healthcare system are all significant.

As Case and Deaton conclude, it is possible that it might be both a particular American trend and one that might be seen elsewhere in the future. They point to the fact that, while the US currently dwarfs other countries in its total number of deaths of despair, countries including Canada, Ireland, Australia and Britain (particularly Scotland), are showing increases. More encouragingly, our analysis of British data suggests that a specific tragedy is playing out with Gen X, and that we are not yet seeing the same generation-on-generation increases in deaths of despair as the US. It is not yet inevitable that Britain will follow America's lead.

Simple answers are wrong

We are programmed to look for patterns and explanations – the countless examples of people seeing the face of Jesus in a tortilla or the Virgin Mary in a grilled cheese sandwich testify to our need to make sense of randomness. This relates to the 'clustering illusion' explained by the Cornell University psychology professor Thomas Gilovich. In one study, he presented the sequence 'oxxxoxxxoxxoooxooxxoo' to hundreds of people and asked them whether they thought it was random. Most believed there was a planned pattern, because when we see clusters, we tend to think there is a design or meaning behind them (it is random).[73]

It takes very little to convince us that there is a reason for patterns, particularly if that reason seems straightforward. We want to know *the* single cause, but this preference for simplicity is not just mental laziness – it also gives us a clear target for action. For example, Europeans in the Middle Ages believed that lice were good for your health, since they were rarely found on sick people. When illness struck, they would therefore deliberately try to catch lice. The reasoning was that people got sick when the lice left, when the real explanation was the lice left when people got sick. Lice are extremely sensitive to body temperature – a small increase in a fever will make them look for a new host. The thermometer had not yet been invented, so this temperature increase was rarely noticed, giving the impression that the lice had left *before* the person got sick. Cause and effect had been reversed, but it felt good to have one source of the problem to blame and one single achievable thing to do.[74]

We've seen some clear shifts in this chapter. There is strong evidence, for example, that mental disorders have increased among sections of young people in some countries in recent years. But there is only superficial evidence that mobile phones or social media are the cause – and there is good reason to think that there are more important, and complex, things going on. It's vital that we resist the lure of these simple answers, as they are likely to distract us from the required actions. The American journalist H. L. Mencken captured the risk in this tendency, when he said: 'For every complex problem there is a simple answer, and it's wrong.'[75]

Causes can also take time to reveal their true nature. The hump of suicide among young people in Britain in the 1980s will have appeared as a blip at the time, but the longer-term picture suggests that it is something more generational, affecting a particular subset of Generation X. It is important that our responses reflect the reality and are not driven by our grasping for an immediate simple answer. Understanding this longer-term view suggests that we should work harder to give that particular cohort the support they need.

The importance of these generational patterns should prompt us to question the view that history jumps rather than crawls. As the work of Case and Deaton suggests, even where the jumps are vitally important, like the 2008 global recession and now COVID-19, the consequences depend on the particular set of circumstances that have developed for different groups over a much longer period. Understanding long-term trends is as vital in times of rapid change as in the quiet periods in between.

Chapter 5

A Healthy Future?

Improvements in health and longevity play out as a series of grinding battles between the ageing process on the one hand and medical and social advances on the other. Our lifecycles exert a powerful force: our risk of dying is pretty high when we are babies and young children, drops to a low in our teens and then increases each year for the rest of our lives. Here's a cheery fact: from our thirties, the probability of dying doubles every decade (sorry if that adds to your midlife misery).[1]

But life expectancy is also highly dependent on what era you are born into. In 1800, for example, the average length of life across the globe was around 30 years; even in the most developed nations it was only around 40 years. Despite the huge economic growth of the Industrial Revolution, this picture didn't change much until the start of the twentieth century, when economic progress combined with advances in medical science, increased healthcare provision and better sanitation to create an extended surge in life expectancy. And this remarkable rise has continued through our more recent past. In 1950, life expectancy was still only 63 years in Spain, 66 years in France and 68 years in Canada, but by 2015 it was at least 82 years in each of those countries.[2]

This has also been a truly global trend, and less developed countries have experienced even more extraordinary improvements. For example, at the start of the twentieth century, life expectancy in India was only around 25 years, but by 2019 it was 70 years. Today, most of the world can expect to live as long as those in the richest countries did in 1950, with the poorest regions having improved quickest recently.

Lifecycle and cohort effects are, then, central to our shifting health. The collective health of whole countries is seldom directly affected by huge shocks – the type of sudden period effect we associate with an economic crash or a terrorist attack. But the COVID-19 pandemic is an extraordinary exception. The pandemic has had a huge impact on global health, despite the unprecedented measures introduced to contain its spread. It seems set to become a true generation-defining moment, with after-effects that will shape the future of whole cohorts. This will take some time to play out, but a generational perspective on the pandemic can also help to understand how it is affecting us *now*.

Firstly, the probability of dying from COVID-19 is fundamentally related to when you were born. In Italy, for example, those aged 75 or over when the pandemic struck make up around 12 per cent of the population, but they account for around 70 per cent of all deaths. The age gradient of fatalities is exceptionally steep: over 70 per cent of Italians are under 60, but they account for only 3 per cent of COVID-related deaths.

The course of the pandemic has also been shaped by the period of history in which it occurred. While COVID-19 is an archetypal historical 'jump', as defined by Nassim Nicholas Taleb, its impact has been influenced by slower evolutions in the economy, society and medical technologies that have shaped our response to it. This becomes particularly clear when you compare the direct health impacts of COVID-19 with the Spanish flu pandemic in 1918. Estimates for the number killed by Spanish flu reach up to 50 million, or around 3 per cent of the 1.7 billion world population at the time.[3]

The huge impact of the Spanish flu pandemic reflects how different a time that was, with poverty, malnutrition, overcrowded living conditions and poor sanitation widespread. Many deaths from the disease were linked to secondary bacterial infections rather than the initial viral infection[4] – antibiotics could have significantly reduced death rates if they had been widely available. We've also seen a transformation in global communication, which has meant that our response has been swifter and more consistent internationally. The actions of many governments in response to COVID-19 have often been very far from perfect, but the suppression of information that existed during the Spanish flu pandemic just isn't possible today.[5]

However, the changes in our health have been far from entirely positive. While our living conditions have improved hugely and medical advances have been extraordinary, other lifestyle drivers of disease have gone in the other direction. We're also seeing new interactions between our health and inequalities that were not present even a few decades ago. If we separate out cohort, period and lifecycle effects, we can see new patterns that show your chances of a long and healthy life are no longer automatically increasing if you are born into some of the less well-off groups in wealthy countries such as the UK.

But let's start with smoking, which is one of the real success stories, where a long-term outlook has been vital to our progress.

Smoking kills

Smoking has killed in almost unimaginable numbers. One estimate suggests that over 100 million people have died prematurely during the twentieth century because of smoking.[6] It is still responsible for around 8 million deaths a year, around 15 per cent of all deaths. In more developed countries, the proportion of deaths from smoking is even higher: in the US, for example, it accounts for more than 480,000 deaths every year, around one in five of those who die.[7]

These awful figures would have been so much worse without a sustained fall in smoking levels. For example, in 2018, only 14 per cent of adults smoked in England,[8] down from 46 per cent in 1976.[9] Smoking levels are down to 14 per cent in the US too, from a similar peak.[10] Of course, this trend is not universal – countries as diverse as Croatia, Egypt and Indonesia have seen an increase in the proportion of people who smoke over the last decade. Global population growth has also meant that the total number of smokers has held up, driven by increases in developing countries. But in the last few years, even the total number of cigarettes sold (a terrifying 5.7 trillion in 2016) has finally started to fall.[11]

Within this overall decline, the generational patterns on smoking are another example of combined lifecycle, cohort and period effects. Taking England as an example, it's clear in Figure 5.1 that every generation is smoking less over time, with each line drifting downwards. But each generation tells its own story. The Pre-War generation has the lowest level of smoking, despite its members having grown up before the links between smoking and cancer were unequivocally proved. This will, sadly, partly reflect higher death rates among those who continued to smoke, but it is also the result of the high propensity of this older generation to give up. One study suggests that over 40 per cent of the Pre-War generation are former smokers.[12]

The relative positions of the Gen X and Millennial lines here are fascinating. At the start of the series, Gen Xers were slightly more likely to be smokers than Millennials, but then the lines cross over, and for much of this period, particularly from 2009 until the last couple of years, Millennials were more likely to smoke. Millennials

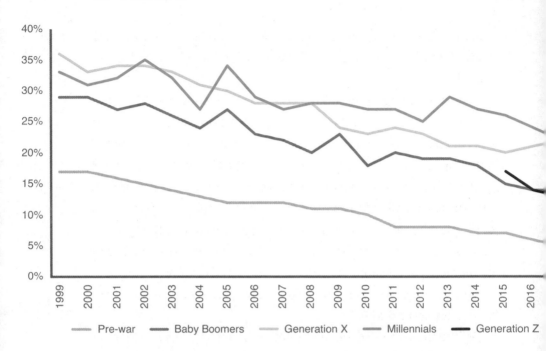

Figure 5.1: Percentage of adults in England who are current smokers[13]

were still giving up during this period: 33 per cent smoked in 1999, and now it's 22 per cent. But they've been quitting more slowly, with a shallower line than other generations, until the last few years. This fits with the 'delayed adulthood' theme that we've seen elsewhere. Some of the spurs to giving up – getting married and having children, for instance – are happening later or not at all. Millennials are acting 'younger', for longer.

The pattern of smoking in the US is remarkably similar to that seen in England, with the same slow decline across all generations, and the same hierarchy between them. American Millennials started out with a similar smoking rate to Gen X in 2000, but this then increased slightly and stayed above Gen X for a number of years, before falling closer into line. The trend of delayed adulthood seems to have played out in the US, too.

But the most important (and encouraging) pattern in both the US and England is the utterly different starting point of Gen Z. In both countries, this cohort is much less likely to smoke cigarettes, with only around 12–13 per cent doing so – an incredible generational break in the habit.

Of course, this trend can partly be explained by the extraordinary rise of e-cigarettes. These relatively new products contain nicotine and flavourings, and create a water vapour that users inhale. Vaping has exploded in the US in particular, with one 2019 study showing that 27 per cent of American 17 and 18 year olds had vaped in the last 30 days. Concerns about this rapid rise in use, combined with a spate of lung conditions and deaths among vapers towards the end of 2019, led to fierce debate about the safety of vaping. As a result, the Trump administration raised the legal age to buy tobacco products, including e-cigarettes, to 21, and banned some flavoured products that were seen to particularly appeal to young people.

This is a tricky public health line to tread, and it is partly a generational trade-off. The health gains from existing smokers switching to vaping are clear – one independent review concludes that they are 95 per cent safer than regular cigarettes[14] – but the counterbalancing risk is that some people who would not otherwise have smoked will develop a nicotine addiction through vaping that leads to tobacco. These concerns have exercised many in the US, including the Secretary of Health and Human Services, Alex Azar, who said: 'We will not stand idly by as these products become an on-ramp to combustible cigarettes or nicotine addiction for a generation of youth.'[15]

Age is key here, as smoking illustrates how we form attitudes and behaviours in our teens and early adult years: around 90 per cent of daily smokers first used cigarettes before they were 19.[16] Vaping presents a generational choice between promoting a product that converts older smokers to a less harmful behaviour on the one hand, and protecting younger generations from an increased risk of starting on the other.

The stakes are high precisely because it seems that we may be turning a corner on cigarette smoking with Generation Z. This success has been built on a long-term series of robust measures, including increases in the legal age of smoking, price rises, bans in public spaces and changes in tobacco packaging, sponsorship and advertising. Some of these measures have been deliberate generational investments, such as the introduction of picture-based health warnings on cigarette packets in Canada in 2000 and entirely plain packaging in Australia in 2012, both measures that have been taken up in a number of other countries. As David Hammond, a professor of public health focused on tobacco control, explains, these measures were *not* primarily designed to get current smokers to quit – rather 'the expectation is that the benefit will accrue and grow over time as children grow up without the positive brand imagery on packages'.[17] This makes sense to me, as an ex-smoker of around 20 years, who still has strong associations with 'my' brand's design. By contrast, such an idea will be completely alien to my children, who will never have seen a designed cigarette packet. The generational investment is paying off.

The last suppers?

Our relationship with alcohol is also highly related to when we were born. In fact, regular drinking is one of the clearest examples of a cohort effect we'll see in this book. Figure 5.2 tracks the proportions of cohorts in England who have said they drink alcohol on five or more days a week over the last 20 years. The lines are incredibly flat, with a strict generational hierarchy and extremely consistent gaps between each.

Around three in ten of the Pre-War generation drink alcohol five or more days a week; as far as we can tell, they always have and always will. I know I shouldn't be impressed, but I can't help thinking that's a great effort for a cohort in which the youngest is now 75 years old. Baby Boomers are not that far behind, at around a fifth. The rate drops to around 10–15 per cent for Gen X, and then down again to Millennials at around 5 per cent. And it has become a near extinct behaviour among Gen Z, with less than 1 per cent drinking this regularly.

Being from a cohort in the middle of this range, I am slightly perplexed by both ends of this spectrum. I can't imagine being part

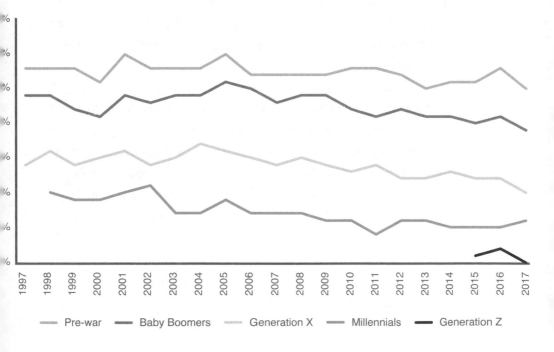

Figure 5.2: Percentage of adults in England drinking alcohol on five or more days per week[18]

of a cohort where so many of my peers have the dedication required to drink nearly every day, but nor can I picture a world where *no one* does.

I was similarly surprised when looking at the generational patterns for those who have 'ever tried' alcohol as teenagers. Looking at Millennials when they were aged 13 to 15, in 2000, around seven in ten said they had tried alcohol. But by 2016 this had *halved*, to 36 per cent of the 13- to 15-year-old slice of Gen Z. That's an incredible shift in just one generation, and this is not just seen in the UK. The Centers for Disease Control and Prevention's Youth Risk Behavior study has tracked alcohol use among young people in the US since 1991, and it shows a similar trend. In that first year of the study, which covered the tail end of Gen X, 82 per cent of high-school students said they'd tried alcohol, but by 2017 this had trailed off to 60 per cent among Gen Z teenagers (a higher figure than in the UK because it includes older kids).

Of course, 'ever tried' and highly regular drinking represent the extreme measures of alcohol consumption. Tracking the total volume of alcohol consumed by each cohort over a long period is less straightforward, partly because the definition of an alcohol 'unit' is relatively new, but evidence suggests that younger cohorts are drinking less overall. For example, in 2014 only a quarter of Millennials drank over 14 units of alcohol per week, compared with 31 per cent of Baby Boomers and 30 per cent of Generation Xers.[19]

The UK and US are far from alone in this trend – total alcohol consumption among current younger generations is falling in Sweden, Germany, Australia and most of the OECD group of richer countries.[20] There are no definitive explanations for why this has happened in so many different national contexts – it is almost certainly a combination of factors. For example, many countries have developed stronger legal enforcement of underage drinking laws, and many have significantly raised taxation on alcohol. Combined with the tighter financial circumstances facing younger people in many countries, this increased expense has made alcohol less affordable for the young.

There is a long-standing academic theory that the popularity of alcohol ebbs and flows in 'long waves'.[21] It may feel like a fixed part of our culture, but levels of consumption actually vary significantly over time. For example, the per capita consumption of alcohol in the UK doubled between the 1960s and the 2000s, but has since fallen back. This fits with the view that, above a certain level, society reaches 'saturation point', at which the harm resulting from alcohol leads to greater concern among both individuals and politicians. Consumption then declines, in tandem with increasingly restrictive government policies that pick up on and reinforce this cultural shift. Eventually, consumption is suppressed to a point where previous concern seems exaggerated, which leads to a relaxation of attitudes and an increase in drinking, and the cycle repeats.

This also fits with what we've seen in the shifting perceptions of risk among the young. As a whole, Gen Zers have a reputation for being 'more mild than wild', reflected in their lower smoking, drinking, criminal behaviour and, as we'll see in the next chapter, sexual activity. But, for the most part, there have been no big increases in their perception of the risk of smoking, sex or illegal drugs. The one exception in the UK is alcohol. In 2018, 70 per cent of Gen Z teenagers saw binge drinking as very risky, compared with 56 per cent of Millennial teenagers in 2004. A quarter of Gen Z teenagers now say even just *having* an alcoholic drink is risky. The fact that this wasn't a question that seemed worth asking in 2004 is a clear sign of how far cultural norms have changed.

Of course, this is good for our collective health. Alcohol was implicated in 5.3 per cent of global deaths in 2016.[22] A more measured attitude to alcohol is a positive change, particularly when it appears to be a long and steady cultural shift rather than a fad.

Just say no

While the downward generational trends in both smoking and drinking are crystal clear, the changes in patterns of drug use are as murky as the bong water at a college party. Headline writers, hungry for a simple message, must find this complexity frustrating, but they still have a go. As one *Vice* article puts it: 'Being a teen today is the same as joining a sanctimonious monk-cult, obsessed with organic food and extreme yoga. Yet, turn the page and teenage ecstasy deaths are spiralling, laughing gas and Spice are all over the schoolyard.'[23]

The actual picture depends on where you're looking and what you're measuring. There are different, and often contradictory, patterns, both within and across countries. Beyond the recent opioid crisis concentrated among particular populations in the US, and the terrible toll drug addiction seems to be taking on some members of Gen X in the UK, there are few clear-cut patterns and no real signs of a consistent generational shift in either direction. Taken as a whole, there have been small declines in harder drug use among recent generations of young people, with marijuana use remaining fairly steady or falling in some countries.

For example, an 'ever used' measure for a collection of illegal drugs – marijuana, cocaine, methamphetamines and heroin – in the US over the past ten years shows a pretty stable pattern across generations. There are some differences between the cohorts and over time, but they are all in a percentage range between early fifties and late sixties, and there is no clear direction of travel.

Looking just at marijuana use among US teens over a longer time period, we can see why there is such confusion in media reporting of generational drug trends. For example, the percentage of American 17 and 18 year olds who had tried the drug in the previous 12 months has gone from a high of around 50 per cent in the late 1970s, through a sustained decline to a low of 20 per cent at the end of the 1980s and start of the 1990s, before bouncing back up and bobbing around 35 per cent from around 2000 until today. It is actually the deep low of the late 1980s and early 1990s that stand out as different, and commentators now seem to be exaggerating relatively small short-term changes.[24]

The lower level of marijuana use in America in the 1980s is mirrored in a steep decline in support for its legalization, as shown in Figure 5.3. These trends in use and attitudes coincided with the height of the country's 'War on Drugs', a key focus of the Reagan administration, and the 'Just Say No' campaign, which lasted for a

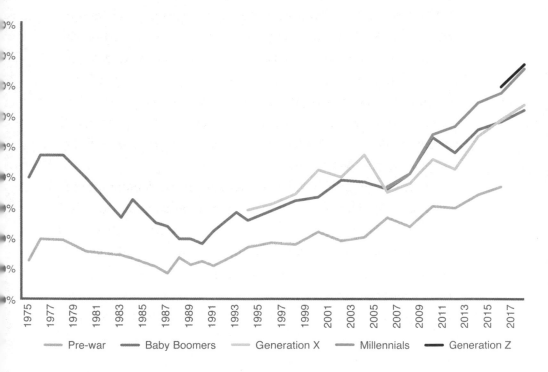

Figure 5.3: Percentage of adults in US who approve of legalizing marijuana[25]

decade from the early 1980s. Support for legalization started to rise again almost immediately after this, an illustration of how attitudes can reflect an interplay between general cultural trends and the tone set by political leaders.

After that more uptight period, the US saw very significant increases in support for the legalization of marijuana among all generations; over 60 per cent of all generations except the Pre-War generation were in favour by 2018. Since 2012, 11 US states have fully legalized it, with many others decriminalizing it and allowing medical use. There's little evidence that this has changed how many people partake, and some studies in states that have legalized marijuana have claimed reductions in opioid use and related deaths.[26] Looking at the generational trends in opinion, relaxation in further states seems a safe bet.

Similarly, six in ten Britons thought cannabis use was 'morally wrong' in 1989, but this collapsed to 29 per cent by 2019. This decline has been driven by a generational change, with a steeper drop in concern between those aged 55 or over at the two different timepoints. This reflects the fact that, over this 30-year period, we are comparing two very different generations of older people, with very different formative experiences – one born in 1934 or before, and one born in 1964 or before.[27]

These changing views of the morality of marijuana are also reflected in the shift in the perception of the risk associated with the drug. In stark contrast with the increased likelihood that young people see alcohol as risky, there have been steep falls in their assessment of the threat posed by marijuana. For example, nearly 80 per cent of American 17 to 18 year olds in the late 1980s thought there was a great risk in regularly using marijuana; this had collapsed to under 30 per cent by 2019.[28] There have been similar falls across many other countries, including the UK and New Zealand.[29] Today's young people are not a particularly drug-fearing generation.

The girth of nations

While the generational breaks in smoking and drinking are extremely good news for our health, the trends in obesity levels are not. The most striking pattern is driven by lifecycle effects. Figure 5.4 shows the slow downward drift of each generation in England as they age. I can track my own generation's progress to fatness in the Gen X line; in 1992, 70 per cent of us were a healthy weight, but now that we are in middle age, only around a quarter of us have managed to maintain that.

Our downward drift means we've joined the previous two cohorts, ending up at a remarkably similar end point to Baby Boomers and the Pre-War generation. I find this a mildly motivating thought: if I

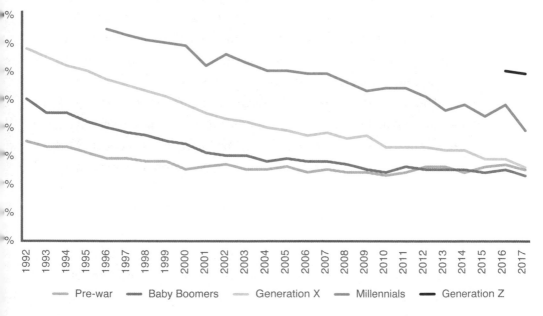

Figure 5.4: Percentage of adults in England with a healthy weight (defined as BMI score between 18.5 and 24.9)[30]

can make it to my fifties at a healthy weight, there is a good chance that I'll stay there. Of course, the reality is more complex and less comforting; the chart only shows an average, with people flowing in and out, including through dying. The harsh truth is that many of us will continue to get flabbier, even while the proportions of those who are at a healthy weight within each older generation seem to remain stable – because the overweight tend to die younger.

Despite the dominance of lifecycle effects, we can also see significant generational differences in our chances of being a healthy weight. Comparing Gen X with Millennials in England, when they were both an average age of 26, 53 per cent of Gen X were a healthy weight, compared with 48 per cent of Millennials. Millennials are the first cohort in England to reach their mid-twenties with a minority being a healthy weight, and the trend seems to be continuing: in the latest data from 2017, 62 per cent of Gen Z were a healthy weight, compared with around 70 per cent of Millennials at the equivalent age. We need to treat this with some caution as this represents just an early slice of Gen Z, but it seems that we haven't reached the bottom of the generational slide into weight problems.

There is a similar pattern among adults in the US when we look at the proportion who are classed as obese, meaning they have a Body Mass Index (BMI) of at least 30. For example, 40 per cent of US Millennials were obese by 2018, compared with around 30 per cent of Gen Xers when they were a similar average age in 2004. It's too early to draw conclusions about Gen Zers, but current data suggests their obesity levels are rising even faster than in Millennials.

However, you wouldn't think these were the trends from looking at the huge number of spurious articles claiming either Millennials or Gen Z to be the 'wellness generation'. Some are unintentionally funny. One article called American Millennials the new 'health-conscious' generation – simply because they watch a lot of videos on 'how to consume turmeric ... apple cider vinegar, cauliflower rice, bone broth and avocado oil'.[31] Another article, inexplicably, pointed to the fact that '54 per cent of Millennials ... expect ancient grain to be included in their foods'. But this kind of thinking also infects more serious analysis, including from one of the most famous financial investment companies in the world. Goldman Sachs suggests: 'For Millennials, wellness is a daily, active pursuit ... "healthy" doesn't mean just "not sick". It's a daily commitment to eating right and exercising.'[32]

These spurious generalizations are damaging, because they distract us from the impact of generation-on-generation weight increases, which has become a global issue. Worldwide, obesity has tripled since 1975; in 2016, 650 million adults were obese, and a further 1.25 billion were overweight.[33] This has serious consequences on our collective life expectancy – a World Health Organization report suggests it 'has the potential to negate many of the health benefits that have contributed to the increased longevity observed in the world'.[34]

There is also growing variation within populations, particularly in more developed countries such as the US and UK: childhood weight is becoming increasingly intertwined with inequality. For example, one study draws on a series of cohort surveys that track UK residents born in a particular year throughout their lives. It compares slices of the population born in 1946, 1958, 1970 and 2001, providing a vitally important resource in understanding how life is really changing between generations. It confirms that children in the latest 2001 cohort are heavier than in previous cohorts. However, it also shows a new pattern of increasing divergence between those born into the highest and lowest social classes, with the latter having significantly higher BMI scores in 2001 than the former, unlike previous cohorts where there was little difference between classes.[35] Being born into lower social classes now is more damaging to your relative chances of making it through childhood at a healthy weight than in the past.

This pattern isn't confined to the UK; in Europe and North America, some of the strongest correlations with childhood obesity are based on income and social class – and the gap appears to be widening. A survey of children covering 34 countries across Europe and North America has shown that the impact on your weight of the social class you are born into nearly doubled between 2002 and 2010. Socio-economic differences, it seems, are becoming a more significant influence on childhood obesity.[36]

On one level, the cause of the generational increase in obesity and its growing link to inequality is straightforward: we have been increasingly consuming more calories than we are burning, and the less well-off have been more affected. However, the stubbornness of childhood obesity levels in the face of endless initiatives, and the fact that they are increasingly skewed between different social groups, reflects how tightly tied outcomes are to particular societal conditions that are difficult to shift. These 'obesogenic' factors can be found in all aspects of young people's lives, and are often transferred between generations. Many more adults who children interact with are now obese or overweight themselves, and there are also important environmental factors, such as the accessibility of safe places to exercise and what food is available at school and home. These conditions shape our young people and are more geared towards promoting obesity than the ones their grandparents experienced, and many are worse for the poor.[37]

When you're born is increasingly interacting with the socio-economic circumstances you're born into. We've already outlined that, in the US, for example, life expectancy has actually started to fall again in the last few years, in the longest downturn since the Spanish flu.[38] As Case and Deaton have demonstrated, this is entirely due to decreases among subsets of the population, particularly white Americans without a bachelor's degree. While the UK has not seen an actual reversal in life expectancy, progress has stalled for the first time in 100 years.[39] The trajectories of different communities are startling, and explain much of the slowdown. For example, we have seen falls in life expectancy among women in the most deprived areas in England, and for both sexes in deprived areas of some regions, such as the north-east of the country.[40] Meanwhile, those in the least deprived areas continue to see improvements in life expectancy. In the US and England, as well as elsewhere in Europe, being born into a poorer background shapes your life in a more negative way than it would have done in the recent past.

Would you still choose to be born now?

The extraordinary medical and social advances of the last century have scored numerous victories in the constant battles with disease and old age. We'll see further gains in the future, as medical innovations continue at pace, and our investment in breaking the smoking habit, the biggest recent cause of preventable death, continues to pay off.

Towards the end of his presidency, Barack Obama regularly returned to this theme of our progress, and the resilience it brings. In his introductory piece to an edition of *Wired* magazine that he guest-edited in 2016, he emphasized his faith in scientific and social innovations: 'We are far better equipped to take on the challenges we face than ever before.'[41] He later expanded on his belief in the benefits this brings to being born today: 'If you had to choose a moment in history to be born, and you did not know ahead of time who you would be – you didn't know whether you were going to be born into a wealthy family or a poor family, what country you'd be born in, whether you were going to be a man or a woman – if you had to choose blindly what moment you'd want to be born, you'd choose now.'[42]

Even at the time of writing, in a world that is largely 'locked down' during a global pandemic, Obama is still correct. Despite the immediate health risks, and the unknown long-term impact of the pandemic, such has been the scale of improvement across the world that choosing now would still be a smart bet.

However, the calculations have gradually been shifting. Firstly, progress in health across society as a whole has faltered, with trends such as the rise in obesity acting as a drag on our gains. Secondly, we have seen starker reversals in health and life expectancy among particular subsets of the population. If you were destined to be a white non-graduate in the US or a woman living in a deprived area of northern England, it is less clear that being born now would be the best choice. This is a shocking thought, particularly when we have grown to take progress for granted. Health inequalities, of course, have always existed, but they are more startling and harder to accept when they are accompanied by actual reversals for significant proportions of the population in wealthy countries such as the UK and US.

While medical and social advances mean we can deal with the COVID-19 pandemic more effectively than we would have done at any time in history, even the best-equipped countries have huge inequalities in terms of vulnerability to both the direct threat of the virus and the longer-term impact of the measures taken to control its spread. The tragic consequences of this were clear from the start of the pandemic: deaths from COVID-19 were twice as high in the most deprived areas of England than in the least deprived – a larger gap in death rates than in normal times.[43]

We expect to enjoy a healthier, longer life than our parents, and we expect our children to enjoy the same. But the actual trend has become clear: when it comes to health, generational progress is increasingly reserved for those who can afford it.

Chapter 6

The Sex Recession, Baby Bust and Death of Marriage

n *Everybody Lies*, Seth Stephens-Davidowitz draws on the vast swathes of thoughts we happily share with Google in our internet searches, but no one else. As you might expect, sex features prominently in the book – it contains insights such as 'Men's top Googled question related to how their body or mind would change as they aged was whether their penis would get smaller' and 'Men make as many searches looking for ways to perform oral sex on themselves as they do how to give a woman an orgasm.'[1]

While these insights are in equal parts grim and predictable, they only give a partial picture. To truly understand our sex lives, we need careful measurement in rigorous and sensitive surveys, and to understand how generations are changing, we need these to go back a long way. We also need to be mindful that people don't always tell the whole truth in surveys, particularly on sensitive subjects like sex, but the good studies provide insights we can't get anywhere else.

Unfortunately, high-quality studies of reported sexual attitudes and behaviour are rare today, and they were even rarer 30 years ago. Instead, we tend to get an endless stream of spurious polls and attention-grabbing headlines, which often attempt to sum up whole generations in pithy but misleading ways. These are sometimes based on serious studies that point to important changes, but it's a reflection of our sensationalist approach to sex that they often over-reach. Taking each generation in turn, here are some of the key messages you might pick up from a casual reading of the articles:

- **Gen Z:** 'The Kids Are Boning Less.'[2] No explanation is required for this article, and the trend it describes is based on a real pattern in the US, as we'll see.
- **Millennials:** Here it gets confusing, as there are two contradictory groups of pieces that both somehow manage to blame Millennials for killing something. The first emphasizes the rise of 'hook-up' culture, aided by new technology, and claims it is killing serious relationships.[3] The second accuses Millennials of killing sex because they are too wrapped up in their devices to be bothered – 'Netflix and chill' has apparently become a literal description rather than a euphemism.[4]
- **Baby Boomers:** 'Silver Shaggers Risk STDs.'[5] These pieces pick up on a genuine trend of higher rates of sexually transmitted disease among Baby Boomers. However, it represents a very niche behaviour, far from the impression of a wave of wrinkly, unprotected orgies given by the headlines.

The eagle-eyed reader will have spotted the gap in the above line-up; Gen X is virtually non-existent in generational discussions of sex, true to its forgotten-middle-child status. There are plenty of pieces on the difficulty of maintaining an interest in sex during midlife, but very little that is about the cohort's unique character. The one piece I found may not be the most rigorous, but it is based on analysis from a US academic, who suggests: 'Generation X ... were influenced by the sexual revolution and ruled by the blowjob, while Millennials embraced anal sex ... and Gen Z is into pegging ... the next generation will likely be the masturbation generation.'[6] I guess being 'ruled by blowjobs' or 'embracing anal' are more colourful generational clichés than being narcissistic or materialistic.

Of course, it's easy to mock, particularly when we still have a slightly embarrassed attitude towards sex. But it's a literally existential aspect of human life, and one that shows significant differences over time and between generations, which can sometimes get lost in the noise. One of the biggest challenges facing many countries over the coming decades is our low or declining birth rates – which will create increasingly unbalanced populations, with many more older people and fewer of working age. The tendency in some commentary is to blame this trend on recent generations of young people, for their supposed lack of interest in sex and childrearing. But this is a gross misreading of a longer-term decline in fertility rates and a simplification of a much more complex pattern.

A future with fewer kids is not the only challenge that our shifting family lives present. As the writer David Brooks points out, the 'nuclear family' of two parents and 2.5 children (or *2point4 Children* as in the title of a long-running British sitcom) seems like the natural order 'even though this wasn't the way most humans lived during the tens of thousands of years before 1950, and it isn't the way most humans have lived during the 55 years since 1965'. This stripped-back model of family life has worked well for some, but not for those with fewer resources, and this has all sorts of knock-on effects.

Nevertheless, the resilience of marriage itself should not be underestimated. As Stephanie Coontz, author of *The Way We Never Were: American Families and the Nostalgia Trap*, points out, people have been unsuccessfully predicting the death of marriage for decades.[7] In 1928, John B. Watson, a prominent child psychologist, predicted that marriage would be finished by

1977. And in 1977, the sociologist Amitai Etzioni suggested that, if contemporary trends continued, by the 1990s 'not one American family will be left'.[8] More recently, and predictably, headlines have accused Millennials of 'killing marriage'.[9] The reality is that the history of marriage has always been a mix of continuity and change.

A sexual recession?

Let's start at the beginning, by looking at trends in first sexual experiences from a US study of high-school students.[10] This shows a clear decline in the proportion of young people aged 15 to 18 who have lost their virginity, from 54 per cent for Generation X in 1991 to 40 per cent for Gen Z by 2017. There are two downward steps in the trend that coincide quite neatly with the periods when different generations were reaching their late teens – the youngest Millennials in the late 1990s and Gen Zers in the mid-2010s. On this measure, it seems perfectly reasonable to believe that 'the kids are boning less'.

We don't have the same sort of studies in the UK, but there are indications that we are seeing a similar pattern, with a higher proportion of young adults in recent generations delaying sex for longer. For example, a study tracking a cohort of people born in 1989 and 1990 and interviewing them at various points as they grow up shows that, by the time they were 25, 12 per cent of these late Millennials were still virgins. This is significantly higher than the levels seen in previous generations, where it used to hover around 5 per cent by people's mid-twenties.[11]

Is this a universal trend across countries, or just a British and American phenomenon? Long-term, robust surveys of teenagers' sexual behaviour are rare, but a study in six African countries, for example, shows a slow but steady rise in the age of first sexual experience over the last few decades, with particularly significant effects in Uganda, Kenya and Ghana.[12] The country that is most widely seen as the archetype of the trend, however, is Japan, where the level and longevity of virginity is of quite a different order. In 2015, 26 per cent of men and 25 per cent of women aged 18 to 39 had no experience of heterosexual sex (disappointingly, Japanese sex surveys don't measure same-sex experiences). As seen with US teenagers, this has been a slow evolution rather than a sudden shift – the figures were already 20 per cent for men and 22 per cent for women in 1992. Reflecting this, long-term virginity is increasingly affecting the oldest age groups within the survey: for example, the proportion of 35 to 39 year olds who have not had heterosexual intercourse roughly doubled between 1992 and 2015, to nearly 10 per cent.

A gradual increase in the age of virginity loss is a relatively narrow measure of declining sexual activity. It tells us very little about the sex lives of most people: after all, virginity is still rare by the time we get to our thirties, even in Japan.

Counting the number of sexual partners people have had in the last year gives a more representative perspective on trends in sexual activity, and we'll begin with those in the US who've had none (Figure 6.1). We can see that the starting point for each line indicates a higher proportion of young adults saying they've had no sexual partners in the last year as you go through the generations, from Generation X (12 per cent) to Millennials (21 per cent) and Gen Z (34 per cent). These are very large increases over the course of just three generations.

But, unlike the trends among teenagers, we can now take a fuller generational perspective. In particular, we can track Millennials further through their lifecycle, with the oldest around 38 by the time of the latest survey in 2018. We get a different picture of their sex lives from this longer view; after years of lagging behind, Millennials

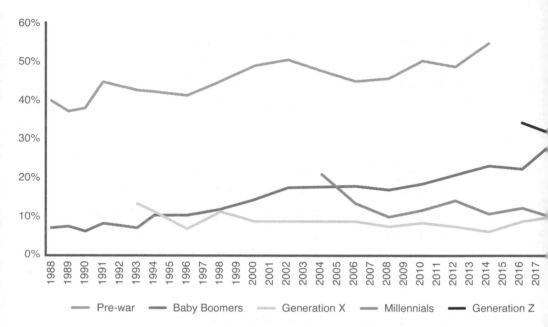

Figure 6.1: Percentage of adults in US who say they have had no sexual partners in the last year[13]

are now perfectly in line with Gen X, with just 10 per cent having had no sexual partners in the last year. Once again, the story of their development is of a delayed path rather than a different destination: they started later and took longer to get going, but ended up in the same place.

However, the chart also makes it clear that Gen Zers have a big gap to close if they are to get back to similar levels of sexual activity to previous cohorts. Even though the Millennial path has shown how powerful human lifecycles are at pulling us back into line, it seems more likely that Gen Z will struggle to close the gap completely. We may be heading for a higher level of sexual abstinence among young adults in the US.

It's a similar picture when we look at how frequently different generations are having sex. Figure 6.2 shows US data on those who have had sex at least weekly over the past year. Each of these lines will be tracking a pretty content bunch of people – once a week appears to be the perfect frequency of sex for a happy relationship. Studies show that couples who have sex less than once a week are less content, but we fail to show real happiness gains from more frequent sex, and this seems to apply equally to men and women, young and old.[14]

The chart shows some fascinating shifting patterns that illustrate how tied up our sex lives are with lifecycle, period and cohort effects. In particular, when Generation X Americans were first measured in 1992 (average age 20), 66 per cent of them were having at least weekly sex. When Millennials were around the same average age in

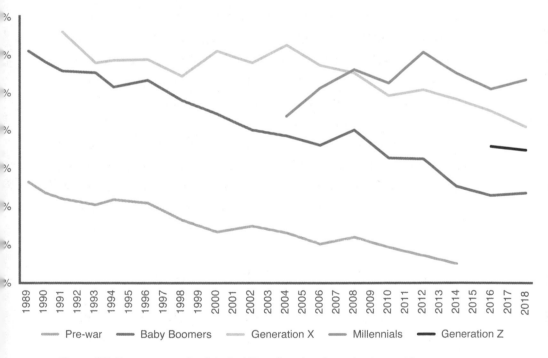

Figure 6.2: Percentage of adults in US saying they have had sex at least once a week in the last year[15]

2006, only 50 per cent were having sex this frequently, which at the time would have looked like a collapse in sexual activity. However, the shape of the Millennials' line is entirely different – rather than falling in these early adult years, it rises until it gets up to around 60 per cent, before stabilizing. By 2018, 53 per cent of Millennials are having sex at least weekly, which is not too different from the 58 per cent among Gen Xers when they were a similar average age of around 30 in 2002. After a slower start, regular sex for Millennials is a bit lower than Gen X, but not a lot. Again, the story for Millennials is mostly of a delayed lifecycle – they came later to regular sex, but ended up in a not dissimilar place to Gen X.

As with their sexual abstinence, Gen Zers have taken a further step down, with only around 35 per cent having sex at least weekly. They are nearly half as likely to be having weekly sex as Gen Xers were when they were young adults. Again, given the different sexual lifecycle Millennials have followed to reach roughly the same point, we can't be sure that this is a complete break from the past – but it seems increasingly unlikely that Gen Z will catch up with previous generations' levels of sexual activity.

Recent changes in our sex lives are often described as a 'sex recession', as coined by *Atlantic* journalist Kate Julian at the end of 2018.[16] Her article focuses on how this 'recession' is being driven by younger generations, with vivid stories of young people forlornly 'swiping left' on dating apps with no real interest in meeting a match, terrified of initiating real-life contact and distracted by their smartphones and internet porn. It gives the impression that a whole generation is giving up on sex, but this is misleading.

Part of the problem with the 'sex recession' term is that it often treats the decline in sexual activity as a single trend that stems solely from changing behaviours among the young, when it has several strands running together. In particular, this portrayal brushes over the fact that older age groups have often seen larger falls in sexual activity. In fact, the frequency with which everyone in the US overall are having sex has declined in recent years, from around 60 times a year in the 1990s to around 50 by the mid-2010s.[17] In Britain, the median number of times adults had sex in the previous four weeks fell from five in 1990 to three by 2010.[18] A similar generalized decline in the frequency of sex has also been recorded in Sweden,[19] Australia,[20] Finland, Spain, Italy[21] and, of course, Japan.[22] The studies show significant differences in which groups are driving the change, but it's actually mainly *not* the young who are to blame. Data from the US, UK, Australia and Finland are broadly consistent in showing that the largest declines in frequency are actually among married people and those in early middle age.[23]

These are long-term, multifaceted declines, where pointing to one generation or individual factors, such as the rise of mobile phones, dating apps or Pornhub, doesn't fit with the timing of the trends.

On top of these period effects, younger generations have also experienced shifts in their lifecycle. Delayed adulthood is writ large in their stalling sex lives. The trends for Millennials have shown how this can be a pause rather than an outright rejection of sex. For example, it's still the case that by the time people in the US and UK reach their mid-thirties (where Millennials are now), one in 20 or fewer remain virgins, which is not hugely different from past patterns.[24] However, Generation Z may be the first generation where this stretched lifecycle snaps and we settle at a lower level of sexual activity – we will get a clearer picture of this in the next few years.

This, I think, gets closer to the point of why 'sex recession' doesn't quite work as a term – it suggests a temporary and unusual phase that we would bounce back from if young people could only get their act together. But a fuller understanding suggests that the causes of the trend are more varied, and it's likely to be more permanent.

Baby bust?

The later start to our sex lives is mirrored in significant increases in the average age at which women give birth to their first child. For example, in the UK it has gone from around 26 years in the 1950s to over 30 years, with a steady upward trajectory starting in the mid-1960s.[25] France, Australia and America followed a similar pattern, although the US settled at a lower 29 years old in 2017. In Germany, the average age decreased from nearly 28 to 26 between the 1950s and early 1980s, but then rose to around 31.

These small increases may not seem dramatic, but they hide very different distributions across age ranges. For example, in England and Wales in 1985, six times as many babies were born to teenagers as to women aged over 40. But by 2015, the number of children born to women aged over 40 was larger than the number born to those aged under 20, for the first time in our history.[26] This same tipping point was reached in Canada and Australia in the early 2010s.[27] Of course, a large part of the explanation is the huge fall in teen pregnancies, but the number of 'geriatric births' (until recently the official medical term for births by older women) have also risen significantly. It's no accident that Bridget Jones, the chronicler of shifting female lives, was 43 in the film *Bridget Jones's Baby*.

As with our declining sexual behaviour, these trends have often been mispresented as a failing of current generations of young people, as headlines like 'Will Childless Millennials Turn America Into Japan?' illustrate.[28] But the reality is that the average age for childbirth has been increasing in almost all countries since at least the 1980s, when Baby Boomers and then Gen Xers were in their prime childbearing years. These are not sudden generational shifts driven by a particular cohort.

As for the number of children people are having, the judgements on today's younger generations are similarly unfair. It is true that birth rates have plummeted globally; the worldwide total fertility rate (the number of children born for every woman of childbearing years) halved from around five in the 1960s to around 2.5 by 2015.[29] But more recent falls have been driven by lower-income countries, with relative stability elsewhere. For example, total fertility rates in the UK have only moved between around 1.7 and 1.9 per woman since the 1980s.[30] It's true that we have had six years of slightly decreasing rates in the UK, while the US has seen small but consistent falls since 2008,[31] but the main pattern in the long-term trends is a much steeper fall in the 1960s and 1970s. The rate in richer countries seems to settle around 1.7; the latest assumption from the Office of National Statistics in the UK is that the average completed family size for each woman will still be 1.78 children in 2043.[32]

Of course, while this is not the generationally driven plunge in the number of children that you might assume from the headlines ('Baby Bust! Millennials' Birth Rate Drop May Signal Historic Shift'[33]), it is significantly below the replacement rate of around 2.1 children. And when this is combined with our increased longevity, it indicates that we are going to see very large and fast increases in the 'old age dependency ratio', or how many working-age people there are compared with those aged over 65.[34] In fact, in the US, this ratio is expected to *double* between 2010 and 2050, from 19 to 36 older people per 100 working-age people. Of course, we need to be careful not to overstate the impact of this: improved health and longer working lives mean that many of these older people won't be 'dependent'. But it is still a huge societal shift.

COVID-19 will also have a significant impact on our birth rates – but not in the way some people have expected. In the initial stages of the 'lockdown' in March 2020, the UK health minister Nadine Dorries even tweeted: 'As the minister responsible for maternity services, I'm just wondering how busy we are going to be nine months from now.'[35]

These expectations were based on a widespread misperception that events which leave people stuck at home, such as blackouts or blizzards, result in more babies. But these myths are not supported by the data.[36] Stress and anxiety in crises generally outweighs the boredom of being at home.

COVID-19 is, it seems, more likely to accentuate the 'baby bust'. The economists Melissa S. Kearney and Phillip B. Levine have drawn on trends from previous recessions and the 1918 Spanish flu pandemic to estimate that there could be between 300,000 and 500,000 fewer births in the US, a loss of up to 14 per cent of all births.[37] Their analysis also shows a 12.5 per cent decline in birth rates nine months after each wave of the Spanish flu pandemic. This was not primarily an economic effect – the economy barely contracted – but was instead driven by the anxiety and public health impacts of the crisis. The Spanish flu affected those of childbearing age more directly than COVID-19 has, so this effect is likely to be less marked this time; however, the current pandemic does seem set to have a significant economic effect, which will have an impact. Birth rates are procyclical, rising and falling with economic growth and decline. Analysis of the 2008 recession suggests that a one percentage point increase in unemployment rates was associated with a 0.9 per cent decrease in birth rates.[38]

A protracted period of social separation and the even longer-lasting economic 'scarring' will mean not just a delay, but a permanent loss. As with so much about COVID-19, it seems it will hasten pre-existing trends; the resulting slowing of birth rates could have long-term repercussions for Western countries that are already struggling to support ageing populations.

Saving ourselves

What do Britney Spears, Miley Cyrus and Justin Bieber have in common? As a Gen X dad of two daughters, who have listened incessantly to their music at times, I could think of a few sweary phrases to connect them. But beyond their responsibility for my aural torture, they've all at one point pledged to 'wait' – before subsequently admitting that they didn't. Miley Cyrus, who originally opined a 'True Love Waits' mindset, later concluded that 'virginity is a social construct'.

The American 'purity industry', which includes elaborate events and the sale of jewellery, books, T-shirts and DVDs, as well as government programmes reinforcing it, appears very alien from the UK's perspective. But when we look at the differences in attitudes to pre-marital sex between the two countries, it's much less surprising.

Each generation in the US, with the exception of the latest figures for Gen Z, is significantly more concerned about sex before marriage than the equivalent generation in Britain, as we can see in Figures 6.3 and 6.4. For example, nearly three in ten US Baby Boomers think pre-marital sex is always or almost always wrong, compared with just 8 per cent of British Boomers. If you looked only at the overall population's disapproval of pre-marital sex in Britain, which has gone from 27 per cent in 1983 to 9 per cent in 2017, you might think this was due to a gradual shift in views rather than the deeply generational trend that it actually is. There has, in fact, been remarkable consistency among the views of most British generations since the question was first asked in the early 1980s: with the exception of the Pre-War generation, only one in ten or fewer of all generations have ever thought it was wrong. Even the Pre-War generation has been slowly catching up with this general view, and now only one in five are concerned, less than half the level of the equivalent American generation.

Some raise concerns about how this perspective impacts on women and their sense of their own value. As Jessica Valenti suggests in *The Purity Myth*, using 'purity' as a shorthand for not having sex

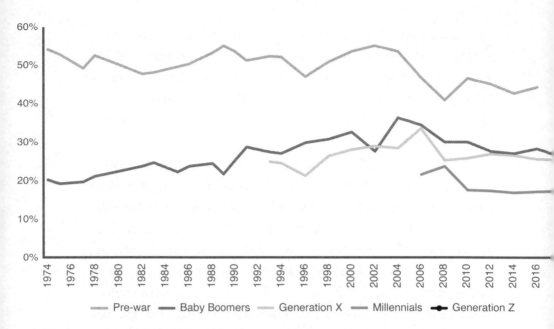

Figure 6.3: Percentage of adults in US who say that having sex before marriage is 'always' or 'almost always' wrong[39]

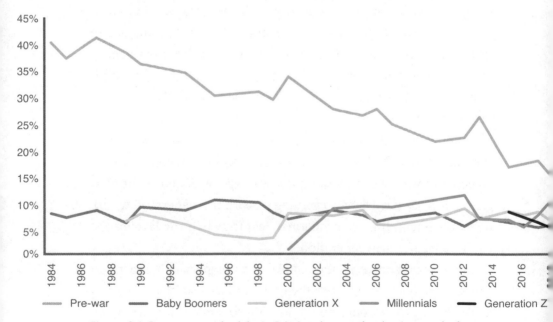

Figure 6.4: Percentage of adults in Britain who say that having sex before marriage is 'always' or 'mostly' wrong[40]

means that women who do have sex before marriage are impure or tainted: 'While boys are taught that the things that make them men – good men – are universally accepted ethical ideals, women are led to believe that our moral compass lies somewhere between our legs.'[41]

The reality is that it's not just Britney, Miley and Justin who fall short – hardly anyone lives up to the ideal. Around 95 per cent of both American men and women in their forties say they had pre-marital sex, and this applies pretty equally across the generations, including those with the highest levels of concern about the issue.[42] That's a lot of regret – or cognitive dissonance – for people to be carrying around.

While so many sexual attitudes seem to be shifting between generations, there is one aspect of sexual behaviour that has remained utterly unchanged over the past 30–40 years, in both the US and Britain: infidelity. It has always been wrong to cheat, and probably always will be. Around nine in ten Americans across all generations have said that it's wrong for a married person to have sexual relations with someone outside their marriage, all the way back to the mid-1970s. While the level of disapproval is lower in Britain, there is incredible consistency between 1989 and 2019 in the majorities who say it is morally wrong to have sexual relations with someone who is married to someone else.[43] In fact, levels of objection in Britain have increased slightly, mostly driven by men coming into line with views among women – a pattern that applies equally across generations. With so much change in sexual attitudes and behaviour, it's strangely striking how universal this one view is across time and generations.

Marriage can wait

But while people value being faithful, it's less clear that they think fidelity requires marriage. All around the world, people are getting married later or not at all, as Table 6.1 shows: for example, the average

age of marriage for French women in 1980 was 23, but by the 2010s it was 32. The average age of marriage in African countries is lower, but the direction of change is the same. Across countries, the age of first marriage for women has generally increased more than for men, closing the age gap and reflecting women's increasing financial independence.[44]

Table 6.1: Average age of marriage for men and women (1980 to 2016)[45]

Country	Gender	Mean age of marriage (1980–2)	Mean age of marriage (2011–16)	Difference (years)
France	Men	25	34	9
France	Women	23	32	9
UK	Men	26	33	7
UK	Women	24	32	8
Sweden	Men	26	33	7
Sweden	Women	24	31	7
Australia	Men	26	31	5
Australia	Women	24	30	6
Japan	Men	29	31	2
Japan	Women	25	29	4
USA	Men	24	29	5
USA	Women	22	28	6
Rwanda	Men	25	27	2
Rwanda	Women	17	24	7

While these figures point to a clear trend, they tell us nothing about changes in the proportions of people who don't marry at all, or the source of the changes across generations. This is clearer when you track generations over time. Figure 6.5 firstly demonstrates how universal marriage has been for the current older generations in Britain, and this is mirrored in other countries: almost all of the US Pre-War generation and over 90 per cent in Britain and France were married at some point in their lives. This fell slightly for American Baby

Boomers, but more for British and French Boomers, to around 85 and 80 per cent respectively. Around 82 per cent of US Generation X have been married at some point, compared with 70 per cent in Britain and 60 per cent in France. But the chart also shows the Millennial line stays much flatter for longer than the Gen X line: marrying in their late teens or twenties was much rarer for Millennials than for Gen X. Millennials did pick up the pace, but by 2017, with many of them well into their thirties, only around 40 per cent were married, compared with 50 per cent of Gen X when they were a similar age.

We can't yet be certain about the future endpoint for Millennials: as we saw with their sex lives, they are late starters. However, by current trajectories, it seems reasonable to expect that, in the end, some 75 per cent of US Millennials will have married at some point, compared with just over 60 per cent of British Millennials and less than 50 per cent of French Millennials. These are big changes, but hardly the death of an institution.

It is too early to say whether Gen Z will continue this trend but it seems likely, as their marriage rates are at least as low as those of Millennials in their early adult years. There are also clear signs that teenagers are deprioritizing marriage over other goals. As Jean Twenge outlines in surveys of high-school students, marriage has slipped down the order of life priorities, with financial and career ambitions on the rise.[46] As Twenge suggests, this is partly due to greater economic uncertainty, but it also reflects a cultural change in perceptions of how marriage fits into our lives. As the sociologist Andrew Cherlin outlines, marriage is no longer a first step in adulthood but a celebration of what a couple has already achieved: 'The wedding is the last brick put in place to finally complete the building of the family.'[47]

Of course, young people are not giving up on intimate relationships; a great deal of the change is explained by increases in people living

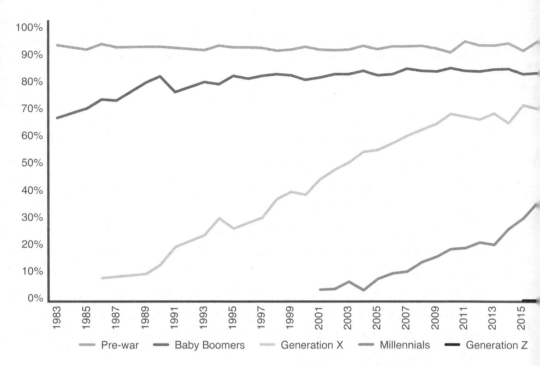

Figure 6.5: Percentage of adults in Britain who were married at some point in their life[48]

as unmarried couples. For example, 25 per cent of British Millennials were living with a partner in 2017, twice the level of Gen Xers at a similar age. This no doubt reflects the narrowing distinction younger generations make between marriage and living together.[49]

This is despite efforts by governments around the world to incentivize marriage. According to the US Government Accountability Office, there are 1,138 perks in federal law available to married couples.[50] Many of them are pretty niche: Title 18 of the US Code, Section 879, for example, makes it illegal to threaten certain individuals guarded by the Secret Service, including the president, the vice president and their 'immediate family'.[51] Jared Kushner, Ivanka Trump's husband, was covered – but Kimberly Guilfoyle,

Donald Trump Jr's partner, was not. This is unlikely to coax Gen Zers down the aisle, but the real benefits include substantial tax breaks, property rights and inheritance rules. Of course, one of a married couple needs to die to get the full value from many of them, which may also explain why they're less enticing to the young.

The shifting state of marriage is not all about delay and decline, however – recent years have seen remarkable progress in the recognition of same-sex marriage. Since the Netherlands became the first country to legally recognize same-sex marriage in 2001, around thirty other nations have followed. There is still a huge distance to travel, but it represents an incredible turnaround in a relatively short period of time.

The extent of the change in attitudes is clear in the generational trends in US support for gay marriage, as shown in Figure 6.6. This is one of the most remarkable shifts we'll see in the whole book: in 1988, barely 10 per cent of people agreed that homosexual couples should have the right to marry, a figure that had increased to over 60 per cent by 2018. Both period and cohort effects are clear in the chart, with every generation moving significantly over time and each new cohort more supportive than the last. This is a clear illustration of both the capability of societies to shift quickly and the power of socialization in our early years, where our views are shaped by the prevailing attitudes when we were growing up.

These two trends – the declining relevance of marriage and its hard-won expansion among a previously excluded group – may seem at odds, but they reflect the increasing diversity of our relationships.

However, as with other aspects of life, this increase in freedom has played out differently depending on your resources.[52] Americans with at least a bachelor's degree, for example, are now more likely to get and stay married than those with lower educational attainment. This is new: in the 1960s, marriage and divorce rates in these groups

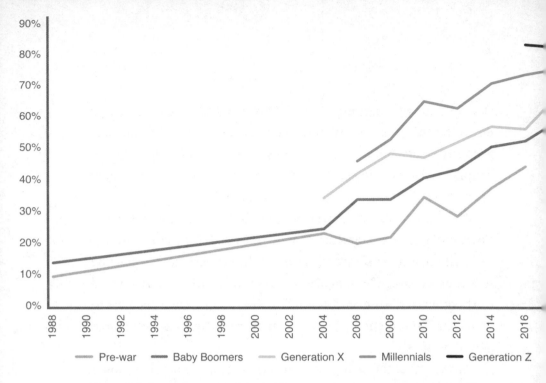

Figure 6.6: Percentage of adults in US supporting homosexual marriage[53]

were nearly identical. Similar divisions between income groups have arisen in other countries too, including the UK.

In our more individualized times, where we are less connected to extended families, affluent nuclear families can buy support that helps keep families together, from childcare to couples counselling. Less well-off families are on their own, and the impact is startling: in the US, college-educated women aged between 22 and 44 have a 78 per cent chance of their first marriage lasting at least 20 years, while women with a high-school education have only about half that chance.[54]

This divergence also transfers across generations, as the shape of families does seem to affect life outcomes for children. Simplistic assertions that a two-parent model is always best are clearly false: studies show that high-conflict two-parent households can be a lot worse for children.[55] But study[56] after study[57] has shown that children in households with both their married parents, on average, do better than the alternatives. Of course, cause, effect and intervening factors are impossible to untangle, and many studies show that the indirect financial implications of single parenthood or relationship break-ups may be more important than the relationship itself.[58] But in the end, stability matters, and it tends to be greater in married households, despite claims that long-term cohabitation is equivalent.[59] Children in France, for example, are 66 per cent more likely to see their parents break up if they are cohabiting rather than married.[60]

Splitting up

It is good news, then, that recent declines in divorce rates suggest that break-ups are becoming rarer. For example, in England and Wales there was a 28 percentage point fall in the number of divorces between 2005 and 2015.[61] In Germany, 2016 saw the lowest rate of divorce since 1993.[62] In the US, the rate fell from a peak of five divorces per 1,000 people in the 1980s to around three by 2017, its lowest since 1968.[63]

This change appears to be at least partly generationally driven, with younger cohorts particularly likely to be divorcing less. In fact, the trend resulted in one of the few positive headlines I've found about Millennials in years of research, from the World Economic Forum: 'The United States Divorce Rate is Dropping, Thanks to Millennials'.[64]

You can see the signs of this when tracking the proportions of British people who say they're divorced or separated. Only around 3 per cent of Millennials were divorced in 2017, compared with 6 per cent of Gen Xers when they were a similar age. Of course, as we've seen, fewer Millennials were married at the same age, but that does not entirely explain the lower divorce rates. Instead, later marriages tend to be less likely to fail, partly because the additional time allows people to build up financial resources and establish careers, reducing some of the key sources of marital stress.[65]

Accordingly, older people seem to be bucking the trend of fewer divorces.[66] In England and Wales between 2005 and 2015, the number of men aged over 65 who divorced increased by 23 per cent and the number of women increased by 38 per cent.[67] Part of the reason for the increased numbers of older divorcees is that there were many more older people in 2015. Looking at the number of men and women divorcing as a proportion of the married older population shows that their divorce rate has remained broadly consistent over the past decade.[68] Of course, in the context of falling divorce rates in other age groups, this bucks the trend and reflects a bulge of divorces among Baby Boomers that is making its way through the age range. In 2008, the peak proportion of divorces was among those in their late forties and early fifties, but by 2018 it had shifted to those in their sixties. There's a similar trend in the US, too: the divorce rate was 12.5 per cent among 55 to 64 year olds in 2017, compared with 5 per cent in 2008.[69]

Many explanations have been put forward for these 'Silver Splicers' – the increased economic independence of women and the shift towards greater focus on individual happiness, to rising longevity prompting panic at the prospect of spending several more decades with the same person. As one sardonic *Guardian* article put it, in the old days, an unhappy partner 'could just die, and avoid all that paperwork'.[70]

There has also been speculation that the COVID-19 crisis will both reverse the trend towards lower divorce rates and encourage the shift to delayed marriage. Some short-term impact on marriage rates is inevitable: most countries banned weddings for several months, and restrictions remain on ceremony sizes. Similarly, the stress of the crisis is likely to be too much for some relationships: Citizens Advice, a UK-based charitable network, reports that visits to its divorce webpage were up 25 per cent in the first week of September 2020 compared with the same week in 2019.[71]

But there are reasons to be hopeful that the longer-term impact of the crisis and its economic fallout will be less dramatic on marriage and divorce rates than on birth rates. Analysis of previous recessions shows limited effects on these rates. There were plenty of headlines[72] that claimed people were delaying marriage as a direct result of the recession in 2008, but the evidence cited generally mistook the long trend towards later marriage for a short-term economic effect. As the University of Michigan economist Justin Wolfers points out, the decline in the rate of marriage following the 2008 financial crisis was at the same rate as in the preceding boom and the previous bust. He concludes: 'The patterns of marriage and divorce rates have remained remarkably immune to the ups and downs of the business cycle.'[73]

Am I the only one who...?

While the pandemic may have put a temporary block on marriage, it has had the opposite effect on the use of internet porn: Pornhub, for example, reported a 22 per cent increase in traffic in the early months of the crisis. This is likely to be playing out very differently for different generations, as attitudes to porn are very generational. Figure 6.7 shows the proportions of each American generation who think that it should be illegal: while over half of the Pre-War generation have consistently called for outright prohibition, this falls to one in five among Millennials and Gen Z. Interestingly, Baby Boomers in particular have become increasingly prohibitive over the years. This seems to reflect a lifecycle effect rather than a general period effect, as other cohorts are not moving in the same direction.

There are signs of a similar 'generation gap' in British attitudes to porn. Back in 1989, four in ten Brits thought the sale of soft porn magazines in newsagents was 'morally wrong'. This halved to only

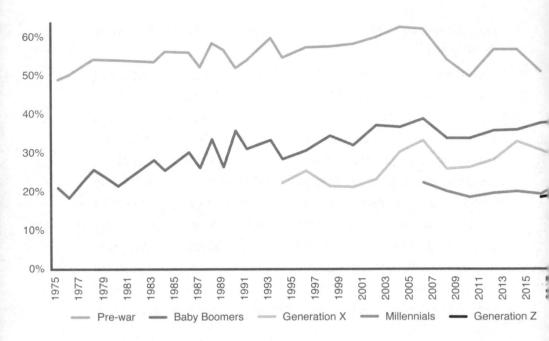

Figure 6.7: Percentage of adults in US who say that pornography should be illegal[74]

22 per cent by 2019 – although this may partly reflect the fact that buying hard-copy porn in a newsagents now seems incredibly quaint, as much as a relaxation in attitudes. However, the change has been driven by a shift among older age groups, with more permissive Baby Boomers replacing the more concerned Pre-War generation, in a similar pattern to that seen in the US.

We Brits are also much more relaxed about full-frontal male nudity on TV than we were in the late 1980s; the proportion of people who disapproved halved from around four in ten to 23 per cent by 2019, with women driving a lot of that change. Male nudity has become much more common on TV in recent years, but there still remains a distinct gender imbalance. As the ardent auditor of TV nudity, 'Mr Skin' (who runs a website that records the number and nature of naked scenes on popular programmes) points out, of the 82 nude scenes in the first seven series of *Game of Thrones*, only 21 were of men, and there were ten pairs of breasts for every penis shown.[75]

While it's clear that our exposure to nudity has increased, it is surprisingly difficult to say exactly how widespread pornography use is, or how this has changed. This is partly because of our ongoing reticence in talking about sexual behaviour, but also the myriad and shifting forms of sexually explicit material – which makes consistent measurement tricky. However, most studies find that between seven and eight in ten men, and between three and five in ten women, have viewed porn in the past few months. Not surprisingly, studies of younger people give higher figures: for example, one Dutch study of 15 to 25 year olds finds that 88 per cent of men and 45 per cent of women had viewed sexually explicit material in the past 12 months.[76] One Canadian academic attempting to study the effects of porn on men's attitudes to women ran into a problem with the control sample for his research design: 'We started our research seeking men in their twenties who had never consumed pornography. We couldn't find any.'[77]

The main driver of this ubiquity of porn use is, of course, the incredible reach of internet porn sites. In 2018, *109 billion* videos were watched on Pornhub alone (which ranks as the twenty-second most popular of all websites among UK internet users, just behind Microsoft.com).[78] Pornhub has analysed their users by demographic – splitting out Millennials and comparing them with Generation X and above. Although it is in no way representative of general use – this is only one website and it is difficult to accurately account for users who do not register their age – the data does offer some insight into pornography use by age, across a range of countries.[79]

Overall, Millennials are easily Pornhub's largest user base, accounting for 60 per cent of their global traffic. However, the Millennial share of the Pornhub audience varies widely from country to country – eight in ten Indian users of Pornhub are Millennials, while in Denmark and Japan, older generations account for 52 per cent of the traffic. However, rather than this suggesting that older Indians have no interest in porn, it is much more likely simply to reflect the much younger age profile of the Indian population, and that older Indians have less access to the internet.

Life stage is also reflected in the viewing habits of different generations. Splitting search terms by generation, the Pornhub data reveals that Millennials are more likely to search for clips that are relevant to their age, such as 'teacher', 'party' and 'college', as well as expressing a knowledge of relatively emergent trends such as 'cosplay' and 'hentai'. But plenty more niche interests are also revealed by searches, including 'humping stuffed animals' and 'snot fetish'.[80] Our private internet porn tastes are one of the clearest demonstrations of 'Ugol's Law', named after the software developer Harry Ugol, who said: 'To any question beginning with "Am I the only one who ...?", the answer is no.'[81]

With a new technology bringing such an easy outlet for these types of fantasies, it is unsurprising that there are many concerns about its impact on our patterns of thought and real lives. There has been a particular focus on younger generations, who are both heavier consumers and in their more formative years.

The first point to make is that we have always seen this pattern with the use of, and reaction to, new communications technologies. John Tierney, a US journalist, calls it the 'erotic technological impulse', and it's a constant throughout history. For example, there is a sketch of a reclining female nude on the wall of a cave at La Magdelaine in France from 12,000 BC. Sumerians wrote sonnets to vulvas, as soon as they discovered how to write cuneiform on clay tablets. Among the early books printed on a Gutenberg printing press was a sixteenth-century collection of sex positions. Ivan Bloch, the German physician who coined the term *sexology*, asserted in 1902 that, 'There is no sexual aberration, no perverse act, however frightful, that is not photographically represented today.'[82]

The growth of internet porn, then, reflects nothing new in human nature, but given the variety and ease of access, it is right that we look carefully at its possible impact. A thorough review in the *Journal of Sexual Medicine* looked at the many different dimensions of the effect of porn on sexual satisfaction, the quality of intimate relationships, aggression and sexual aggression towards women, lowered libido and erectile dysfunction.[83] The key words used throughout the review are that the evidence is 'mixed' or 'inconsistent', with a number of 'flawed' studies showing a negative impact and just as many showing no effect, while some even show positive outcomes. The authors also point out that divorce rates have fallen and numbers of sexual crimes have declined while the viewing of porn has exploded. They find little relationship between how these increasingly positive outcomes vary across countries and levels of porn use. The review is called 'Pornography Viewing: Keep Calm and Carry On', which is a fair summary of their view of the evidence.

Of course, this is not to say that porn does not have any negative effects. Part of the problem with the media reporting and the political discussion of porn is that it is presented as something that can have only good or bad effects, but not both or neither. In practice, just as there are many different kinds of porn, people engage with it for many different reasons. The meaning individuals give to porn, and the ways in which they use it, seem likely to be crucial in determining whether it is a positive, negative or neutral thing in their lives.

The most thorough studies of the impacts on children and young people present a similar picture. A literature review of over

40,000 academic studies by the Children's Commissioner in the UK concludes that there are very few robust conclusions around the effect of pornography on children and young people. The assessment confirms how much is still unknown, and echoes a review by the Dutch government which concludes that evidence confirming harmful effects on minors is just 'not available'.[84]

It's too late to panic

When looking at our shifting sex lives and family structures, gaining a proper understanding of period, cohort and lifecycle effects is especially important – these issues are so emotionally charged, and moral panics can mess with our memory of the past and colour our judgements of the present. There is a reason why therapists spend so much time carefully unpicking our sexual and family experiences: the private choices and very personal impacts involved, combined with the moral and religious overtones surrounding each, make them difficult subjects to consider.

This also means that we tend to blame current generations of young people for a decline in sexual activity, birth rates and marriage, and we fret that new innovations are damaging them. The reality is a much more interesting blend of consistency and change both within and between generations, driven by long-term period effects, delayed lifecycles and generational shifts. Panic over porn and the death of marriage, as well as the blame that is directed at young people for the 'sex recession' and low birth rates, are all misplaced.

Nevertheless, low birth rates still present one of our biggest challenges, as our populations tip inexorably from young to old. If we think we have reason to focus on the balance between contribution and support, young and old, right now – just wait until the middle of the century. The problem is there are no apparent solutions. As Darrell Bricker and John Ibbitson outline in *Empty Planet,* none of the interventions introduced to encourage higher birth rates, from subsidized childcare to tax breaks, seem to have much traction in the face of powerful forces such as increased education, urbanization and choice.[85] This is not a sudden baby bust that we can turn around, but the end of a long-term trend driven by some of the largest changes of the last few decades.

In the shorter term, we face similarly intractable problems with the families we already have. We need to avoid a fake nostalgia for a supposed 'golden age' of the nuclear family, as Stephanie Coontz points out. We forget that 'during its heyday, rates of poverty, child abuse, marital unhappiness and domestic violence were actually higher' than in our current, more diverse times.[86] But that is only half the story. The fact that we have a rosy view of the past doesn't mean we're in a better place now, and this is particularly true for those with fewer resources.

Just as with too-low birth rates, tiny targeted interventions to increase marriage rates are rightly dismissed as an inadequate approach to deal with the increasingly unequal consequences of our diverse family structures. Robert D. Putnam has suggested a huge raft of measures, from direct financial support for poorer families, reduced incarceration and an increased focus on rehabilitation, improved early childhood education, school and community college investment, and neighbourhood regeneration. Analysts at the Brookings Institute similarly conclude that the answer, rather than directly supporting marriage, is encouraging the factors that lead to stability in families and planning in parenthood – which mainly comes down to increasing education and raising incomes for those at the bottom.

The task is not to attempt to bolster a constantly changing institution, but to improve how family life can support opportunity across future generations as a whole, not just those who already have resources. Putnam suggests that the programmes that achieved this in the decades following the Second World War had at their heart a 'commitment to invest in other people's children. And underlying that commitment was a deeper sense that those kids, too, were our kids.'[87] This is a generational challenge about how we see our collective future.

Chapter 7

Manufacturing a Generational Culture War

'**N**ot cool, University of Manchester. Not cool.'[1] This was how Jeb Bush, former governor of Florida, responded to a 2018 story about a student union that had 'banned' applause at their events. Students had argued that clapping might trigger anxiety among some audience members, and that there were quieter ways for people to show appreciation. Students were encouraged to instead use 'jazz hands' – the British Sign Language gesture for applause, where you lift both hands up and wave them.

It may seem odd that such an eminent American politician felt compelled to comment on a minor decision by a handful of students thousands of miles away. In fact, former Governor Bush was making a self-deprecating reference to his own excruciating experience of 'silent applause', when he had to ask his audience to clap after a flat speech during his unsuccessful campaign for the 2016 Republican presidential nomination.[2] But the joke was missed in the international media storm that blew up around the story. Overnight, the University of Manchester's jazz hands became a *cri de coeur* among those who despaired at the character of today's youth ('What A Load Of Clap' was a popular headline), without any hint of Bush's irony (Piers Morgan tweeted 'Britain's losing its mind'). One professor opined that 'it symbolises our culture's slide into infantilised decadence, where enfeeblement is celebrated and learned helplessness indulged'.[3]

It's not just students in Manchester who have been the subject of such attention: whenever similar incidents crop up, whether at US political conferences[4] or Australian schools,[5] the furore is similar. The reason is that it provides a simple but vivid example of a complicated issue that is seen entirely differently by different groups. On one side, these sorts of measures are just a sensible attempt at the inclusion, in this case, of autistic people for whom applause, as the University of Manchester disability officer said, can feel like a bomb going off.[6] On the other side, it's a sign of a generation that is coddled in a way that will cause them to be utterly unprepared for the real world.[7]

The clapping controversy is one, admittedly slightly ludicrous, example of the 'culture wars', which are most often presented as being waged between the 'snowflake' young and the 'out-of-touch' old. The culture wars are increasingly the prism through which we see generational differences, so it's important to figure out whether we are experiencing any real sea change in the attitudes and beliefs of today's youth.

The first point to recognize is that there is *always* tension between generations, and this is a good thing. We can think of it as a type of 'demographic metabolism', as outlined by the Canadian demographer Norman B. Ryder in the 1960s. Ryder regarded society as an organism where this metabolism makes change inevitable. As both Karl Mannheim and the French philosopher Auguste Comte conclude, social, political or technological innovation would likely stall if we lived forever, as individuals get stuck in their ways. As Ryder says: 'The continual emergence of new participants in the social process and the continual withdrawal of their predecessors compensate the society for limited individual flexibility. The society whose members were immortal would resemble a stagnant pond.'[8]

Despite the benefits of generational change, it is a constant challenge for society to cope with this unending churn of membership, and, as Ryder puts it, 'the incessant "invasion of barbarians"'.[9] While this may seem like a harsh description of our delightful children, Ryder means that each new entrant is, by definition, not 'configured' to the attitudes and behaviours of their parents' society. Traumatic shocks, like wars, economic crises or pandemics, may utterly change the direction of new generations in their formative years, but there is *always* cultural tension between generations. As Ryder says, we are 'pulled apart gradually by the slow grind of evolutionary change'.

This is also the impression we get when we look at the actual data: there have been some incredible changes in our cultural attitudes over the last few decades, but this did *not* start with the arrival of Millennials or Gen Z. Instead, we can see that there is often not a great deal of difference between generations, except for the oldest. High-profile examples of extreme views and behaviours are amplified, but they do not reflect a break across generations as a whole. Rather than a cohort effect, this looks more like a period effect, where the greater polarization in society today sensitizes us to differences.

More than this, painting all young people as battling for 'social justice' misses the fact that less 'progressive' values persist in significant minorities of them. Generational analysis is to some extent part of the problem, as it can give the impression of an unstoppable march towards greater liberalism. In reality, cultural change is neither smooth nor unidirectional. Social values change as a result of a constant and messy struggle both between and within generations, and a fuller understanding of cohort, lifecycle and period effects is vital.

The beloved community

The Black Lives Matter (BLM) protests around the world, at the height of a global pandemic, will be remembered as one of the most extraordinary events of recent times. The murder of George

Floyd in Minneapolis sparked an outpouring of anger about racism and violence against black people around the world. It also had a particularly strong generational element in the profile of campaigners (at least two-thirds of protestors in four major US cities were 34 or under[10]) and the methods of protest and organization. BLM started in 2013, first as a hashtag following the acquittal of George Zimmerman in the killing of Trayvon Martin, and quickly evolved into a movement with a loose organizing structure and Gen Z leaders. The president of BLM Greater New York, 19-year-old Nupol Kiazolu, made the generational nature of the protest clear to the government: 'You've fucked with the last generation ... Young people have been carrying every single movement we've seen across the world, so it's time for adults to step aside and uplift us.'

This is not new, however: young activists have always played a leading role throughout the history of civil rights struggles. John Lewis, one of the most important figures in the fight for racial equality in America, was only 23 when he spoke alongside Martin Luther King at the March on Washington in 1963. His own speech possessed the same urgency that comes from emergent generations, ending: 'We will not and cannot be patient.'[11] In his final essay before his death in July 2020, Lewis urged the protestors to continue with non-violent direct action: 'When you see something that is not right, you must say something. You must do something. Democracy is not a state. It is an act, and each generation must do its part to help build what we called the Beloved Community, a nation and world society at peace with itself.'[12]

The discrimination faced by minority ethnic groups that sparked such passion is rooted in attitudes, beliefs and values. At its heart, it is based on how people see different races. Long-term survey measures can help us understand how views have changed, but it is difficult to gain a true measure of racial prejudice from surveys, particularly over a long period. 'Social desirability bias' in surveys refers to people responding, to some extent, in the way they think they're expected to or that puts them in a good light. This happens with all sensitive social issues, but it's likely to be particularly marked with measures of racism, given the highly charged nature of the issue.

For a while, it seemed like we may be able to access our unconscious bias through a tool called an Implicit Association Test, where the speed at which we associate good and bad things with different racial groups was supposed to provide a 'window into our souls'.[13] The only problem is that it doesn't really work: people who score highly on the test don't seem to be any more racist in practice than people who don't.[14] The same people can also achieve very different scores at different times, as journalist Jesse Singal points out in an article on the test: 'If a depression test, for example, has the tendency to tell people they're severely depressed and at risk of suicidal ideation on Monday, but essentially free of depression on Tuesday, that's not a useful test.'

Despite their limitations then, surveys of attitudes remain key measures of racist views. Some simply ask whether people think of themselves as prejudiced against other races, or whether they think people in the country as a whole are. In Britain, a long-time series survey has asked these questions, with incredibly stable responses: around three in ten have said they are a little or very prejudiced since 1983, with no discernible generational pattern.[15] But it's difficult to judge the meaning of this, as our standards of prejudice will have shifted.

Perhaps more useful are 'social distance' questions, which ask people how comfortable they are connecting with people of other races in specific ways. In Britain, respondents were first asked whether they would 'mind if a relative married a person of black or West Indian origin' back in 1983, when 51 per cent of all respondents said they would, which was a balance between the two quite different views of the Pre-War and Baby Boomer generations. The overall figure had more than halved to 22 per cent by 2013 and generational differences remained important, as we can see in Figure 7.1. In particular, a lot of the Pre-War generation retained their view while Baby Boomer concern halved, and Gen X and Millennials came into the population with few saying they'd mind. The good news is that the very high levels of concern we've seen in the recent past will fade away with the oldest generation. However, generational analysis also makes it clear that these attitudes won't entirely disappear: significant minorities of younger cohorts are holding onto this mindset.

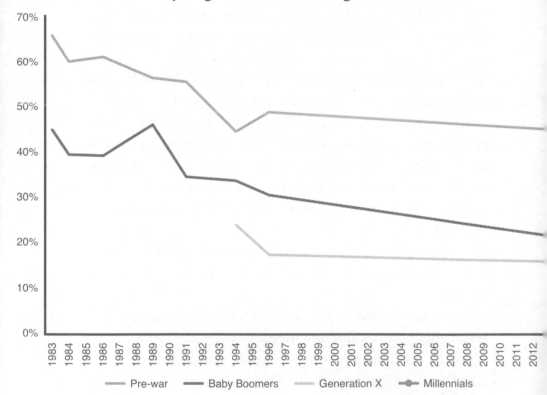

Figure 7.1: Percentage of white British adults who say they would mind if one of their close relatives were to marry a person of black or West Indian origin[16]

The decline in concern about interracial marriage in the US has been much more dramatic than in Britain, and more uniform across generations, as Figure 7.2 shows. The US started worse off in 1990, with 58 per cent of respondents expressing discomfort with interracial relationships (the equivalent figure in Britain was around 50 per cent), but ended at a lower level, at around 9 per cent. And this issue is very generational, with a 30 percentage point gap between the Pre-War generation and Millennials and Gen Z. People in the Pre-War generation have changed their views an awful lot over this period, but being socialized at a different time continues to be

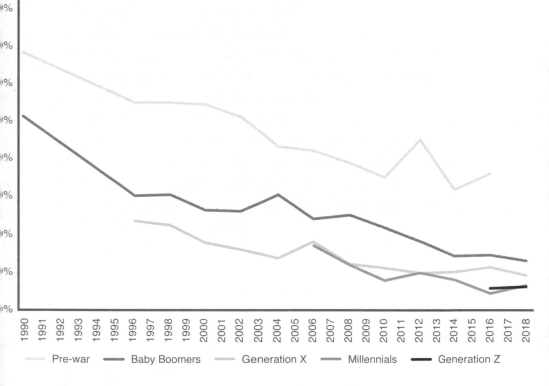

Figure 7.2: Percentage of adults in US saying that they would oppose having a close friend or family member marry a black person[17]

a strong influence for many. There is not, however, much of a gap between other generations.

In both the US and Britain, it is shocking how recently overtly racist attitudes were widespread in each country, and residual racist preferences are holding on in significant minorities of people, including among younger generations. However, more positively, we've come a very long way in a relatively short period of time. These changes in attitudes are also reflected in real-life behaviours; in the US, interracial couples accounted for 17 per cent of marriages by 2015, compared with 3 per cent in 1967.[18] In the UK, around one in ten couples are from different ethnic backgrounds, also a rapid increase in recent decades.

The experience of ethnic minority groups shows how discrimination is hanging on, however. For example, one direct way to understand prejudice in employment is through randomized controlled trials of job applications. Researchers can set qualification and experience levels to be the same on different sets of resumes and vary one characteristic that will indicate which ethnic group the candidate is from. Names are commonly used. Sending out large numbers of these mocked-up applications across job types reveals whether the responses from employers vary by these characteristics. This measures a tiny slice of possible prejudice, but the experimental design removes a lot of the uncertainty of interpretation. And unfortunately, these studies tend to show that racial prejudice in employment practice is widespread and unchanging. One meta-analysis of over 20 studies in the US between 1989 and 2015 shows that white candidates were 36 per cent more likely to get call-backs than black candidates with otherwise identical characteristics, and there was no real change over this period.[19]

These underlying judgements of people's capabilities on the basis of race are also visible in the survey data. A different survey question in the US asks people about the characteristics they associate with different racial groups – for example, whether they are hardworking or lazy. There has been an improvement over the last three decades, from around four in ten people believing black people to be 'lazy', to around a quarter now, but it is a shallower decline than for prejudicial views on marriage and more consistent across generations. The fact that 23 per cent of Millennials and 19 per cent of Gen Z still think black people are lazy is startling. Some suggest that holding onto these stereotypes about how hardworking different ethnic groups are has allowed racist attitudes among a segment of the population to simply shift focus. This framing, of there being a difference in *application* rather than *abilities* between races, is perhaps more socially acceptable now. It allows people to explain the different outcomes across ethnic groups without the need to acknowledge continued discrimination, in an individualistic culture where effort is rewarded.[20]

The BLM movement has shone a spotlight on racial discrimination, while other identity-driven divides have been central to societal tension over the last decade. In particular, major political events and trends have been driven by divisive debates about immigration: high or low 'nativist' views were among the strongest predictors of voting patterns in the 2016 (Trump vs Clinton) election;[21] immigration control was a core motivation in the pro-Brexit vote;[22] and views on immigration have been linked to the rise of right-wing populist parties across Europe.[23]

As with race, concern about immigration is often deeply generational, and nowhere is this more true than in Britain. Figure 7.3 traces the proportion of people in each generation for whom immigration is one of the top issues facing the country, and shows how generationally divisive it became in a short period of time. In the late 1990s, hardly anyone saw immigration as a top concern in Britain – but it shot up as European immigration increased in the early 2000s. It was then often the top issue for the country, peaking just before the European Union

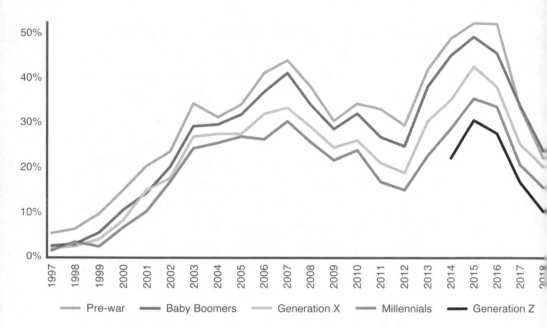

Figure 7.3: Percentage of adults in Britain picking immigration as a top issue facing the country[24]

(EU) Referendum in 2016 before falling away again. While the flow of changes during this period was similar across the generations, the levels of concern were utterly different. At the peak of this gap, the Pre-War generation was twice as likely to identify immigration as a top concern than Gen Z. Britain is far from alone in this generational divide on immigration: the same is seen in the US and Europe.

In 2015 and 2016, there was an expectation among some liberal commentators in the UK, the US and across Europe that this generational difference pointed to a more open future. Indeed, some of my analysis was used in a paper called 'Britain's Cosmopolitan Future',[25] which was published in 2015, a year before the EU Referendum. The paper identified various reasons to believe that Britain was moving towards more outward-facing attitudes: greater diversity, huge increases in university graduates, urban expansion, the decline of traditional institutions like political parties, new communication technologies and so on. The report ended with a warning that the political parties should embrace 'the emerging cosmopolitan majority' or face inevitable electoral decline.

A similar perspective was emerging in the US. Doug Sosnik, Bill Clinton's former political director, borrowed a phrase from the physicist Freeman Dyson when he called 2016 a 'hinge moment' at which the trends of urbanization and growing ethnic diversity would result in an acceleration of generational difference. Writing about the 2016 presidential election, Sosnik said, 'The candidate running for president in 2016 who best understands how the country is changing and runs a campaign based on the America of the future rather than the America of the past is most likely to be our 45th president.'[26]

The reality turned out quite different. We voted for Brexit in the UK, where some of the most powerful factors in explaining the UK's vote to leave the EU were a concern about the speed of cultural change.[27] The winning campaign in the US literally looked backwards as it aimed to make the country great 'again'.

Whether the analysis was wrong or just premature is one of the key debates of our time. One of the risks of only looking at generational trends is that the gaps between cohorts can make the future seem more predictable than it really is. But, of course, period and lifecycle effects still matter. The surge in immigration in the UK, and the huge growth in media and political attention on the issue, increased *all* generations' levels of concern about it. And we still change as we age, which dampens generational effects. Figure 7.4 traces concern about immigration by the Generation X age group compared with the 16 to 29 age group in each year of the study. In the late 1990s, these groups were exactly the same, but as Gen Xers have aged, their concern about immigration has gradually increased compared with people in that age group today.

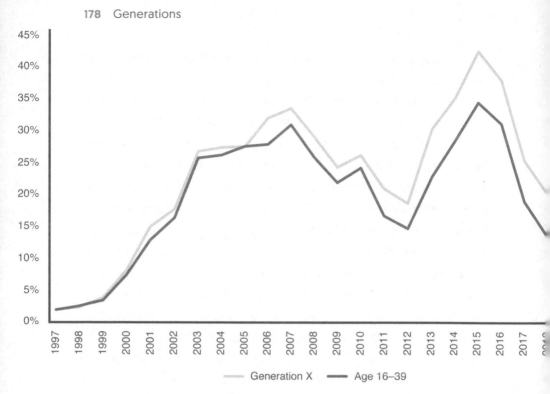

Figure 7.4: Percentage of adults in Britain, in the 16 to 29 age group and in Generation X, who say immigration is a top issue facing the country[28]

The battle of the sexes – and the ages

Our views of gender roles over the last few decades have played out with similar dynamics, and the overall transformation is equally remarkable. It is hard to imagine that, as recently as 1987, 48 per cent of the British population believed that 'the job of the man is to earn money, the job of the woman is to look after the home and family'. Now only 8 per cent of people say they hold this view.

If you looked at this change just across the population as a whole, it would seem like a gradual and consistent shift across British society. However, 'generational replacement' effects play a central role. In particular, members of the Pre-War generation have remained distinct in their views from all other cohorts – a large part of the decline in the belief that 'a woman's place is in the home' is the result of this generation's declining proportion of the population.

Many of this Pre-War cohort will have grown up when women were much less likely to be working: only 24 per cent of women worked in Britain in 1914, and the figure was still only around 50 per cent in the 1960s.[29] More generally, we have lived through what the economics professor Claudia Goldin calls a 'grand gender convergence' in the latter half of the twentieth century; there has been a narrowing in the gap between men and women not just in labour force participation, but in hours worked, occupation types, education levels and earnings.[30] Significant gaps remain, but the main point here is that the oldest generations grew up before many of these advances had begun.

This socialization effect means that the generational divide is much stronger than the gender divide. When we split the Pre-War generation into men and women, there is only ever around a 5 percentage point gap between them throughout the period – much smaller than the 20 percentage point gap between this cohort and the rest. Generation trumps gender on this measure, and Pre-War women are more distinct from their daughters and granddaughters than from their male peers. As one feminist writer puts it, progress seems to falter along a 'mother–daughter' divide: 'The contemporary women's movement seems fated to fight a war on two fronts: alongside the battle of the sexes rages the battle of the ages.'[31] This generational divide in the struggle for gender equality seems set to decline, as all other generations are tightly grouped in their views.

This is also true in the US; again, only the Pre-War generation stands apart, with Baby Boomers through to Gen Z expressing almost identical views, as we can see in Figure 7.5. The US question asks people whether they agree that 'it's much better for everyone involved if the man is the achiever outside the home and the woman

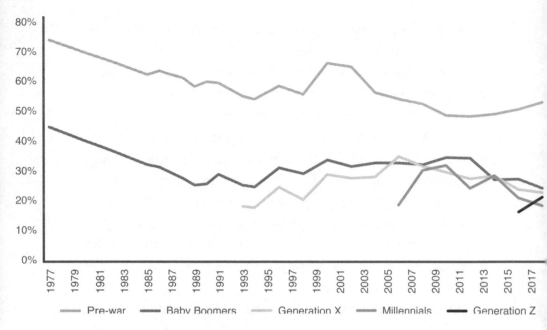

Figure 7.5: Percentage of adults in US who agree that it is much better for everyone if the man is the achiever outside the home and the woman takes care of the home and family[32]

takes care of the home and family', which is a slightly softer wording, and may partly explain why agreement with the sentiment is higher than in Britain. But it's unlikely to be the full reason – the change over time is also very different.

Over the period as a whole, agreement has dropped steeply, from 66 per cent in 1976 to 25 per cent in 2018. But this is not nearly as dramatic a decline as in Britain. The difference in endpoints – 25 per cent agreeing in the US, but only 8 per cent in Britain – is the result of the decline in agreement stalling in the US at the end of the 1980s, and starting to rise slightly during the 1990s, before drifting down again in the 2010s.

This coincides with a time in the US when people were trying to figure out whether women really could 'have it all'. A 1990 article in *Newsweek* came up with the term 'mommy wars' to describe the supposed clash between women who stay at home and women who work outside it. These tensions persisted for many years in political and cultural debate: in November 2003, an episode of *Dr Phil*, an American talk show, physically separated the studio audience to literally pit working and stay-at-home mothers against each other, reinforcing the simplistic polarization that has been common in the media and commentary.[33]

A much deeper and more consistent polarization is seen in long-term generational trends on attitudes to abortion in the US, as shown in Figure 7.6. From the 1970s onwards, around half – or more – of Americans have consistently said that a married woman should *not* be able to get a legal abortion just because she does not want more children. Gen Z is slightly less likely to hold this view, but over 40 per cent of this youngest group still do. The issue splits the country down the middle, regardless of generation. This is an extraordinary level of consistency on a social issue over a long period of time. It is also entirely different from Britain, where public opinion has shifted substantially: in the early 1980s, two-thirds of the population felt that a woman should not be allowed to have an abortion if she simply did not wish to have the child, a figure that had fallen to around a quarter for all except the Pre-War generation by 2016. There are no obvious distinctions between the other British generations: all except the oldest have changed their views similarly.

The explanation for this difference between the two countries is again tied to the much greater connection with religion in the US than the UK, and how this interacts with political identities. Attitudes to abortion are a clear dividing line between Republicans and Democrats in the US, with 82 per cent of the latter believing that abortion should be legal in most cases, compared with 36 per cent of the former. The issue formed a key plank in the early development

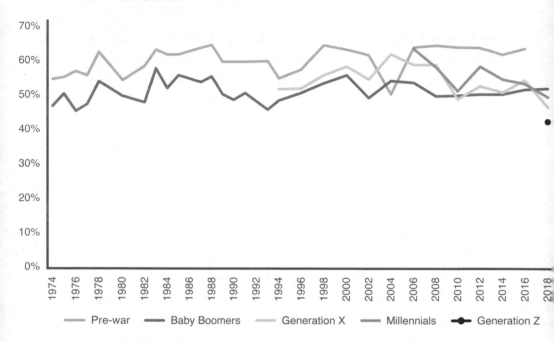

Figure 7.6: Percentage of adults in US who believe it should not be possible for a pregnant married woman who does not want more children to get a legal abortion[34]

of the US 'culture wars', a term first popularized by the sociologist James Davison Hunter, who proposed that American politics had experienced prolonged and intense polarization between orthodox, conservative values and progressive, liberal values. The gulf between these two ideological worldviews, Davison Hunter argued, had created two irreconcilable tribes. This idea remains disputed,[35] and as with many elements of the 'culture wars', we need to be careful not to exaggerate the depth of division on abortion in the US – there is more nuance and less distance between Americans than you may expect. For example, one poll, which gave people the options of 'pro-life', 'pro-choice', 'neither' or 'both', found that around four in ten said 'neither' or 'both'.[36] For a large chunk of the population, it's a complex and contingent issue, and we risk talking up divisions by caricaturing perceptions.

Beyond binary

If abortion was one of the earliest bases of the culture wars in the US, sexual orientation and more recently gender identity have become the most contentious areas in recent years across several countries. Attitudes to same-sex relationships have, however, been changing over a much longer period, and are now less divisive in many countries. We can see the extent of this change in Figures 7.7 and 7.8, which show how people responded to the same question in Britain and the US, going back to the 1970s and 1980s.

A number of things stand out from this comparison. Firstly, there have been incredible increases in the proportions of all generations who think homosexuality is 'not wrong at all', in both Britain and the US. This is a significant period effect – we've all shifted, starting from around 1990 in both countries. It seems quite extraordinary that, as recently as 1987, only 11 per cent of Brits thought homosexuality was not wrong at all, compared with 69 per cent in 2018. I was a teenager in the late 1980s, and that's not how I remember the general attitude at the time, which shows the strength of our tendency to re-write history based on our values today.

We can also see that the US started in an almost identical position to Britain in terms of attitudes to homosexuality, with the figures for both Baby Boomers and the Pre-War generation being very similar. But while the direction of the trend has been the same, the US has not moved quite as far; by 2018, 58 per cent thought homosexuality was not wrong, compared with 69 per cent in Britain.

Distinct generational patterns within the US and Britain are the key to explaining this difference. When you were socialized has a lasting impact on your attitudes, as is seen most clearly in the

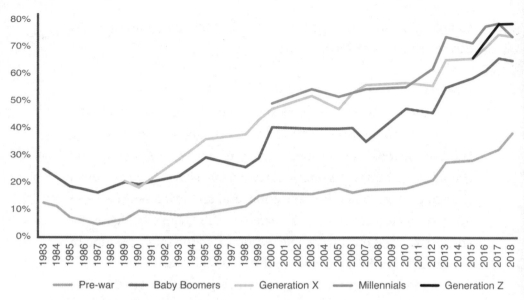

Figure 7.7: Percentage of adults in Britain who view sexual relations between the same sex as 'not wrong at all'[37]

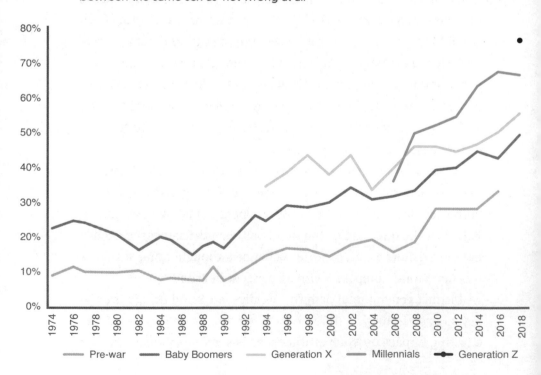

Figure 7.8: Percentage of adults in US who view sexual relations between the same sex as 'not wrong at all'[38]

Pre-War generations in each country. Their views on homosexuality have not shifted nearly as much as other generations', reflecting the fact that their formative experiences were at a time when active discrimination was embedded in many laws and institutions. Homosexual sex was a criminal act in the UK until 1967, when it was only partially decriminalized, and there was a similarly incremental change in the recognition of homosexuality in the US, over the same period. It's no surprise then that the views of the Pre-War generations in Britain and the US have remained remarkably similar. The same is true at the other end of the spectrum; British and American Gen Zers also have practically identical views – 80 per cent of them think homosexuality is not wrong at all.

The two countries, then, have drifted apart over the past couple of decades as a result of differences in attitudes in the middle, among Baby Boomers, Generation X and Millennials. In Britain, these generations have grouped together at the more permissive end of the spectrum, but in the US they've remained spread out, with Gen X tracking closer to Baby Boomers. For example, 75 per cent of British Gen X say that sex between two people of the same sex is not wrong at all, compared with 57 per cent of American Gen X.

There are a number of explanations for this growing separation, but key among them is again likely to be the very different connection with religion seen in those middle-aged cohorts in the two countries. Analysis by the Pew Research Center shows how much the acceptance of homosexuality is related to religious belief around the world, with a pretty straight line connecting the two. Majority-Muslim countries, such as Egypt, are at one end of the spectrum, with secular European countries, such as Sweden and Denmark, at the other end. There are exceptions – for example, Russia is much less accepting than its level of religious belief would suggest, and Brazil is much more accepting. The US is actually more accepting than you'd predict from looking at religiosity levels alone, but the strength of religious connection in these middle generations keeps it much less open than a lot of Europe.[39]

This international analysis is also an important reminder of how varied attitudes to homosexuality are around the world. The range is extraordinary, from around 5 per cent thinking homosexuality is 'morally unacceptable' in countries such as Denmark and Norway, up to 93 per cent in Indonesia. There are many countries where large proportions morally object, from Russia and Turkey at around 70 per cent, to Brazil and Mexico at around 40 per cent. *Where* you are born is still a much bigger determinant of attitudes to homosexuality than *when* you were born.

While trends in attitudes towards different sexual orientations over time and across countries are well documented, it is much more difficult to get consistent and insightful measures of actual sexual identities and behaviours over a long enough period to identify generational differences. However, it is clear that the changes in individual sexual identity have not been nearly as dramatic as our changes in attitudes. The most basic measures of identity, typically collected by official statistics agencies, mostly show a steady upward drift in people identifying as other than heterosexual. In the US, for example, it has increased from around 2.7 per cent in 2008 to 5 per cent in 2018, mainly driven by more people identifying as bisexual.[40] There is a clear generational difference in both countries: younger cohorts are more likely to identify as other than heterosexual – up to 10 per cent of American Millennials and 4 per cent of Gen Z in the UK.

Of course, such binary classifications are very blunt measures of our sexual identity, let alone our behaviour or attraction. Questions that allow people more of a spectrum get a very different response. For example, one 2015 US study by an advertising agency reports that only 48 per cent of 13 to 20 year olds (roughly Generation Z) identified as 'completely straight', compared with 65 per cent of people aged 21 to 34 (roughly Millennials).[41] When a similar question was asked in the UK in 2021, the results were almost identical, with just over seven in ten of the general population identifying as exclusively heterosexual, but only 54 per cent of 18 to 24 year olds doing the same.[42]

We should know by now that age-based gaps can only give us a limited insight into generational change; only long-term trends can show whether the behaviour of newer generations is similar or different from previous generations. Sadly, these are not available. Unfortunately, this generally does not stop the over-reach in the media: one particularly eye-catching headline from *Vice*, drawing on the results of the US study cited above, declared: 'Teens These Days Are Queer AF, New Study Says'.[43] The presentation of these simple age breakdowns as generational characteristics is part of the problem: comparing reported figures for Baby Boomers with Gen Z looks like an utter revolution in sexual attraction, but we can't tell how Baby Boomers would have responded when they were young, or how Gen Z will when they reach their sixties.

The lack of consistent long-term trends is surprising, because questions that regard sexual orientation as a spectrum rather than a discrete categorization have a long history. Alfred Kinsey, one of the pioneers of understanding sexual attraction in the US, developed a scaled approach from 0 (completely heterosexual) to 6 (completely homosexual), which he and colleagues used in thousands of interviews exploring men's sexual behaviours, and then published in his 1948 book *Sexual Behavior in the Human Male*.[44] As Kinsey famously said: 'Males do not represent two discrete populations, heterosexual and homosexual ... The world is not to be divided into sheep and goats.'

While his survey techniques were unorthodox and less structured than modern approaches, his findings suggest that things may not have changed as much as we might think. His research showed that, in 1948, 37 per cent of US males had had some homosexual experience during their lives, that 13 per cent were predominantly homosexual for at least three years (as Kinsey correctly recognized, sexual attraction and behaviour are not constant states), and that 4 per cent were exclusively homosexual throughout their lives.

We are likely seeing important but relatively gradual increases in more diverse sexual identities, attractions and experiences, combined with a greater willingness to report our attitudes and behaviours – rather than the revolution in sexual fluidity that some suggest. For example, there was a significant rise in women reporting same-sex experience in the UK, from 2 per cent to 8 per cent between 1990 and 2010.[45] The researchers attempted to unpick whether this was a real change or due to women being more willing to report what they got up to. Their conclusion was that the change between 1990 and 2000 was partly due to more honest reporting, but the rise between 2000 and 2010 was mostly real.[46]

As well as sexual identity being viewed as less binary, there have been fractious arguments about gender identity and fluidity. Early discussion of attitudes to gender identity focused on transgender equality. A 2014 *Time* magazine cover story with the headline 'The Transgender Tipping Point: America's Next Civil Rights Frontier'[47] emphasized its generational nature. A trans woman interviewed for the article, who didn't begin her transition until middle age, 'is certain she could have had a completely different life if she had been born later'.

The discussion has quickly developed from a focus on transgender rights to broader issues around gender identification, and the generational framing has become even more prominent. Gen Z in particular is often picked out as the 'gender-fluid generation',[48] and for some good reasons, when you consider how much more direct contact Gen Zers have with people who identify as non-binary than other generations. According to a Pew Research Center survey, over a third of US Gen Zers say they personally know someone who uses non-binary pronouns, compared with 12 per cent of Baby Boomers.[49] In the UK, only 27 per cent of British Gen Zers say they've never met anyone who uses non-binary pronouns, compared with 68 per cent of Baby Boomers.[50]

Some attitudes follow similarly steep age gradients – but it's not always as clear-cut as the generational framing suggests. Roughly twice as many young people as older people in Britain think that 'a person should be able to identify as a different gender to the one they were born in', and there's a similar split on whether passports should include a category for people who do not identify as male or female.[51] Support is higher in the US: half of women and four in ten men agree that there is a spectrum of gender identities, but there are no strong age differences on this question.[52] Indeed, your political party is a more reliable indication of attitude towards gender identity among Americans than age; 64 per cent of Democrats agree that whether a person is a man or a woman can differ from their sex at birth, while only 19 per cent of Republicans do.[53]

The rapidity with which this new front has emerged and is changing makes even current opinion difficult to ascertain, so predicting future generational trends is impossible. However, it seems clear that it isn't a 'fad' of youth, as some argue.[54] I am naturally suspicious when older generations respond to any emergent trend in this way – we have seen a similar tendency with some of the biggest social shifts of modern times. H. G. Wells said that some of his contemporaries believed 'the vote for women was an isolated fad, and the agitation an epidemic of madness that would presently pass'.[55]

Equally, the trajectory of attitudes to gender identity is far from set or entirely generationally driven. The issue raises complex questions that are still only emerging, which each generation is still working through, including the youngest. Drawing on the Pew Research Center survey results mentioned above, one American sexology commentator suggests that, 20 years from now, our current 'bickering over bathrooms will seem quaint'.[56] This is too dismissive of some real debates that are playing out, and too simplistic a reading of how cultural change both ebbs and flows.

Rise of the nones?

The continued power of religion to shape wider beliefs has been clear in many of the issues already covered in this chapter. It is, then, vitally important to understand how it's changing – particularly as general attachment to religion is one of the most clear-cut generational traits that we'll see. Of course, individuals fall in and out of religious belief all the time, but not a lot changes within each generation as a whole, as we can see in Figure 7.9, which shows how many of each cohort in Britain say they have no religion.

The generational gaps are huge: 70 per cent of Gen Zers say they have no religious affiliation compared with under 30 per cent of the Pre-War generation, and each of the lines are pretty flat. The challenge facing organized religion in Britain is almost entirely generational, which makes the decline slow; it's mostly changing as one cohort dies out and is replaced with another with a lower level of belief. But this also makes it inevitable. You can't stop these sorts of generational tides without an event on the scale of a 'second coming'.

As frightening as this picture is for religious institutions, it hides an even greater challenge facing Christian faiths in a number of Western countries, including Britain. The figures for religious

1985 1986 1987 1988 1989 1990 1991 1992 1993 1994 1995 1996 1997 1998 1999 2000 2001 2002 2003 2004 2005 2006 2007 2008 2009 2010 2011 2012 2013 2014 2015 2016 2017

——— Pre-war   ——— Baby Boomers   ——— Generation X   ——— Millennials   ——— Generation Z

Figure 7.9: Percentage of adults in Britain who say they have no religion[57]

identification among younger generations would be even worse without the increase in non-Christian faiths among the British young, largely due to immigration. When we look at association with the Church of England in Britain, the dire situation is even clearer. Only 2 per cent of the youngest generations identify as Anglicans, compared with nearly 40 per cent of the Pre-War generation. And to add to the woe, even the older generational lines show signs of decline, with the Pre-War generation, Baby Boomers and Gen X each drifting down over time.

But the generationally driven death of organized religion is not quite as certain as this suggests. While 'cultural' Christians (those who identify but don't practise) might be dying out, those who remain are much more consistently committed. This is a process that the sociologist Grace Davie has likened to the shift from a 'conscript army' to a 'professional force'.[58] She explains how Christianity in countries like Britain has moved from having 'large numbers of people involved whether they liked it or not, to a professional army which people join voluntarily ... Broadly speaking, I contend that the professionals are rather more committed than conscripts.'

This is largely supported by the data: the changes in regular attendance levels in Britain are not nearly as varied across generations and are not collapsing nearly as much. Even on this most generational of issues, different cohorts are not as far apart as it may seem at first. British Baby Boomers have always been lax church-goers, and continue to be, with only around 10 per cent attending services weekly, while Millennials have settled at a similar level. Gen X, however, has seen a significant increase in regular church-going, tripling to around 15 per cent. As the parent of a child nearing secondary school age, I suspect that this has something to do with the continued role of religion in school selection, where many schools require parents and children to attend services to qualify for places. Of course, a more important driver of the overall relative stability of these trends is that they cover all faiths and are bolstered by the growth of non-Christian religions in the UK, where attendance tends to be more regular.

The US has an *entirely* different relationship with religion than Britain, with each American generation twice as likely to say they identify with a religion than their British counterparts, as Figure 7.10 shows. There is a similar generational hierarchy to Britain, but even among Millennials, the most godless US generation, only 34 per cent say they have no religion, compared with 68 per cent in Britain. Even so, the fixation on the 'rise of nones' in America is understandable: levels of religious identification may be much higher than in Britain, but the country is still experiencing a powerful mix of significant cohort and period effects.

Figure 7.10: Percentage of adults in US who say they have no religion[59]

There is, of course, a lot of 'conscript' rather than 'professional' religious attachment among Americans. While eight in ten have a religious affiliation, only around a quarter attend a weekly religious service. However, this is significantly higher than in Britain, particularly among Baby Boomers; 10 per cent of that cohort in Britain attend weekly services, compared with 30 per cent in the US. But again, the differences between generations *within* the US are much lower.

Looking beyond anglophone and northern European countries also turns the narrative of religious decline on its head. As the Archbishop of Canterbury Justin Welby, the most senior bishop in the Anglican church points out, the domestic decline in Britain masks a very different picture elsewhere: 'In global terms, a typical Anglican Christian is an African woman just over the age of thirty living on less than $4 per day.'[60] Overall, Pew Research Center projects that Christians will account for 31 per cent of the global population in 2050 – the same level as now, due to population growth in these Christian developing countries. The global Muslim population, 23 per cent in 2010, will reach 30 per cent by 2050. The proportion of religiously unaffiliated people will fall from 16 per cent to 13 per cent of the world's population, as Europe's global population share also declines.[61]

These patterns can be seen playing out in a question that asks whether people see themselves as religious. Germany has a similar pattern to Britain, with a clear generational hierarchy; older cohorts are more religious than younger cohorts, and only half of Germans as a whole see themselves as religious. But in other Christian countries, such as Italy and Brazil, around seven in ten see themselves as religious, across all generations. The picture is the same in non-Christian countries, such as India and Turkey. Northern Europe is not the norm in an increasingly religiously diverse world.

The generational culture wars

It is startling to observe how far our attitudes to race, gender and sexuality have shifted in the last few decades. That they have moved so much so quickly should be celebrated, particularly as it is not something we would have foreseen 30 or 40 years ago. That these issues remain a source of conflict is more predictable. Such conflict is built in through the constant arrival of new participants in society – it may be a natural part of our societal 'metabolism', but we will always fear the young 'barbarians'. This longer-term perspective also shows that we *always* feel that things are changing too fast for us to keep up. In 1914, the US commentator Walter Lippmann wrote: 'We are unsettled to the very root of our being … We have changed our environment more quickly than we know how to change ourselves.'[62]

The overall impression we get is not of a sudden shift with the latest generation of young people, but rather a remarkable change among most generations over the last three or four decades. Generational effects are essential to understanding culture change, but the gaps between today's young and most other generations are not as large or unusual as they are often portrayed. Of course, we shouldn't downplay the differences entirely; there are important distinctions, and these show up most on emergent issues, as we would expect. For example, support for the BLM protests is roughly twice as high among the youngest compared with the oldest age groups, and in the UK, the young are roughly twice as likely to be 'ashamed' of our imperial past than older groups. But these gaps are no different in scale from those seen between the Pre-War generation and Baby Boomers on race. Even on gender identity, the 'cultural warrior' label is a poor fit for large sections of the young, and other characteristics have a stronger effect on their views.

Once again, our tendency to focus on one explanation for change hides a richer and more complex reality. Lifecycles are important, and we do seem to shift our position on issues like immigration as we age. Period effects also have a say – for example, in how they moved all the generations' views of women's roles in the US in the 1990s against what looked like a solid generational tide.

Perhaps most importantly, greater division across society as a whole, driven by polarizing politics and social media environments, has sensitized us to high-profile but unrepresentative examples of 'woke' and 'unwoke' behaviour. People of all generations are identifying more with their own group and differentiating themselves more from the 'other' group, which leads us to focus on behaviours that would have attracted less attention in the past. The 'war on woke' seems to be more a result of this change in the general environment than a distinct break in the attitudes of our current generation of young people. By exaggerating differences, we are in danger of falling into a behaviour that we claim young people today are guilty of: 'catastrophizing'.

Overly simplistic generational analysis is part of the problem. Generational replacement is a key driver of cultural change, with older generations being replaced by cohorts socialized in very different times. However, this can give a false sense of certainty; we need to remember the power of shocks that can change our trajectory, and lifecycle effects that return younger generations to well-worn paths. The generational trends are also sometimes wrongly translated as 'job done', which skirts over the fact that less liberal attitudes persist in significant minorities of younger generations, and that inequalities continue to exist.

For example, the writer Douglas Murray shows a palpable frustration about new expressions of inequality, such as a focus on 'toxic masculinity': 'Why would the ... rhetoric become so heated when the standards of equality have so much improved? Is it because the stakes are so low? Because people are bored and want to assume the heroic posture amid a life of relative safety and comfort?'[63] It is perfectly reasonable to question the usefulness of emergent concepts, but doing so should not lead to a dismissal of continuing injustice. The persistence of discriminatory attitudes and the gaps in outcomes on the basis of gender, race and sexuality deserve more attention than that.

There is a further risk with emphasizing this generational framing, and in particular ascribing so much responsibility to emerging generations of young people. Barack Obama, for example, has repeatedly outlined his particularly strong faith in the 'next generation' whose 'conviction in the equal worth of all people seems to come as second nature', while implying that their parents and teachers never truly believed the same.[64] This is no doubt intended to be a positive encouragement, but it brings its own risks. The trends in our attitudes don't suggest that current generations represent a real break with the recent past on issues including gender, race and sexuality. Lionizing coming generations not only misrepresents reality but also encourages a false sense of separation.

Chapter 8

Constant Crises

'Events, dear boy, events.' This was the British prime minister Harold Macmillan's reported response when he was asked what he thought would blow his government off course.[1] The reply succinctly captures the tendency of politicians to view their actions as moment-to-moment survival in the face of the unpredictable. In 1886, the British politician Joseph Chamberlain wrote, 'In politics, it's no use looking beyond the next fortnight.' Today, a fortnight seems positively luxurious, with the advent of 24-hour news and social media. As the former Australian prime minister Malcolm Turnbull suggested, 'It's a 60-second news cycle now, it's instantaneous.'[2]

Of all the areas examined in this book, politics is the one most obviously determined by sudden, unexpected period effects – but that does not mean that 'events' are all that matters. Indeed, it is important to fight that perception, not least because it reinforces the sense that we are constantly teetering on the edge of crises – with challenges as significant as trust in politics or even support for democracy. In fact, there is substantial continuity and resilience in our political system, partly because many of the most important patterns in our political behaviour are driven by a combination of slower cohort effects and our own predictable lifecycles.

Each of the powerful generational trends we've seen in previous chapters end up expressed in our political views: the changing attitudes between cohorts shift the political debate and help determine individuals' connection with particular political parties. Clearly this is not a one-way relationship – politics also shapes our views. 'Thatcher's children', those who came of age in the 1980s in the UK and show a greater tendency to be right-leaning than neighbouring cohorts, represent a generation carrying with them some imprint of the political context in which they grew up.[3] Similar patterns have been identified in the US, including some that work in the opposite direction: those who turned 18 during the Nixon presidency were more likely to vote Democrat than the average American in elections decades later.[4]

We also change as we age. There are numerous versions of the saying, 'If you're not a liberal when you're 25, you have no heart. And if you're not a conservative by the time you're 35, you have no brain.' The quote has been attributed to various people over the decades, but it is about as clear an assertion of the importance of lifecycle effects as you'll see. Our generational data shows that the effect is not nearly as absolute as the saying suggests, but it is still an important fact of political life.

In recent years, a number of political predictions from pundits and commentators have been confounded, and our tendency to focus on just one of the cohort, lifecycle or period effects is part of the reason for these misses. Age and generation are increasingly important in understanding our politics, but we need to avoid the temptation of looking for one simple explanation.

Grey votes vs youthquakes

The importance of a generational perspective doesn't just apply to the electorate – it's also helpful in understanding the changing profile of political leadership. In particular, the US stands out among Western democracies for its current drift towards a 'gerontocracy'.

Donald Trump was the oldest president to be inaugurated, at 70 years old – until Joe Biden, at 78. President Biden joins Nancy Pelosi, the 80-year-old House speaker, and Chuck Schumer, the 71-year-old Senate majority leader, at the top of the US political hierarchy. As an article in the *Atlantic* put it, most of these individuals 'came into the world before the International Monetary Fund and the CIA; before the invention of the transistor and the Polaroid camera'.[5]

An ageing political class may seem like a natural consequence of increased longevity and health in later life, but the US is in fact an outlier; since 1950, the average age of heads of government in the OECD has steadily declined, from over 60 to around 54 today[6] – a quarter of a century younger than President Biden.[7] This is largely because of the unusual presidential system in the US, where the enormous resources and political capital required to run for office take much longer to build up. The particularly large US baby boom, and the good fortune of this generation in the growth years, has meant they've been difficult to dislodge by the subsequent, smaller cohorts, but this is starting to shift. The slow but relentless force of generational replacement saw a jump in both Gen X and Millennial members of the 116th Congress in 2019,[8] so that they made up 38 per cent of congressmembers – but that progress seems to have stalled with the 117th Congress in 2021, as Baby Boomers made up almost 70 per cent of incoming congressmembers.[9] We're still waiting for a generational 'hinge moment' in the balance of US political leadership.

However, we need to be mindful of the implied ageism and bias in discussions of 'gerontocracies'. It is not the case that older representatives are bound to act in or appeal to the interests of their own generation: the popularity of Bernie Sanders (79) and Jeremy Corbyn (71) among young people in the US and UK is undeniable.

More generally, the idea that older leaders are not interested in young people or future-focused issues such as climate change is, as we'll see, patently false. Joe Biden made an explicit cross-generational appeal to young Americans during his campaign: 'I view myself as a transitional President ... it's a transition to your generation. The future is yours and I'm counting on you.'[10]

Simplistic interpretations that leaders or electorates consistently act in their generational self-interest are, therefore, deeply flawed. But, in the end, politics is a 'numbers game', and the greater your electoral weight, the more likely it is that political agendas and outcomes will bend towards your interests.

This is a simple function of just two factors: how many of you there are and how many turn out. The first of these factors has clearly worked against younger generations in recent decades across a number of countries. The demographic bulge that followed the Second World War was significant in a large number of nations, including the US, the UK, Canada, Australia, New Zealand, France and most other western European countries.[11] Increased longevity has also helped to 'grey' the electorate. Taken together, these effects have resulted in potential voting power moving steadily up the age range, and this is set to continue: for example, in the UK the median potential voter was 46 in 2010, but will be 50 by 2041.[12]

This demographic advantage is multiplied because older groups are also more likely to vote than younger ones. Figure 8.1 compares self-reported turnout rates of those aged under 30 with those aged 65 or over, and shows a particular imbalance in the UK, Ireland and the US, while the gap is much less marked in Spain and actually reversed in Belgium (the only country in the chart where voting is compulsory). When we combine this unbalanced turnout with the ageing profile of the UK, the median actual voter was 49 in 2010 and 52 in 2019. This results in millions

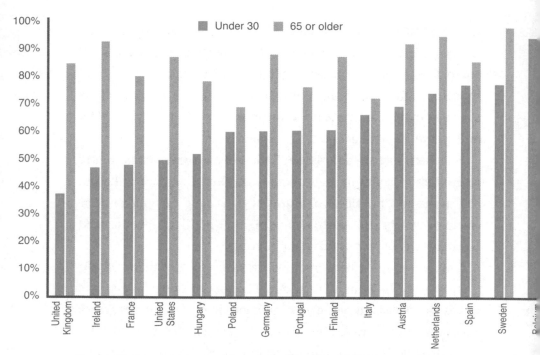

Figure 8.1: Percentage of adults aged under 30 and 65 or over who say they voted in the last national election, Europe and US[13]

of extra votes for older cohorts in elections, which is best seen when we compare single-year birth cohorts within generations. For example, at the 2015 UK general election, each Millennial who voted was joined by an average of 400,000 people born in the same year as them, while each Gen Xer and each Baby Boomer was joined by 485,000 and 530,000 people respectively.[14]

The electoral dominance of older generations may feel like a constant, but in generational terms it's relatively new in many countries, such as the UK. It is true that Baby Boomers were less likely to vote in their youth than the Pre-War generation, but the gap was relatively small. The real break came with Generation X in the 1990s, when there was a 25 percentage point gap in claimed turnout between them and the oldest group. It continued to grow with

Millennials; by 2015, there was a 40 percentage point gap between the oldest and the youngest cohort.[15]

Our awareness of this generational gap makes us sensitive to any sign that it may be reversing. For example, during the 2017 UK general election, there was much discussion of a 'youthquake', where the Labour leader Jeremy Corbyn seemed to be mobilizing younger generations: he was, for example, greeted like a rock star as he strode onto the Pyramid Stage at the Glastonbury Festival. Detailed analysis following the election showed the impact was not quite as earth-shaking as some claimed: there *was* a significant increase in turnout among younger groups, but it was most marked among those in their thirties, and not of the order suggested by some breathless articles at the time.[16] However, the trend in the last few elections has been towards higher claimed turnout among younger generations, particularly from the dire levels seen in the 2000s.

This is mirrored in trends on whether people in Britain see voting as a duty. In 2010, only 40 per cent of British Millennials thought voting was a 'civic duty', compared with 80 per cent of the oldest generation. But by 2017, following two fractious referendums and two general elections, Millennial commitment to voting had increased to 65 per cent. Plenty of political scientists had been extremely worried about the health of the electoral system – and rightly so – but a few short years changed that picture significantly.[17] This is likely to be at least partly related to the tumultuous experience of so many vital political contests in the space of a few years: voting is a habit that younger generations in the UK have had an unprecedented opportunity to develop recently. Events really do matter in politics.

In the US, Bernie Sanders is a similar left-leaning political figure with strong appeal to younger voters. Sanders lost in the Democratic primaries to Joe Biden in 2020, despite having huge leads among young Americans in some states – up to 52 percentage points in Arizona, for example.[18] But turnout worked against him, with voting rates among young people falling from the 2016 primaries.[19] Even if he had been successful and become the Democratic candidate, the challenge of relying on this youth advantage would have followed him into the presidential race. Analysis by the political scientists David Broockman and Joshua Kalla showed that Sanders would have required an 11 percentage point rise in the youth vote, over and above any general increase in turnout, just to match the other Democratic candidates' showing against Trump.[20] This sort of increase is unprecedented in US presidential elections.

As in the UK, the reason why it is risky to rely on the support of the young in the US is the marked gap in voting levels between generations, as shown in Figure 8.2. However, the pattern is quite different, with US generations showing more movement as they age. For example, only around 50 per cent of US Baby Boomers claimed to vote in the late 1970s, but this is now 80 per cent. In the UK, this trend has been much less dramatic, with Baby Boomers starting out at around 75 per cent and ending up at 88 per cent. This powerful lifecycle effect helps explain the relative stability of US turnout, which has hovered around the mid-50 to low-60 per cent level since the 1970s (with the 66 per cent turnout at the 2020 presidential election representing a level not seen since 1900). In contrast, UK turnout has fallen from a peak of 84 per cent in 1950 to 67 per cent in 2019, mostly due to growing gaps between the generations. While youth turnout is a problem in both countries, in the US the electorate seem to grow out of it.

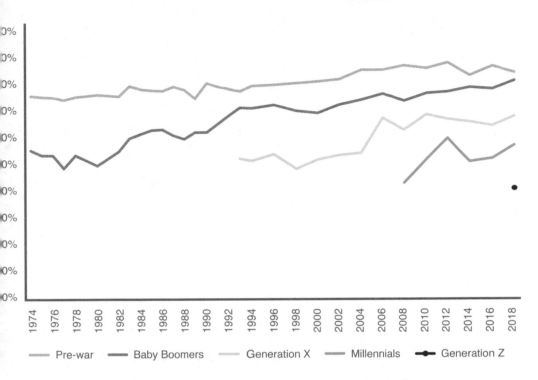

Figure 8.2: Percentage of adults in US claiming they voted in the last presidential election[21]

The slow death of political parties?

The US does, however, face more of a generational challenge regarding connection with political parties. As Figure 8.3 shows, there are worrying long-term trends for the two main parties, with only around four in ten American Millennials identifying as either a Republican or Democrat, compared with six in ten in the Baby Boomer and Pre-War generations. This is a significant shift, but a longer-term perspective shows that it's not entirely new: in the mid-1970s, when Baby Boomers were young, there was nearly as large a gap between them and the Pre-War generations. It has been this oldest Pre-War generation that has held up party attachment, until a steep decline in the latest measure in 2018. The loss of that bulwark

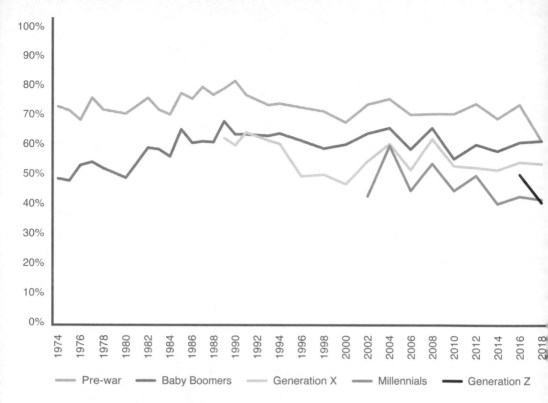

Figure 8.3: Percentage of adults in US identifying with either Republicans or Democrats[22]

Pre-War generation has had a big impact on overall levels of political attachment in the US: the slow but relentless process of generational replacement means that identification with the two main parties has fallen from 63 per cent to 51 per cent in the last 44 years.

A similar question in a European survey asks whether people feel close to one particular party. This only goes back 14 years, but the pattern is similar. The generational lines are very flat, with each successive generation sticking at progressively lower levels of party attachment. The overall impact on party identification over this shorter period is less dramatic, but it is also drifting downwards, from 52 per cent in 2002 to 45 per cent in 2018.

There are a number of structural reasons for this decline, including the weakening of affiliations with religions and labour organizations, which previously delivered large numbers of party supporters.[23] It also seems likely to be related to the cultural changes we've already seen: the rise in individualism makes buying wholesale into one political party for life less likely.

But it's also clear that the outright rejection of political parties is a long way off. And, as with so many aspects of politics, generational trends can be reversed by 'events'. Figure 8.4 tracks the proportion of people in Britain who see themselves as supporters of a particular party. In the 2000s, it seemed like there was a generationally driven collapse in party attachment, to a *much* greater degree than seen in the US or across Europe as a whole. In 2009, for example, fewer

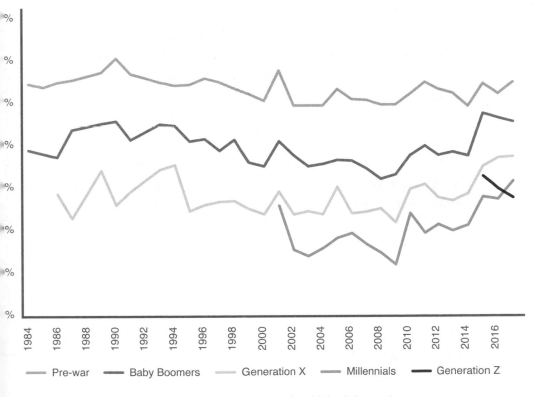

Figure 8.4: Percentage of adults in Britain who think of themselves as supporters of any one political party[24]

than one in ten Millennials thought of themselves as a supporter of a particular party, with members of the Pre-War generation five times as likely to count themselves a party supporter. Overall, we'd gone from 51 per cent of the population saying they were a supporter of a party to *just 29 per cent* in two decades. As one political scientist puts it: 'Millennials ... regard it as the duty of politicians to woo them. They see parties not as movements deserving of loyalty, but as brands they can choose between or ignore.'[25]

However, in the frenzied political period between 2014 and 2017, just as turnout and the feeling that voting was a civic duty increased, party attachment also started to grow for all British generations, including Millennials. In a few eventful years, party support rose back up to 40 per cent across the population. This is still a very low level of party identification, historically and internationally, but it illustrates the dangers of prediction in politics based on apparently settled generational trends.

Demography and destiny

While the political turbulence of the last few years has been positive for party engagement in the UK, I suspect few people would recommend it as a strategy for reconnecting people with politics, not least because it has come with the emergence of age as a clear electoral dividing line. The 2017 general election produced the biggest age gap in party support ever measured in the UK. This fell back slightly in the 2019 election, but it still produced an incredible age gradient. Only 21 per cent of 18 to 24 year olds voted for the Conservatives, and only 14 per cent of those aged 70 or over voted for Labour. Conversely, two-thirds of the oldest group voted Conservative, and over half of the youngest went with Labour.

Looking at long-term generational support for the two main parties shows just how rapid and unusual the shift has been.

As Figure 8.5 indicates, there had been little generational basis to Labour Party support since at least the 1980s, with the lines for each generation staying close together – until a generational explosion in 2017, when over half of Gen Zers said that they identified with Labour, compared with barely 20 per cent of the Pre-War generation.

The Conservative vote has always been more related to age, but the generational difference has also expanded hugely in recent years. This has not been due to a collapse among the young so much as an increasingly fervent level of support from the oldest cohorts, who are now three times more likely to back the Conservatives than the youngest generations.

The reasons for such dramatic swings are related to short-term political events as much as generational tides. Labour partly gained its younger vote from the collapse of the Liberal Democrats, while the Conservatives gained from the decline in the UK Independence Party. The age gradient of party political support was reinforced by the result of the referendum to leave the EU as well. The Leave–Remain divide between the generations is huge, and has grown over time: in 2019, 67 per cent of Gen Zers said that they would have preferred to remain in the EU, compared with 29 per cent of the Pre-War generation.

Whatever the short-term cause, the long-term future of the Conservative Party looks bleak, with a supporter base that is skewed towards generations that are leaving the voting pool, and away from those who are arriving in it. However, the death of the Tories has been predicted many times before, and there are reasons to be sceptical.

Firstly, as we've just seen, these patterns can change quickly thanks to the period effect of 'events'. Secondly, the greying of the electorate and generational gaps in turnout have made the older lines in these charts more valuable over time – and, as we've seen in the predicted increase in the median voter age, this is set to continue.

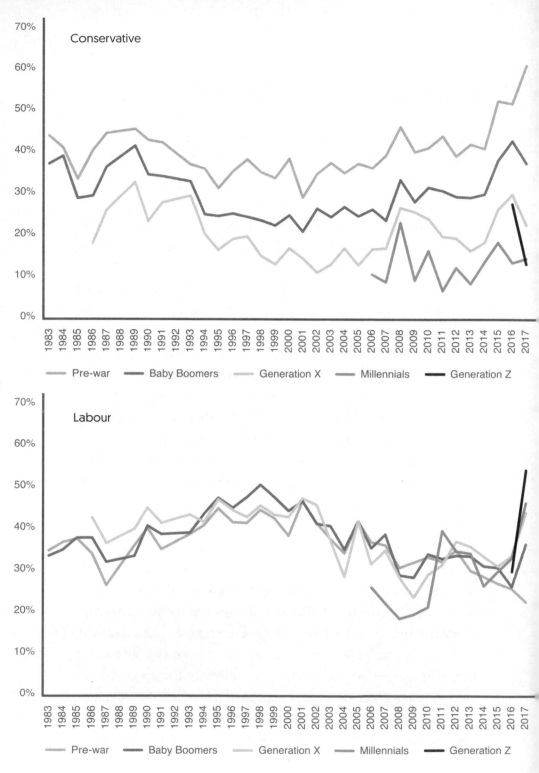

Figure 8.5: Percentage of adults in Britain identifying as Conservative and Labour party supporters[26]

Thirdly, there is significant truth in that much-mimicked saying about conservatism growing with age. Figure 8.6 compares the proportions of two groups who say they would vote Conservative: Generation X and those in the 18 to 29 age group in each year of the study. In the late 1990s, these groups were exactly the same, but Gen X has aged, while the other group has been constantly refreshed with new members. As a result, and as we saw with concern about immigration in Figure 7.4 in the previous chapter, the two lines have grown apart, with Conservative support growing more among the ageing Gen X than among 18 to 29 year olds. This could, of course, be a cohort effect as much as a lifecycle effect. But statistical analysis by political scientists James Tilley and Geoffrey Evans suggests that ageing in itself is important. They find that the ageing effect was

Figure 8.6: Percentage of British adults in 18 to 29 age group and in Generation X who would vote for the Conservative party if there was a general election tomorrow[27]

worth around 0.35 per cent to the Conservatives each year, which may not sound like a lot, but is very valuable over the course of a political lifetime.[28]

Looking internationally can give a wider frame of reference for your problems – and the generational patterns for the Conservative Party should provide some relief for the US Republican Party or 'Grand Old Party' (GOP). Articles on 'The GOP Generational Time Bomb' abound,[29] and yet more claim to explain 'Why Millennials Hate Us',[30] or even suggest that 'Darwin Is Coming for the GOP'.[31] Niall Ferguson and Eyck Freymann argue in an essay entitled 'The Coming Generation War'[32] that a generational framing is the best way to understand the future trajectories of the two parties, and that the mid- to late 2020s may be the point at which the Democrats' demographic advantage will tell.

However, comparison with the UK Conservative Party suggests that this is far from a certainty. It is true that only 36 per cent of 18 to 29 year olds voted for Trump in 2020, but this is a *significantly* better showing among the young than achieved by the UK's Conservative Party.[33] More generally, the Republican candidate's support was not as skewed towards the oldest groups: 46 per cent of those aged between 30 and 44 voted for Trump, compared with 52 per cent of those 65 and over, a much flatter gradient than in the UK. This age pattern is, if anything, less skewed by age than the 2016 election.[34]

Figure 8.7 shows a clear generational hierarchy in identification as a Republican, but at its largest the gap between oldest and youngest has been around 15 percentage points. In the UK, that gap is twice as large. This is not to dismiss the demographic challenge facing the Republican Party: this is a new generational pattern, and, in a finely balanced two-party system, even a relatively small structural change in the balance of votes could prove decisive. But it's good to keep it in perspective.

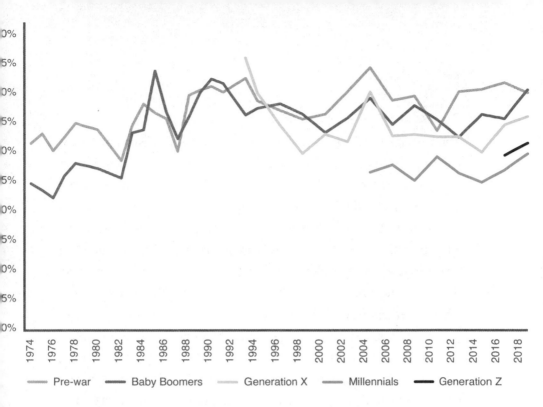

Figure 8.7: Percentage of adults in US that think of themselves as Republicans[35]

More generally, Ferguson and Freymann are right to highlight that a generational framing is becoming increasingly prominent in political contests – and not just in the UK and the US. For example, the 2019 Australian federal election brought generational difference to the fore. The election unexpectedly returned a Liberal–National Coalition to power, dividing the population by age to an extent not seen before: less than a quarter of under-35s voted for the Liberal Party and only 29 per cent of the over-65s voted Labour, both historic lows.[36] The campaign and manifestoes included overt generational pitches: for example, in his 2019 response to the budget, the Labour leader Bill Shorten said that 'the intergenerational bias that the tax system has against young people must be called out'.[37] A stronger generational focus in elections is starting to look like an international trend.

A new crisis of trust?

This new age-based division is often framed as being driven by a loss of trust among younger generations, who are rejecting a political system that has let them down. Indeed, a 'new crisis of trust' is an almost constant feature of politics in media reports and commentary. A series of global studies by Edelman, an international PR firm, that tracks trust annually almost always declares yet another dramatic decline: 'Trust in Government Plunges to Historic Low';[38] 'Global Implosion of Trust';[39] 'Record-Breaking Drop in Trust in the US'.[40] And nearly as often, other reports and headlines blame plummeting trust on younger generations: 'Millennials Have Stopped Trusting the Government'.[41]

I am often invited to give talks to explain these new crises of trust, whether in religion, banking, business, social media, charities, the police, universities or, of course, politics. In just about every case, the evidence I present is not as bad as audiences expect. Our natural human tendency is to pay more attention to negative information – we tend to remember the vivid, worrying stories and trends, particularly when they are about our own industry or interests – and to recall the past more fondly than the present. This means that even unchanging levels of criticism can feel like a new trend.

This last point is important to understanding our levels of political trust: our lack of trust in politicians is problematic, but it's a *long-term condition* rather than a sudden, acute crisis. For example, less than one in five people in Britain trust our politicians to tell the truth – but this is the same as when the survey started four decades ago. And, rather than declining trust being driven by younger generations, Millennials were slightly more trusting than older generations when they first entered adulthood – although this has mostly been knocked out of them in recent years. This is not to say that 'events' don't have the potential to immediately affect trust: the 2000 'expenses scandal' clearly undermined trust in politicians for a few years, but we're now back at exactly the same (very low) level of trust that we saw prior to this. Britain is far from alone in its political leaders being trusted by only small minorities of the population. The overall pattern and level of trust in politicians is similar across a collection of around 20 countries in Europe, with consistently low levels over the last 16 years and not much difference between generations.

The truth is that we've been disappointed in our politicians for a long time. The philosopher Onora O'Neill makes the vital distinction between trust and trustworthiness, pointing out that 'Nobody sensible simply wants more trust. Sensible people want to place their trust where it is deserved. They also want to place their mistrust where it is deserved. They want well-directed trust and mistrust.'[42] We have long thought that mistrust is well directed at politicians, a case powerfully made by Nick Clarke and his co-authors in *The Good Politician*,[43] which reviewed long-term surveys and 'Mass Observation' (which is based on analysis of essays from a cross-section of the public) from as far back as the 1940s. As they point out, even in August 1944, with the Second World War reaching a climax, when a polling company asked, 'Do you think that British politicians are out merely for themselves, for their party or to do their best for their country?', only 36 per cent of respondents chose the last option. This view is backed up by their detailed analysis of how people have thought about politicians through the ages, with common narratives in the mid-twentieth century suggesting that politicians were 'out for themselves' and 'good talkers' (which was not a compliment).

What stands out is a growing discontent with governments' ability to deliver, rather than a new crisis of trust. As Figure 8.8 shows, the proportion of Americans saying that they have 'hardly any' confidence in the people running their government increased to 45 per cent in 2018, three times the level seen in 1977. This is a record high, although this long-term view shows that it was nearly as bad in

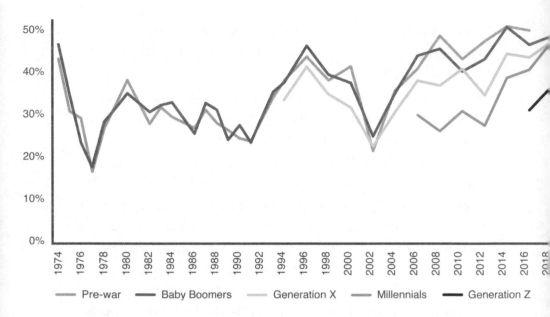

Figure 8.8: Percentage of adults in US who say they have 'hardly any' confidence in people running the executive branch of the federal government[44]

the mid-1990s and in the early 1970s (the American public's response to the September 11th attacks makes the short-run trend look much worse than it is). This is not driven by younger generations, however. Quite the opposite – the most striking pattern is that Millennials and Gen Z enter adulthood with a higher level of confidence than older generations, although that has quickly eroded for Millennials in particular. The tendency is for confidence in government to be lost through repeated disappointments.

Does this lack of confidence in governments reflect a threat to democracy as a whole? Many recent books have questioned the long-held assumption that once 'democratic consolidation' has taken hold and countries have developed democratic institutions, a robust civil society and a certain level of wealth, their democracy is secure.[45]

Instead, these analyses outline how democratic 'backsliding' can creep up on us slowly. The Economist Democracy Index rates 167 countries across factors such as electoral processes, civil liberties and political cultures, and the 2019 version found the lowest rating for the health of democracy since the index started in 2006.[46] In the US, Barack Obama mentioned the word 'democracy' 18 times in his short address to the 2020 Democratic National Convention, highlighting the sense of threat he felt: 'Because that's what's at stake right now. Our democracy.'[47]

While the danger is real, it's important that we challenge some of the eye-catching claims that suggest that the public are suddenly and uniquely losing faith in democracy today.[48] We get a rather different perspective when we look at the long-term picture. Figure 8.9 tracks satisfaction with the way democracy is working in three different countries across many decades. Firstly, this confirms that it really matters which country you are looking at. Satisfaction with democracy is extremely high and increasing in Sweden, but the situation could hardly be more different in Spain, where it collapsed following the 2008 financial crisis. This highlights another of the repeated themes in this chapter: major events really matter. This sensitivity to crises may seem to indicate a fragile attachment to democracy, but the trends also show a remarkable longer-term resilience to deep shocks. For example, German faith in democracy recovered markedly from extremely low levels in the mid-1990s, following reunification. While we shouldn't downplay the risks we face today, long-term trends show that things have been at least this bad before. Younger cohorts today tend to be *more* satisfied than older cohorts, contrary to claims that it's the young who are losing faith quickest.

Previous lows in public faith also coincided with deep concerns from politicians and commentators. The introductory remarks in *The Crisis of Democracy*, written in 1975 by French academic Michel Crozier and his colleagues, could have been written today:

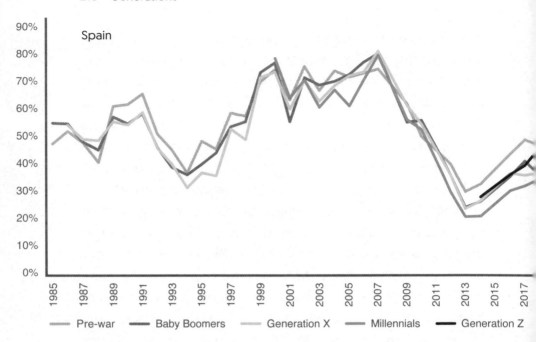

Spain

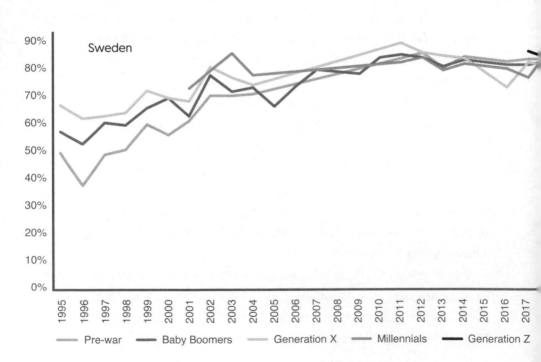

Sweden

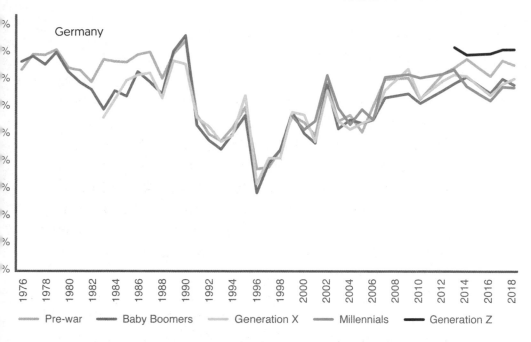

Figure 8.9: Percentage of adults saying they are satisfied with how democracy works in their country[49]

'Is democracy in crisis? This question is being posed with increasing urgency by some of the leading statesmen of the West, by columnists and scholars.'[50] Some of their quoted sources would easily fit in comment pieces now: 'In recent years, acute observers ... have seen a bleak future for democratic government. Before leaving office, Willy Brandt [West German chancellor between 1969 and 1974] was reported to believe that "Western Europe has only 20 or 30 more years of democracy left in it; after that it will slide, engineless and rudderless, under the surrounding sea of dictatorship".' A few years after this was written, satisfaction with democracy in Germany reached record highs, and satisfaction levels today are once again approaching those levels, 40 years on. None of this is to say that we don't need to bolster democratic support, but rather that long-term trends remind us that we can be too quick to believe that all is lost.

Millennials rising...

Strauss and Howe predicted that Millennials would ride to the rescue of American politics. They expected that generation to come of age 'so willing and energised' that they would deliver on their belief in politics as a 'tool for turning collegial purpose into civic progress'. According to Strauss and Howe, Millennials' high level of civic commitment would bring risks, as their 'youthful hunger for social discipline and centralised authority could lead Millennial youth brigades to lend mass to dangerous demagogues', but their political power was not in question because they would 'confound pundits with their huge turnouts'.[51] I doubt many Millennials will recognize this portrait of their generation.

This may be an extreme example of an inaccurate political prediction, but it illustrates the pointlessness of long-term fortune-telling in politics using simplistic generational caricatures. A key conclusion from the data presented in this chapter is that political trends are a complex blend of cohort, lifecycle and period effects. Political punditry often ignores this fact, preferring grand schemes or themes, and this helps to explain why so many political pundits make so many bad predictions.

By separating these effects more carefully and taking a long-term view, we can get better answers to some of the big questions in politics. The death of political parties is slow and exaggerated, and can be turned around by a series of events. Support for democracy is not a generational characteristic; while we may see differences in how groups feel about specific leaders or policies, our support for the fundamental aspects of our political system remains strong. As for our mistrust in political leaders, this is a chronic condition, and one that young generations grow into rather than instigate.

Age and generation are undoubtedly more important dividing lines in a number of countries than they were in the past. However, this isn't just due to demographic or cultural trends – political parties and leaders have played a role in shaping this trend. As Ferguson and Freymann point out, it makes complete sense for the Republican Party to take 'campus politics national' by accusing their opponents of an obsession with 'safe spaces, trigger warnings and gender-neutral pronouns' that are an 'alien parallel world' to many older voters.[52] On the other hand, it's understandable that Joe Biden, following Barack Obama's lead, should place such emphasis on appealing to the next generation.

The trend of parties becoming more reliant on particular age groups for support brings risks, not just to them, but to politics more generally. When one side thinks they have demography on their side, the other will respond by exaggerating the extremism of their opponents, in order to pull their shrinking base closer towards them. And as this generational caricaturing grows, each party will find it increasingly difficult to ask their supporters to engage in the trade offs that avoid further polarization. This is the root of the growing generational aspect to the culture wars in both the US and UK: as the Resolution Foundation points out, 'generational locks' are emerging in political support, and they're difficult to shift once they're in place.[53]

This may seem like normal political tactics, but the scale of the generational divisions it could create would be a significant barrier to a collective vision for the future. Setting old against young, even if on the basis of a dubious reading of actual divisions, is a dangerous path. All the evidence we've seen suggests that generational differences on the actual issues are not nearly as great as they're often made out to be – but a concerted political effort could change that.

Chapter 9

Consuming the Planet

I n a speech to political and business leaders, the legendary conservationist David Attenborough captured the unique challenge of addressing climate change by arguing, 'What happens now and in these next few years will profoundly affect the next few thousand years.'[1] Unfortunately, our political and economic systems are particularly ill suited to addressing threats that need urgent action to avoid long-term consequences. This is not a new shortcoming, caused by 24-hour news, Twitter streams and financial markets that crash in seconds. Rather, our pathological short-termism is more fundamental, driven by how humans struggle to focus on the future.

The Australian philosopher Roman Krznaric neatly summarizes the problem in *The Good Ancestor*, when he writes: 'We treat the future like a distant colonial outpost devoid of people, where we can freely dump ecological degradation, technological risk and nuclear waste, and which we can plunder as we please.'[2] He draws a parallel with the British colonization of Australia, which built on the legal concept *terra nullius* – 'nobody's land' – to justify its actions. Krznaric suggests that we currently see the future as *tempus nullius* – 'nobody's time' – to allow us to ignore the impact of today's actions on tomorrow's world.

This is not to say that we are incapable of taking a longer view. In fact, one of the defining characteristics of humans is our ability to envision the future and the many alternatives it brings. As the psychologist Daniel Gilbert describes, 'our brains, unlike the brains of almost every other species, are prepared to treat the future as if it were present'. We are the 'ape that learned to look forward'.[3] But simply because we *can* think about the future does not mean we always do. As Krznaric suggests, there is a tension between our ability to think 'short and long' – and short tends to win out. In evolutionary terms, longer-term thinking is something that we're still learning how to do. This idea is supported by studies in which people record whether they are thinking about the past, present or future during the course of a day: while we spend 14 per cent of our time thinking about the future, 80 per cent of these future thoughts are about the same or the next day. Other studies show that beyond the next 15 to 20 years, our futures seem blank.[4]

Of course, one obvious reason we don't spend so much time trying to plan for the distant future is that it is really hard to control. John Maynard Keynes once wrote, 'It is not wise to look too far ahead; our powers of prediction are slight, our command over results infinitesimal. It is therefore the happiness of our own contemporaries that is our main concern; we should be very chary of sacrificing large numbers of people for the sake of a contingent end, however advantageous that may appear.'[5]

There is also an emotional aspect to our reluctance to plan too far in advance, as the writer Nathaniel Rich outlines: 'If human beings really were able to take the long view ... we would be forced to grapple with the transience of all we know and love in the great sweep of time. So we have trained ourselves, whether culturally or evolutionarily, to obsess over the present, worry about the medium term and cast the long term out of our minds, as we might spit out a poison.'

While it is understandable that we would want to avoid this long view as individuals, our political systems are *required* to confront it. The Irish philosopher Edmund Burke saw governments as custodians of the contract between generations. For him, society is a partnership in science, art and 'every virtue', 'not only between those who are living, but between those who are living, those who are dead and those who are to be born'.[6]

The multiple challenges facing our planet are the clearest illustration of our struggle to match this Burkean ideal. Instead, our short-term consumer culture reinforces our natural tendency to 'think short' and distracts us from long-term challenges. These are powerful effects, so it shouldn't be surprising that they also shape younger generations, but that's not what we're led to believe by the general perspective of the media and commentary. Two of the most destructive generational myths are that young people are rejecting consumer culture for more sustainable alternatives and that older people don't care about our planet's future. The former gives a false sense of comfort that there is a coming behavioural sea change that will halt climate change, and the latter carelessly discards the current and potential support of vast swathes of the population.

You can understand why the simplistic 'battle of the age groups' framing has taken hold, not least because this is a theme emphasized by Greta Thunberg herself. There have also been some remarkable instances of youth action, most notably the global climate strikes that involved over 1.6 million young students in more than 300 cities, but the highest-profile environmental campaigners span as wide an age range as you can get. Even a cursory glance at climate change marches shows that it is far from a universally young movement: at one Extinction Rebellion event in London, people charged with offences by the Metropolitan Police were aged between 19 and 77.[7] Our generational analysis of attitudes and behaviours shows that, while there are clear differences between generations on some measures, they are frequently wildly overblown.

Climate change is the most obviously generational issue we'll see in this book – not because it's a source of division between young and old, but because our response requires a truly generational perspective.

We still think short

Starting with the fundamental question of whether people recognize that the world's climate is changing, a major European survey has shown that there is no real age divide in the recognition of climate change. Around half of the Pre-War generation think the world's climate is definitely changing. That figure rises to around six in ten among Gen X, the generation most likely to hold this view, with the younger generations slightly less likely to be certain.

The picture changes, however, when Europeans are asked whether climate change is a natural or man-made process. There is a clear generational hierarchy here: just over half of Gen Z think it is man-made, compared with around a third of the Pre-War generation. In contrast to much of the rhetoric, we are a long way from either universal acceptance of anthropogenic climate change among the young, or universal denial among older generations. More generally, large proportions of all age groups, including the young, remain unconvinced. This is despite the overwhelming evidence of change, where the 20 hottest years on record since 1880 have all occurred since 1998[8] – and the near-unanimous consensus, from 97 per cent of climate scientists, that human activity is the dominant cause.[9]

Longer-term surveys paint a picture of gradually increasing concern and relatively small generational difference. For example, Figure 9.1 shows that the proportion of people in the US who think a rise in world temperatures caused by the greenhouse effect is either

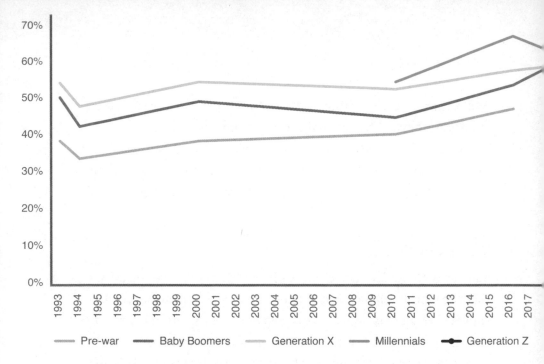

Pre-war	Baby Boomers	Generation X	Millennials	Generation Z

Figure 9.1: Percentage of adults in US who think that the rise in world temperature caused by the greenhouse effect is 'extremely' or 'very' dangerous[10]

very or extremely dangerous has increased from 47 per cent to 61 per cent over the last 25 years. There is a generational hierarchy, with younger cohorts feeling a greater sense of threat – but the differences aren't huge, with levels of concern among Baby Boomers catching up in recent years, and only the Pre-War generation lagging behind.

A similar pattern is seen in a survey that asks people what they think are the most important issues facing their country, from a list that includes everything from the economy and crime to health services. In Britain, environmental issues have featured relatively far down the list for most of the last 20 years, with less than 10 per cent of the population mentioning them. In contrast, the top issues, whether these were the economy, health services, immigration or Brexit, were regularly chosen by 60–70 per cent of people as the most important. The issue dominating our lives in 2020, COVID-19, was chosen as a top issue by over 80 per cent of Brits at its peak.

These questions of 'salience' illustrate the power of our 'present bias' in how we respond to threats: longer-term issues tend to be swamped by more immediate challenges. For example, when the pandemic hit, the reported salience of all other issues, including environmental concerns, plummeted. Prior to the COVID-19 crisis, there had been signs that worries about environmental issues were growing. As Figure 9.2 shows, concern peaked in Britain in 2019, due to a rise among all generations except the Pre-War cohort. However, it was still a relatively low priority, and similar to the level of concern seen in 2007, before the financial crisis shifted our attention to more immediate worries.

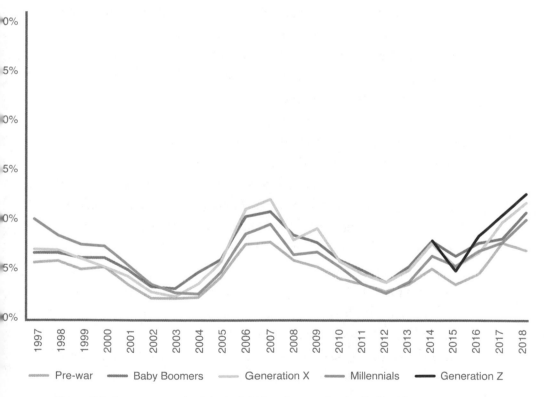

Figure 9.2: Percentage of adults in Britain who say that 'pollution/the environment' is one of the most important issues facing the country today[11]

A different international study has, since 2010, asked a similar question on top worries, and some countries show slightly more marked generational gaps than Britain. In each of Canada, Australia and the US, Gen Z was the most concerned group, followed by Millennials: around three in ten of the youngest generation select climate change as a top concern, compared with around 15 per cent of Baby Boomers. But again, this is not a clear generational break.

This is also clear in longer-term British and American surveys that ask whether governments should spend more or much more on protecting the environment (the UK) and whether the government is currently spending too little (the US). Again, younger cohorts in both countries tend to want governments to do more. For example, in Britain, 54 per cent of Gen Z want spending to increase, compared with 32 per cent of the Pre-War generation. In the US, Millennials are the generation most likely to think the government is spending too little. However, if we exclude the Pre-War generation, the generational gaps in the US are not that dramatic, partly reflecting the degree to which climate change views in the US are politically aligned. Despite some signs that younger Republicans are pulling away from older Republicans, party gaps still outweigh age. For example, a Pew Research Center study shows that only 52 per cent of Republican Millennials and Gen Z think the government is doing too little to reduce the effects of climate change, compared with 90 per cent of *all* Democrats.[12]

The standout pattern in the overall trends, however, is that demands for environmental spending have not increased consistently and seem to be vulnerable to more immediate concerns. In both the UK and the US, there was a spike in calls for more investment in the second half of the 1980s, but this faded away when the early 1990s recession hit. As Figure 9.3 tracing US opinion shows, momentum was starting to grow again in the 2000s, but the 2008 financial crisis set environmental spending back as a priority. This cyclical pattern

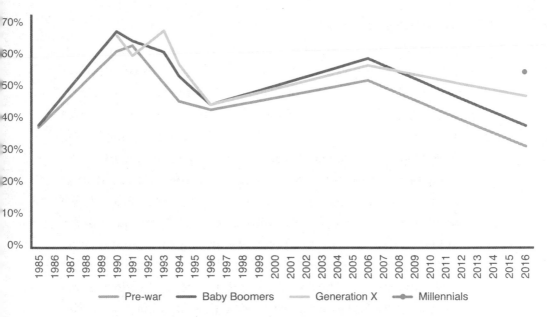

Figure 9.3: Percentage of adults in US who say that the country spends too little on protecting the environment[13]

is at odds with some commentary suggesting that the 'good news is that environmental issues seem to be behaving like issues such as gay marriage, criminal justice reform and marijuana legalisation', with inexorably growing support for change, driven by younger people.[14] As we've seen, the generational patterns on support for gay marriage and the legalization of marijuana are *very* different from the endorsement of environmental spending: we are a lot less certain about the future than this interpretation suggests.

Of course, tackling climate change is not just about government spending; as awareness of our myriad effects on the planet has grown, there have been claims that younger generations in particular are expressing their environmental concern in more direct ways, shifting their own behaviour and consumption patterns to reduce their impact on the planet.[15]

The end of car culture?

One of the most effective environmental actions we can take as individuals is to stop using our cars. According to a Swedish study, this would save 2.4 tonnes of CO_2 per driver per year, significantly more than, for example, shifting to a meat-free diet (which saves 0.8 tonnes of CO_2 per person per year).[16] So it seemed to be good news when, for a number of years in the late 2000s and early 2010s, young people appeared to be shunning cars. For example, in 2010, adults aged between 21 and 34 bought just 27 per cent of all new vehicles sold in America, down from a peak of 38 per cent in 1985.[17] Understandably, this caused concern among car manufacturers and a flurry of comment pieces on its possible meaning and implications: it was 'The End of Car Culture', as *The New York Times* put it in 2013.[18] The evidence seemed stark in just about all well-off countries: compared with previous generations, younger cohorts were delaying getting a driving licence, were less likely to own a car, were driving fewer miles, and in some countries they were using public transport more.[19] Two separate articles in the *Atlantic* in 2012[20] offered two groups of reasons behind the drop-off: economic factors, where young people could no longer afford to own cars in the wake of the financial crisis, and wider cultural factors, including a preference for city living, less interest in the status of car ownership, being comfortable with sharing rather than owning, greater use of technology to connect with others, delayed marriage and child-rearing, and a greater concern for the environment.

However, as we've seen previously, patterns that look like permanent cohort shifts can be due to a delay rather than a rejection, and are often tied to broader changes in how generations live. For example, a 2019 paper[21] shows that US Millennials own 0.4 per cent fewer vehicles per household than Baby Boomers did at the same age – but, after controlling for a range of variables including income levels, educational attainment, geography and family formation, this difference disappears. The same pattern is seen with car use: when the researchers control for the same economic and life stage factors, 'vehicle miles travelled' data shows that American Millennials are, if anything, *more* active car users than older generations. As the paper concludes, 'the results suggest that while Millennial vehicle ownership and use may be lower early on in life, these differences are only temporary and, in fact, lifetime vehicle use is likely to be greater'.

Similar studies in other countries have found the same sort of pattern – that changes in car ownership and use are not as dramatic as they first seem, and shifting lifestyles and delayed lifecycles are important explanations.[22] This can also be seen in our generational analysis of car ownership. Figure 9.4 shows that Irish Millennials' car ownership, for example, continued to increase throughout their twenties and thirties, until, in 2018, they almost matched Gen X levels of ownership when the latter were a similar age in 2005.

Analyses that point to delay rather than rejection have not stopped the suggestion that Gen Z is taking its turn at 'killing the car industry', but such claims seem to be mostly a result of the same pattern of younger generations owning cars later in life. It's definitely the case that our relationship with cars is changing, but the death of car culture is exaggerated – partly as a result of confusing period, lifecycle and cohort effects.

COVID-19 and its economic fallout have already caused further swings. The car industry was one of the harder-hit sectors in the early stages of the pandemic, with global sales of just over 70 million new vehicles in 2020, 18.5 million lower than estimates at the start of the year – roughly equivalent to all new car sales in the UK, Japan and the US combined.[23] The medium-term effects of the pandemic are still emerging, but early signs from China point to a sharp recovery in car use, as commuters shun public transport. By the middle of April 2020,

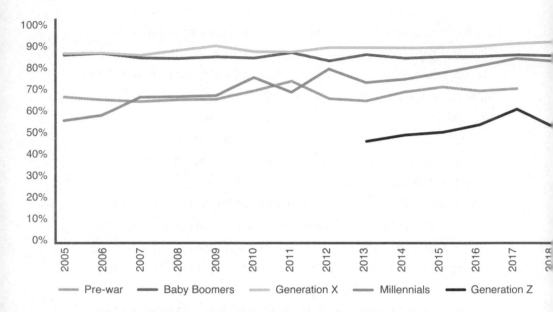

Figure 9.4: Percentage of adults in Ireland owning a car[24]

congestion in major Chinese cities was 90 per cent of pre-lockdown levels, while subway use was at just 50 per cent.[25] Sellers of cars wasted no time in trying to capitalize on anxiety regarding public transport; a newspaper advert in Germany showed a huge face mask across the front of a VW Tiguan, each ear loop stretched over a wing mirror, with the tagline 'safety first'. We may see some lasting decreases in traffic, as remote working seems likely to settle at a higher level than pre-COVID, but it seems unlikely that a long-term effect of the pandemic will be to encourage greater use of public transport.

On purpose

The exaggeration of generational difference on sustainable consumption extends way beyond car use. In recent years, headlines and comment pieces have painted a vivid picture of how young people's focus on environmental and social purpose has changed their patterns of consumption and affected their relationships with brands. Firstly, Millennials were billed as 'the green generation',[26] where 'sustainability is their shopping priority' and they 'make efforts to buy products from companies that support the causes they care about'.[27] This swiftly moved on to Gen Z: we were told that 'Purpose-driven, sustainable brands are the ones who will capture the hearts, minds, and wallets' of a generation who 'wants to know about your values, ethics and mission'.[28]

But there is just about no evidence that these assertions reflect real differences in those generations' priorities. A British study has covered a wide range of ethical behaviours since the 1990s, ranging from boycotting products due to the behaviour of the company behind them, choosing a product because of the company's principles, seeking out information on how responsible a company is, and paying more for ethically sourced products.[29] Each behaviour shows a similar pattern: younger generations are no more likely to say they have behaved in these ways than older generations, and in some cases they are less likely. For example, a fifth of Baby Boomers say they have boycotted a product because the company had not behaved responsibly, compared with 16 per cent of Millennials. And Generation Xers are more likely than Millennials to say they would pay more for products that are ethically sourced.

Of course, these patterns may be a feature of age rather than cohort: we may become more prepared to act on our principles as we get older, or perhaps we get richer and more willing to spend on the right sort of products. However, the length of this study allows us to compare cohorts at the same age and get a generational view. For example, in 1999, when Generation Xers were a similar age to Millennials in 2015, Gen Xers were actually slightly *more* likely to say they would choose a product service because of the behaviour of a company (17 per cent, versus 12 per cent for Millennials).

There appear to be similar patterns in other countries. A European study that started measuring the prevalence of product boycotts in 2004 confirms that this is more common in middle age. Germany is pretty typical of the pattern in a number of European countries; as Figure 9.5 shows, Gen Xers and Baby Boomers are most likely to have boycotted a product in the last 12 months. Gen Zers currently lag a long way behind – but as the line for Millennials suggests, this behaviour seems to increase as we get older. While the claims that this trend is driven by new waves of young activists seems wrong, we shouldn't downplay how much more common this behaviour is

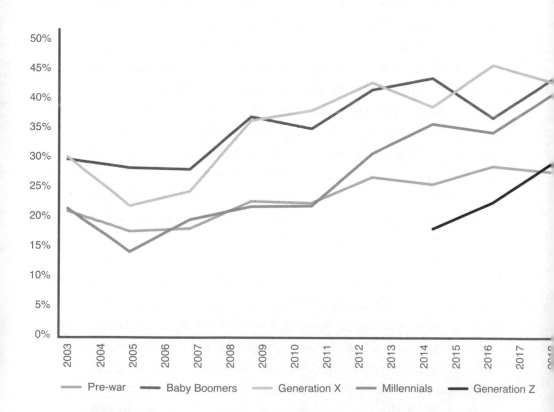

Figure 9.5: Percentage of adults in Germany who say they have boycotted certain products in the last 12 months[30]

becoming in some countries: in Germany, there has been a significant increase among all except the oldest cohorts over the past decade. Brands should be increasingly mindful of direct consumer action, but they should also recognize that this is not solely, or even mainly, driven by younger generations. On this measure, 'cancel culture' seems to be more of a middle-age thing.

However, the differences between countries on these measures are often bigger than those between generations, both in terms of levels of boycotting and the trends – yet another example of 'country before cohort'. For example, there is a huge range in the levels of claimed boycotting behaviour among Generation X across countries, as well as very different trajectories. Nearly 60 per cent of Gen X in Sweden have boycotted a product in the last year, following a steep increase over the past 14 years, compared with under 10 per cent of Gen X in Poland, a figure that has barely changed in that time. In the UK, Generation Xers are closer to Poles than Swedes on this behaviour, with one in five having boycotted a product – a pretty flat trend.

The overblown claims for young people's 'brand activism' reflects the influence marketing agencies have on the creation and dissemination of generational myths. Endless reports and press releases create a sense of change that's not justified by the facts, and yet these consistently gain significant attention. In a chapter that began with the existential threat to our planet, it may seem strange to examine these spurious trends, but in many ways that's the point: our consumer culture reflects and reinforces our natural tendency to emphasize the short term and the novel at the expense of the distant but more meaningful. The assertion that younger generations are escaping this consumer culture and rejecting brands and advertising is not just wrong, it's dangerous. Younger generations are perhaps even more entwined in modern brand-driven consumerism than older generations, which means a generationally driven sustainable future is much less certain than peddled myths suggest.

Generational marketing exists less to discover true social trends and more to help sell the marketer's value to companies, and so they often end up finding problems that don't really exist. Articles claiming that brand loyalty is 'not such a biggie for Millennials'[31] offer various pieces of advice on how to advertise to a generation that is 'notoriously fickle'.[32] One of the challenges in identifying truly generational consumer insight is that the long-term data required to isolate cohort effects doesn't really exist – but even snapshot surveys show that there is no evidence to support such claims. According to the Ipsos Global Trends survey in 2019, for example, 43 per cent of Millennials and Gen Zers say they always try to buy branded products. Baby Boomers seem less concerned, at 32 per cent. There is also little difference between Gen X, Millennials and Gen Z on whether they are 'more likely to trust a new product if it's made by a brand they already know' – three-quarters of each generation agree, with Baby Boomers slightly more sceptical.

It is not just the generational death of brand loyalty that is exaggerated. The idea that traditional advertising fails to impress younger cohorts is also often raised, in claims such as 'only 1 per cent of Millennials said that a compelling advert would make them trust a brand more'.[33] Of course, drawing conclusions about advertising impact based on self-reported attitudes is not advisable – we're poor at identifying and reporting our reactions, and there are big gaps between our stated intentions and actions. As is often the case with headline-chasing research, this study also looks at Millennial opinions in isolation, overlooking the high probability that we might see similar findings across all generations. Indeed, when research is conducted across the whole population, Gen Z and Millennials say they pay *more* attention to advertising than other cohorts. There is a pretty straightforward age gradient, which applies across various types of media, with younger generations saying they pay more heed. For example, 52 per cent of Gen Z say they pay at least a little attention to cinema ads, compared with 48 per cent of Millennials, 41 per cent of Generation X and just 31 per cent of Baby Boomers. And it is not just that younger generations are more likely to notice adverts on a wider variety of media types – they are more likely to say they *like* adverts. For example, 35 per cent of Gen Z say they like adverts on their mobile phones, compared with 19 per cent of Baby Boomers.

A similar repeated assertion is that personal recommendations rather than advertising are key to Millennials' purchasing decisions. Typical headlines include bold statements like 'Millennials Trust People Over Brands'[34] and call the generation 'leaders in word-of-mouth recommendations'.[35] At first glance, this seems to correspond with the research – Millennials do say they are more influenced by social media, known peers, opinion leaders and experts than other generations claim.[36] But, again, it's a misdirection: younger people tend to say they are more influenced by *all* sources – including traditional advertising. Data from the US, for example, shows that Millennials claim to draw on a more varied pool of resources before they make decisions about brands. It's true that American Millennials are more likely to say they are influenced by experts, family and friends than Generation X and Baby Boomers, but they're also more likely to say they are influenced by communications from businesses, whether through traditional media or online.[37] The underlying theme here seems to be a greater use of multiple sources, rather than personal recommendations replacing traditional communications and advertising. Younger generations are very much *not* rejecting these key tools of consumerism.

A long-time project

Our consumer culture is inextricably linked to both our reliance on short-term thinking and our slow and partial recognition of the severity of the environmental emergency facing the planet. Most obviously, as Al Gore argues, 'governing institutions have been suborned by vested interests obsessed with short-term gain rather than long-term sustainability'.[38] As George Monbiot suggests, this creates a 'cannibal economy' that undermines the future.

Underlying this, however, is the more general human characteristic to be drawn to the immediate and present, and our corresponding struggle to focus on the longer term. As Monbiot writes, 'It was easier [for people] to pretend that the science was wrong and their lives were right than to accept that the science was right and their lives were wrong.'[39] We *can* think 'long', but we don't find it easy, and we're surrounded by an economic and political context that discourages it.

Given these powerful forces, it should be no surprise that younger generations haven't entirely broken free. It's true that the young show greater concern about the environment according to some measures, but the differences are not huge and they have not translated into markedly more sustainable behaviours. The impression given by endless articles and analyses is of a clean generational break. This is not just misleading but dangerous, as it suggests that we can rely on young people to both demand action from governments and take direct action themselves.

The focus on the young also grossly exaggerates the lack of concern felt by the old. I feel the same unease as the sociologist and writer Anne Karpf about the 'unthinking ageism' that has crept into some portrayals of the environmental movement. The Gen Z singer Billie Eilish said in an interview: 'Hopefully the adults and the old people start listening to us [about climate change]. Old people are gonna die and don't really care if we die, but we don't wanna die yet.'[40] This particularly blunt way of putting it reflects a more general attitude that caricatures whole cohorts of the older population as uncaring about the environment or future generations. This is not just wrong – it also ignores the growing demographic weight and financial power of the older population. Support for a greener future depends on uniting the generations, rather than dividing them. There are clear ways to do that, starting with including older people in the conversation about climate change and appealing to the greater focus on 'legacy thinking' that we develop as we age. As the gerontologists Elizabeth Hunter and Graham Rowles suggest, 'Few of us are comfortable with the idea that we live, we die, and that is it. We want to believe that there is a purpose in life and that we will make a mark of some kind ... This is the fertile ground from which the desire for legacy sprouts.'[41]

We will need all the help we can get to keep the focus on climate change in the aftermath of the COVID-19 pandemic. In the early stages of our response, scientists were hopeful that 'lockdowns' around the world would result in a significant reduction in CO_2 emissions. This initially seemed justified, with global emissions in April 2020 down by 17 per cent on the previous year. But that optimism was short-lived, as even a partial return to normality increased emissions significantly – they were only 5 per cent down on the previous year by June, and were predicted to be between 4 and 7 per cent down over 2020 as a whole.[42] Given the incredible changes in our lives, as Bill Gates says, 'What is remarkable is not how much emissions will go down because of the pandemic, but how little.'[43]

Of course, the most important effects of COVID-19 will be seen over the longer term, and there are some encouraging signs on this. Investment in more sustainable growth is a core element of a number of the emerging 'Build Back Better' plans across countries and institutions: for example, the EU's 'Next Generation' recovery fund proposes that 25 per cent of EU spending is set aside for climate-friendly expenditure.[44] However, such plans certainly shouldn't be taken for granted; a further theme of our long-term analysis is how easily environmental concerns are knocked back by more immediate priorities, particularly during economic downturns that increase our focus on the here and now.[45] It's about to get even harder to think long.

Chapter 10

Us and Them

Generational thinking, as we understand it today, is a relatively new way of explaining social change. Many of the foundational works were written during the turbulent years following the First World War, an event that 'dug a chasm between the generations'.[1] It's no surprise, then, that conflict is at its very heart. It is clear in the irreversible rage in Wilfred Owen's preface to his *Poems*, at 'the willingness of the old to sacrifice the young':[2]

> My subject is War, and the pity of War. The Poetry is in the pity. Yet these elegies are to this generation in no sense consolatory. They may be to the next. All a poet can do today is warn.[3]

This same sentiment also deeply affected sociologists and philosophers who were trying to make sense of the First World War's consequences for relationships between generations. The Spanish philosopher José Ortega y Gasset, for example, believed that history was a series of epochs, where each new generation considered itself either heir to a valuable heritage or born to destroy it.[4] Karl Mannheim also saw conflict as central to how generations are formed and act. Firstly, he said, a generation needs to have common experiences and a shared identity that create some sort of affinity. Mirroring ideas on class formation and conflict, he suggests that this sense of identity leads to competition with others: a generation is not just a coherent social identity 'in itself' but 'for itself'.[5]

This framing also infects a lot of recent discussion on generational relationships, where futures have been 'stolen' by one generation and need to be forcibly taken back by another. As we've seen throughout this book, this attitude doesn't reflect how most of the public see intergenerational relations. And there is at least one obvious reason for this discrepancy between theory and observation. Our familial attachments, both up and down the generations, remain stronger than our connections to our peer groups. This may seem blindingly obvious, but it is often strangely absent from the type of commentary that pits one generation against another. It leads to rather absurd analysis, such as a piece in the German magazine *Der Spiegel* that presented the conflict between old and young as a major issue in the financial crisis, where older people were living at the expense of the young, and how 'it's high time the next generation took to the streets to confront their parents'.[6]

There are other obstacles that tend to limit generational conflict, too. In particular, age is a uniquely problematic characteristic to base division on – compared with class, gender or ethnicity – as we *all* inevitably pass through the different age categories. We know, for instance, that the support afforded to older people is an indicator of what we'll receive when we are old, so we'll probably be a little more cautious about going to war against it. Of course, our generational membership is a characteristic that *doesn't* change; as we've seen, many in our current generations of older people have likely had a better deal than future generations of old will – but our own unstoppable lifecycles are still likely to give us reason to pause.

The view that serious generational conflict is either imminent or justified reflects our tendency to explain phenomena as being caused by a single factor, in this case a generational effect. But as we've seen, we gain a better understanding of our changing societies when we unpick cohort, lifecycle and period effects. Our analysis of the nature, scope and potential of generational conflict is richer when we recognize each of these elements: that generational self-interest is real but also moderated by our love for our grandparents, parents, children and grandchildren; that the inevitability of our lifecycles means we have a connection to older age groups based on self-interest that we don't have across other societal divisions; and that period effects can alter the relationship between generations in significant ways. On the last of these, we've already outlined the unprecedented separation of the generations into increasingly distinct communities. In this chapter, we'll see this change mirrored in a separation of our digital lives. The potential of periods of rapid technological change to increase the importance and difficulty of maintaining intergenerational connections was recognized by Mannheim in the early twentieth century, and is no less relevant today.

If we look at these effects together, we can see that it's not intergenerational warfare we should be most worried about, but a drifting apart of age groups. This powers the stereotypes that exaggerate the divisions between generations, and means we miss out on a host of positive benefits from generational connections.

Our generation?

But let's start with Mannheim's first generational question – whether we identify as part of 'our generation'. The Pew Research Center explored this in the US in 2015, and finds that lots of us do – although it depends on which generation you're in.[7] At one end of the spectrum, only 40 per cent of Millennials say they identify with that label, compared with 58 per cent of Generation X and 79 per cent of

Baby Boomers (this survey was too early to test Gen Z identification). Given these results, it's no surprise that many people, particularly Millennials, see themselves as belonging to different generations from the one dictated by their birth year: a third of US Millennials see themselves as Gen X (we may be a forgotten generation, but, for many people, it's still better than being a Millennial). I particularly admire the chutzpah of the 8 per cent of Millennials who think they're part of the 'Greatest Generation', the label used in the US for those born in the 1920s or before. I'm sure this is not an attempt to claim credit for fighting in the Second World War or living through the impact of the Great Depression – but if you're asked to pick a generational label, why not pick the one called 'Greatest'?

The Pew survey goes on to ask people how well they think the term applies to them, and the pattern is similar: 70 per cent of Baby Boomers think it describes them well, 38 per cent of Gen X think the same about their label, as do 30 per cent of Millennials. So, while it varies across groups, generational identity, even as summed up in simple labels, is not trivial. When a British study asked people what they would say was most important to their identity (not including their family or job) if they were introducing themselves to someone, the top answers were their interests, values and opinions. But the next important thing was their 'age or generation', ahead of their nationality, and way ahead of social class, ethnicity and religion. Although this question combines age and generation in a single category, it suggests that we see when we were born as an important indicator of our identity.[8]

At first glance, we also seem to have strong images of the key characteristics of other generations. In a survey across 30 countries conducted for this book, the top and bottom five characteristics chosen for each generation show the distinct traits people associate and don't associate with each one, as shown in Figure 10.1. And it

Gen Z

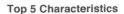

Top 5 Characteristics   **Bottom 5 Characteristics**

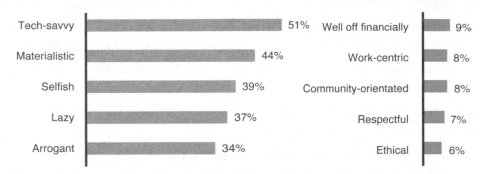

Top 5		Bottom 5	
Tech-savvy	51%	Well off financially	9%
Materialistic	44%	Work-centric	8%
Selfish	39%	Community-orientated	8%
Lazy	37%	Respectful	7%
Arrogant	34%	Ethical	6%

Millennials

Top 5 Characteristics   **Bottom 5 Characteristics**

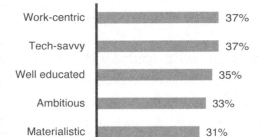
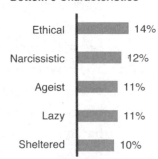

Top 5		Bottom 5	
Work-centric	37%	Ethical	14%
Tech-savvy	37%	Narcissistic	12%
Well educated	35%	Ageist	11%
Ambitious	33%	Lazy	11%
Materialistic	31%	Sheltered	10%

Baby Boomers

Top 5 Characteristics   **Bottom 5 Characteristics**

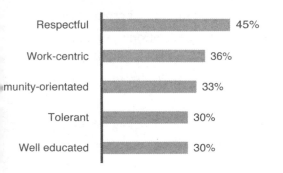
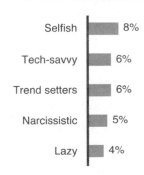

Top 5		Bottom 5	
Respectful	45%	Selfish	8%
Work-centric	36%	Tech-savvy	6%
munity-orientated	33%	Trend setters	6%
Tolerant	30%	Narcissistic	5%
Well educated	30%	Lazy	4%

Figure 10.1: Perceived characteristics of generations[9]

isn't great news for Gen Z. On the plus side, half of the public say Gen Zers are tech-savvy, but that's the only positive in a top five that includes materialistic, selfish, lazy and arrogant. It's true that Gen Z are not well off financially, and it may even be fair to say they're not yet work-orientated – after all, lots of them are still in education – but, more damningly, very few people see them as community-orientated, respectful or ethical.

Perhaps surprisingly, given the 'Generation Me' and 'snowflake' images that are thrust on them, Millennials receive less of a character assassination. Like Gen Z, they are also seen as tech-savvy and materialistic, but next come more positive characteristics – they're work-centric, well educated and ambitious. Again, like Gen Z, they're not widely seen as ethical – but nor are they seen as narcissistic, ageist, lazy or sheltered.

However, even this positive report card can't compete with the praise showered on Baby Boomers – for being respectful, work-centric, community-orientated, tolerant and well educated, with hardly anyone thinking they're selfish, narcissistic or lazy. Sure, they're not seen as tech-savvy or trend setters, but that's a small price to pay for such a positive picture. This may come as a surprise to Baby Boomers who have seen the social media portrayals of them 'ruining everything'. It does, however, fit with how they see themselves, at least in the US. A different study asked generations whether they had a favourable view of their own and other generations, and Baby Boomers were by far the most positive: 83 per cent said they were favourable towards their own generation, compared with 53 per cent of Gen X and 57 per cent of Millennials.[10]

Gen Z, then, is clearly the weak link. Gen Zers even agree with that characterization themselves: their top-five descriptors for their own generation are almost identical to the population's as a whole: tech-savvy, materialistic, lazy, ambitious and selfish. So, given this contrast in generational characteristics, is society set to plummet downhill, as a venal younger generation replaces upstanding older cohorts? Surely this younger group will take at least some of their distinct and heinous deficiencies with them throughout their lives?

Millennials, on the other hand, seem to have completely turned around their image. We asked the same questions about Millennials and Baby Boomers in 2017, and Figure 10.2 compares what people thought about Millennials then with two years later. Millennials had already established their tech-savvy credentials in 2017, but in contrast with their current image as work-centric, well educated and ambitious, at that point they were regarded as materialistic, selfish, lazy and arrogant. Although there are only two years between the studies, they show a remarkable transformation in the perceived character of a generation.

Of course, this is no more a 'generational rebirth' of Millennials than Gen Z is destined to be the worst-regarded generation ever. Both of these patterns are nothing but a reflection of our timeless denigration of young people. In the 2017 study, it was a little too

illennials in 2017 versus 2019

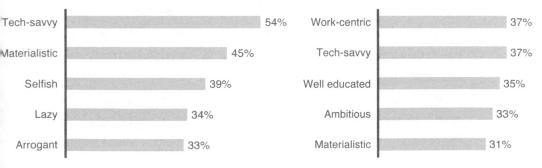

17 Millennials Top 5 Characteristics		2019 Millennials Top 5 Characteristics	
Tech-savvy	54%	Work-centric	37%
Materialistic	45%	Tech-savvy	37%
Selfish	39%	Well educated	35%
Lazy	34%	Ambitious	33%
Arrogant	33%	Materialistic	31%

Figure 10.2: Perceived characteristics of Millennials in 2017 and 2019[11]

early to ask about Gen Z, as they were still coming through as a recognizable cohort and label. Millennials, then, were the newest generation identified, and a shorthand for 'young'. As soon as Gen Z becomes an option, we transfer our negative stereotypes about youth to them – in an almost identical way, if you look back to Figure 10.1. Our apparent generational splits in how we see each other are nothing of the sort – they are age-based clichés that don't stick over time. Beyond our tendency to judge the young negatively, we mostly see each other as pretty decent. Even Millennials.

This is not as trivial and obvious as it seems. Firstly, generations are very often labelled as embodying a particular characteristic, and then expected to take it with them through life. For example, according to some high-profile generational analysis, Millennials were supposed to be either 'narcissistic' or 'civic-minded', depending on who you listened to. Secondly, even though we've seen in this book that Millennials are often generally very similar to previous young cohorts, I genuinely expected the negative image to stick to the 'Millennial' label. I've always felt sympathy for them, for their double whammy of tough circumstances and being denigrated on an unprecedented scale . When I saw the results, I was surprised that their bad reputation hadn't followed them.

This is good news, as it suggests that the public don't actually buy into the simplistic view that whole generations can be summed up for the rest of their life in just one or two words. On the other hand, this means that we can expect the 'Generation Me' magazine headlines to continue for each new cohort of young people *forever* – we're incredibly susceptible to believing that today's youth are worse than any previous versions. A 1969 US newspaper article talked about the (now sainted) Baby Boomer generation in similar terms: 'With all this smuggery, self-righteousness and self-pity, there is a temptation to tell the young pups off. But as a matter of fact, current American youth has indeed had a great crime committed against it. It is the worst-raised generation in our history.'[12] Expect to see a very similar piece in 2069.

Disconnecting cohorts

One of the key reasons that Millennials have been piled on so much is that they were growing up just as our lives turned digital. The explosion of social media gave us a new outlet for sharing shallow stereotypes in memes and 140 characters or fewer. These technologies have not just made it easier to complain about each other – they also mean that different generations live in increasingly separate digital spaces.

A signal of how central to our lives these new technologies, particularly the smartphone, have become is seen in the endless surveys that ask what we'd rather give up – according to one headline finding, 'One in 10 Millennials Would Rather Lose a Finger Than Give Up Their Smartphone.'[13] Four in ten of all Americans say they would give up their dog or their partner for a month before their phone,[14] two in ten say they would give up their toothbrush (urgh) or shoes (?) for a week[15] and, depending on which dubious survey you pick, between a third and a half of people would forgo sex for between one week and three months.[16] Less speculative and more meaningful questions on our actual behaviour with our phones also illustrate our attachment: four in ten Americans sleep with their phones right next to their bed, and a similar proportion say they always or often browse the internet or use apps within ten minutes of waking up.[17]

The speed with which smartphones have become central to our lives is also clear from Figure 10.3. Hardly anyone had access to smartphones in Britain in 2008; today, there is near-universal ownership among Gen Z, Millennials and Gen X. Gen Zers have known little else, while Millennials' experiences over the course

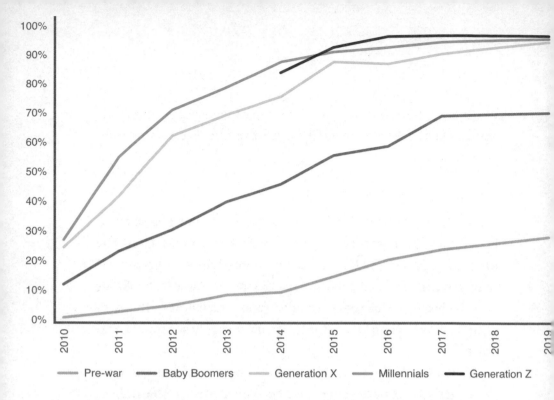

Figure 10.3: Percentage of adults in Britain who own a smartphone[18]

of their adult lives have varied. Around seven in ten British Baby Boomers own a smartphone, while the Pre-War generation continues to nudge upwards, to 30 per cent. Although those last statistics are likely to be down to how difficult it is to get a 'dumb' phone these days as much as the attractions of a smartphone.

This doesn't look like a huge separation between the generations – but the gaps in how different cohorts *use* their smartphones are much greater than blunt ownership measures suggest. For example, a technology time-use diary survey run by Ofcom, the UK communications regulator, showed that in 2016, Millennials spent an average of nearly 1,500 minutes (around 25 hours) on their smartphones each week, compared with less than half that for Gen X. The oldest group, aged 55 and over, spent half as much time again as Gen X, at around 300 minutes a week. So, while British Gen Z and Millennials may be only around 30 per cent more likely to own

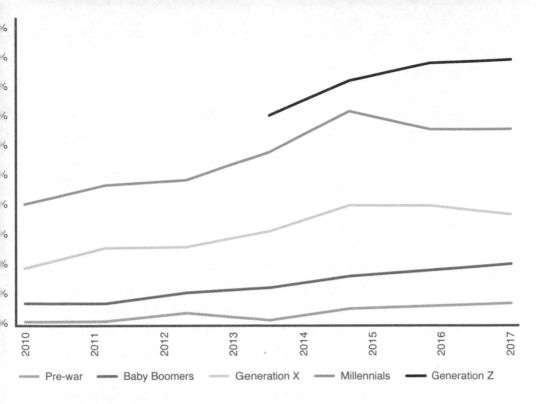

Figure 10.4: Percentage of adults in France using online social networks every day[19]

a smartphone than their parents and grandparents, they spend five times as long using them.[20]

It's not just the intensity of use that varies between generations, it's also the types of things we do when we're online. In particular, social media use is one of the most generationally differentiating things we'll look at in this book. Taking France as an example, Figure 10.4 shows that nine in ten Gen Zers use social media every day – while only 7 per cent of the Pre-War generation do the same. Millennials are a fair way behind Gen Z, and Gen X are a further big step down. And, unlike with smartphone ownership, Baby Boomers are much closer to the Pre-War generation than the youngest cohorts.

The different ways in which young and old interact through technology is the source of a key disconnect in real life. When Italian academics interviewed older people as part of a study on age-based stereotypes in mobile phone use, one 79-year-old respondent said of

their 13-year-old great-nephew: 'I meet them, they say "Hello aunt!",
I greet them and ... down! They bend over the phone and then there
is no more conversation.'[21] But, of course, there is a decent chance
the 13-year-old *is* still in a conversation – it's just not with their
great aunt. This capability to be physically present but constantly
connected elsewhere is new: it's an ability us older generations may
have wished for during our own boring visits to relatives – but it has
consequences for intergenerational connection.

It's not just that different generations have different levels of
social media use – they're also on different networks. Each of the
platforms has its own distinct generational profile, as we can see in
Figure 10.5, based on analysis of a dataset of 30,000 interviews by
Ipsos, from Britain in 2019. Snapchat, for example, has a particularly
steep generational gradient: half of Gen Z say they use the platform,
compared with just 16 per cent of Millennials, 5 per cent of Gen
X, 1 per cent of Baby Boomers and just 0.1 per cent of the Pre-War
generation. Instagram use is also very skewed to the young, but
Facebook, Twitter and WhatsApp have much flatter user profiles
across generations: while Gen Zers are seven times more likely to
be on Instagram than Baby Boomers, they're only twice as likely to
be on WhatsApp or Facebook.

Of course, the use of particular technologies and platforms by
different generations is incredibly fluid, and it will have changed
again by the time you read this. Facebook provides a prime example.
It started out in 2004 as solely for college students, but in just a
few years the focus of commentary had shifted to ask, 'Is Facebook
for old people?',[22] and, just as quickly, to answer it: 'Facebook is
officially for old people'.[23] On the surface, this seems just wrong, as
younger generations are still the most likely to ever use the platform.
However, the intensity of Facebook use among younger generations
has declined substantially. This is hardly surprising: at a time when

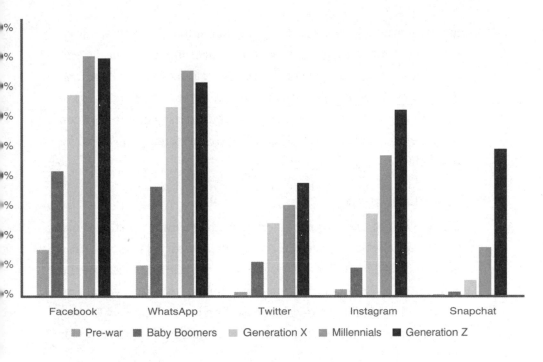

Figure 10.5: Use of social media platforms among adults in Britain[24]

digital spaces are vital for young people to explore their individual and group identities, it makes sense to gravitate away from platforms where their parents' generation are increasingly posting embarrassing photos and messages. The greying of the 'blue app' has inevitably led to a satirical response from young people, with two American 20 year olds setting up a Facebook 'group where we all pretend to be boomers', which has nearly 300,000 members.[25] The content is a mix of capitalized political rants ('MY GRANDSON FORGOT TO CALL ME ON MY BIRTHDAY. THANKS OBAMA'), disgusting medical queries ('Good home remedies for anal tremors?'), inappropriate use of graphics ('TOM IS DIVORCING ME', above an image of party balloons) and Minions gifs. While it's mostly good, satirical fun, it's also a case study in how quickly darker stereotyping can appear in our segmented digital world. The group administrators have admitted they sometimes struggle to moderate the strong homophobic and racist undertones in many of the posts credited to Baby Boomers. While there may be elements of truth in these sorts of portrayals, they exaggerate the real-world degree of cultural separation between the generations and show how easily extreme stereotyping can take hold online.

'Coronials' rising

The COVID-19 crisis has provided an unwelcome boost to these generational clichés, whether that meant memes about Baby Boomers hoarding toilet rolls or refusing to wear facemasks, or the selfishness of 'Generation Me' in continuing to party and complain. As one clickbait *Daily Telegraph* headline put it: 'The Self-Pitying "Woke" Generation Needed a War – and in Coronavirus They've Got One'.[26]

However, the potential for the pandemic to increase generational division reaches way beyond sensationalist comment pieces. Of all the possible types of global crises, it is hard to think of one with characteristics that would greater test intergenerational connection. This starts with the literal separation of different generations, through lockdowns and restrictions that have kept us apart. We've learned a new language of 'shielding', 'cocooning', 'self-quarantining' and 'bubbles'. Given the much greater risk that the disease poses to the old, it's been this group who have had to be particularly cautious, which has accentuated the trend towards separation. As the British actress Joan Collins tweeted, a particularly harmful aspect of this is 'bolstering the existing belief among the general public ... that the old should keep out of everyone's way'.

It is the young, however, who will be more affected by the long-term impact of these extraordinary restrictions on how we've had to live, with the disruption to their education and through the coming economic impact. In Ireland, more than half of 18 to 24 year olds who were working before the coronavirus pandemic claimed the pandemic unemployment payment in the summer of 2020, compared with just over 20 per cent of 25- to 34-year-old workers.[27] In Britain, 16 to 25 year olds were more than twice as likely as older workers to have lost their job, while six in ten saw their earnings fall.[28] And this is before the long-term economic impact, the 'scarring' of career and economic progression that we know will affect the young more than the old.[29]

The differential impact on generations reaches way beyond education and employment into social relations and mental health, partly because of the very different physical living conditions for different age groups. For example, as we saw in Chapter 2, older age groups have risen up the housing ladder more easily than younger generations – so much so that one report on English living conditions during the pandemic finds that older people's homes are twice as spacious: those aged 65 and over have 50 square metres per person, compared with 26 square metres for 16 to 24 year olds. The same report also finds that young people in England are three times more likely to live in a damp home than older people, and more than one-and-a-half times as likely to have no garden or to live in a derelict or congested neighbourhood.

But, despite these very real differences in experiences, not one of the niche caricatures of intergenerational conflict represents actual behaviour during lockdown. As the journalist James Ball neatly summed up in a tweet: 'Millennials and Gen Z are supportive of lockdown largely to protect *others*: their parents, grandparents, vulnerable people their age, etc. Lockdown has a high cost on them, and they're willingly bearing it. Mocking them as scared for their own sake is a cheap shot that misses.'[30] This has also been reflected in the reactions of many in older groups. Dorothy Byrne, editor-at-large at Channel 4 and a 67 year old with underlying medical conditions, wrote in *The Guardian*:

> Over the past weeks, I've been deeply moved by the sacrifices younger people are making ... society is taking part in a remarkable exercise to keep those like me alive. In my own street, many people have lost their jobs ... Three of my lovely young neighbours were immediately told they would be evicted. One might expect people facing hardship to turn inwards; instead, they came round and asked me if they could do my shopping. You often hear about Britain's intergenerational divide. Indeed, one constantly reads that the young resent the old ... But I've never bought the narrative that pits one age group against another. Younger people resent a political class that has failed them, yes, but they don't resent me.[31]

Others made the point that older people were also deeply concerned about the young – and that the actions we were all taking to protect older groups was not just the result of our love for individual members, but also the value they bring to society, as outlined in a letter to *The Times*:

> Sir, Help! I opened the paper today to find a letter from my 81-year-old mum ... announcing she would prefer a younger person to take her ventilator should she become seriously ill with Covid-19. Although I am in favour of living wills and sensible decisions about life and death, may I remind my mother that she still tutors maths, runs her residents' association, provides emergency care for dogs

and grandchildren and makes unbeatable Christmas cakes. The over-80s have become very noble in the face of the coronavirus, underestimating their value to society. We are not just protecting them out of love – we need them.

These individual stories and perspectives are key to countering some of the stereotypes that have taken hold. We will see very many reports, evaluations and inquiries on what exactly happened during the pandemic in the months and years to come, but in the meantime it is important not to give in to a fake sense of old/young division. As Alex Evans, author of *The Myth Gap*, says: 'This is a moment when early drafts ... count for a lot ... stories *create* our reality as much as they describe it, and can all too easily become self-fulfilling prophecies, especially in conditions of high uncertainty. So it matters a great deal that we nurture stories right now about how generations are coming together ... and rally around a new, hopeful, shared agenda.'[32] This can help to set the tone for what comes next, and how we might plot our way back to recovery.

A generational perspective on the crisis and its aftermath is crucial, but it's currently being set out in a very simplistic way. Completely unsurprisingly, the race to attach generational labels to the pandemic has already begun. We've had the 'Coronials', the 'Illenials' (which doesn't make much sense, given that the impact on young people's physical health is largely minimal), the 'Quaranteens' (I quite like that one) and, inevitably, a tech-related one, 'Generation Zoom', after the video-conferencing app. Of course, this is a ludicrous game to play so early in a crisis that will undoubtedly shape generations in ways that we can't yet see.

I am very suspicious of this sort of generational naming. However, I completely disagree with the suggestion that COVID-19, far from being a generational event, is 'as close to a homogenous and constant period effect as we could ever observe'.[33] One of the defining features of the pandemic has been how differently the consequences have been experienced by different groups, with age being a key factor. In fact, this is *the* most generational event in just about all our lifetimes, because when we were born has played a key role in shaping how we've been affected so far, and this will continue to be the case for years to come. This characterization of the pandemic as a uniform period effect completely misses the point of how generational impacts work.

Throughout all the focus on age groups during the COVID-19 pandemic, you may have noticed that, as usual, the middle-aged have been *almost entirely* left out. We are, of course, in the thick of it, juggling kids, parents and working from home, but we're not the primary focus of either the short-term health threat or the long-term implications. It's not surprising, then, that some of us tried to take advantage of that 'forgotten middle child' position to focus on our real passions, as one tweet suggested: 'I would open pubs for 35 to 45 year olds exclusively first. The youth can't be trusted not to go silly and the elderly are at risk if they catch the lurgy. Clear sweet spot of age which can be trusted. Rest of you stay safe at home please, give us a month to check it's safe out.'[34]

Building connection in a disconnected age

As I write this, vaccines to protect against COVID-19 are being rolled out across the world. While the signs are encouraging, I am unsure what the world will look like in even a few months' time. But for all our sakes, I hope the vaccines and treatments we've developed at breakneck pace allow the generations to mix freely again soon. Maintaining personal connections across age groups has been shown time and again to be incredibly important, both on a personal level and at the societal level. Anthropological studies looking at age-mixing among children and adults show older kids who spend time with younger ones learn to be nurturing, while the younger ones learn how to be less dominant, and both groups benefit from spending time with adults from outside their family. Kids who only play with their exact peers, on the other hand, are more likely to be competitive.[35]

As part of his eight stages of adult development, Erik Erikson coined the term 'generativity', to describe the concern felt by older people about their responsibility for establishing and guiding the next generation.[36] Marc Freedman suggests that our focus on legacy may come initially from our drive to pass on our genes, but 'as we move through and beyond midlife, generativity ripens into a broader concern for the next generation, for all the children who will outlive us'. Erikson contrasts generativity with self-concern, the inability to see beyond a narcissism that denies our own mortality and prevents us from seeing ourselves as part of something greater. David Brooks talks about how we similarly shift from a focus on 'resume virtues', the 'skills you bring to the marketplace', to 'eulogy virtues', the ones we want to be remembered for: 'whether you were kind, brave, honest or faithful. Were you capable of deep love?'[37]

In Chapter 2, we outlined the importance of reversing age-based segregation in where we live, and the small steps already being taken to bring us back together. Many other initiatives attempt to increase meaningful contact between age groups while also providing commercial services, including schemes that find spare rooms in older people's homes for young people in university towns: Nesterly in Boston is one such service.[38] John W. Gardner, the former Secretary of Health, Education and Welfare in the US, developed the idea for an 'Experience Corps' to connect older people to public elementary schools. It was launched in the 1990s by collaborators Marc Freedman and Linda Fried, and focuses on helping students read by the time they get to the third grade. Freedman says he often gets asked: 'Was it a corps designed to bring the *experience* of older people ... to benefit young people or was it a corps designed to provide older people useful and meaningful *experiences*? To which I'd say yes and yes.'

The Cares Family is a group of community networks in the UK that represent another take on this same balance of benefits, with a mission to 'find connection in a disconnected age'. The founder Alex Smith describes how the idea came to him in 2010. When standing as a candidate in the local council elections, he was out canvassing and met Fred, an 84-year-old neighbour who hadn't left his house for three months. Alex pushed Fred in his wheelchair to the polling station, and the next day returned to help him get a haircut. As the pair became friends, it was clear that this was a truly mutual relationship: Fred felt less lonely through his interactions with Alex, who in turn felt more connected to his community. The Cares Family started in North London, before opening branches in South London, Manchester, Liverpool and East London. Altogether, the initiatives have connected 22,000 people in programmes that reduce isolation, improve relations across the generations, and help people feel happier, closer to their community and that they have someone to rely on in times of need. These careful, thoughtful initiatives are inspiring – but not enough, in the face of the powerful trend pushing us apart. They deserve more support, and governments need to take more of a lead, by starting to see connection across the age groups as a core objective.

The efforts of these social entrepreneurs stand in stark contrast to the opportunistic use of the narrative of generational conflict to sow division. Steve Bannon's 2010 documentary *Generation Zero* provides a prime example of the latter. It is a bizarre film that is often literally painful to watch, with loud dramatic music and rapidly interspersed videos of setting suns, butterflies emerging from cocoons, riots and statues of Christ on the cross. The core message, which focuses on the lack of responsibility and foresight that led to the 2008 financial crisis, is reasonable if unsurprising.

But the film goes on to connect the causes and consequences of the crisis to the thesis in Strauss and Howe's *The Fourth Turning*, in order to blame the crisis on the liberalism of the 1960s generation and signal an inevitable reckoning to come. It builds a sense of impending decline and doom through the heavy caricaturing of generations and eras: the 1990s was apparently a time of 'bad manners' and 'cynicism'. The documentary is the culmination in a long line of thought, beginning with the 'pulse rate hypothesis' of history, developed by a number of philosophers and sociologists at the turn of the twentieth century, which 'sought the regularities of the universal rhythm of generations'.[39] This is seen as the more extreme end of generational thinking in its attempt to 'impose biological rhythms on socio-historical phenomena'.[40] But Strauss and Howe turned this universal rhythm idea into a prophecy of an inevitable unravelling, on which Bannon hung his unnerving documentary.

The problem with this framing is not just the crass stereotyping of whole groups of people, or even the selective reading of history to fit a narrative – but the idea that this looming crisis is inevitable. This removes any sense of agency in how we might change our course and falls victim to our propensity to always believe we're on the verge of chaos. As the British author and academic Noel Annan writes, 'All generationalists believe their own generation is lost.'[41]

The reality is that generational change is an inevitable mix of harmony and tension, where conflict of some sort is built in. Ortega suggests that 'the concept of the generation is the most important one in the whole of history', precisely because it constitutes the mechanism by which 'history moves, changes, wheels and flows'.[42]

In practice, the lack of real resentment between generations is partly due to the strength of love between them. The Harvard Study of Adult Development launched in 1938 and followed men from a wide variety of backgrounds for over three-quarters of a century. One of the study's findings stands out above all others: relationships are the crucial ingredient in well-being, particularly as we age. As George Vaillant, the Harvard professor who led the study for four decades, writes, 'Happiness is love. Full stop.'[43] And this is particularly the case where love spans the generations: those in middle age and beyond who care for the next generation are three times as likely to be happy as those who don't. This may seem like just another cosy idea, but the importance of these roles in our society is getting increasing attention, and this will only be accentuated by the COVID-19 crisis. Bill Gates, for example, suggested that we introduce a 'tax on robots', in order to fund the training and employment of people to fulfil these roles: 'let us do a better job of reaching out to the elderly, having smaller class sizes, helping kids with special needs. You know, all of those are things where human empathy and understanding are still very, very unique. And we still deal with an immense shortage of people to help out there.'[44]

Marc Freedman has outlined how activities that bring the generations together result in every dollar being 'spent twice', because both generations benefit from it. But as he says: 'In the long run, the love may well be what matters most ... every emotion is also felt twice.' Our forced separation during the pandemic has made it even clearer what we're missing – contact, not conflict.

Chapter 11

The End of the Line?

For such a famously warm-hearted Christmas movie, Frank Capra's *It's a Wonderful Life* addresses some very dark themes. Much of the first half of the film focuses on the suffocation of small-town life, with George Bailey's attempts to escape thwarted by his sense of obligation. George seems to be from a different era from his carefree younger brother. He is an archetype of a 'civic-minded generation' brought up in pre-war America (he was 'born older', as his father tells him). Inevitably, as he grinds along this single-track life, he hits a midlife crisis that only divine intervention (or a major hallucinatory breakdown, depending on your view) can snap him out of. By the end of the film he has come to terms with his lot, shaped by the age and circumstances he was born into.

The spur for George's revelation is seeing how his small town of Bedford Falls would have been different without him. In the end, *It's a Wonderful Life* is compelling because this vision of an alternative reality raises big questions, before answering them in a reassuringly Christmassy way. How is our own character and life course shaped by our formative experiences? And what do we add to the world before we're gone for good?

It turns out that George's presence changed a lot. He saved his brother's life, who in turn saved a whole platoon of men during the war. He stopped a grief-stricken pharmacist (who'd just received word that his son had died in the Spanish flu pandemic) from inadvertently poisoning a customer. He saved the soul of his town by preventing a run on the bank.

George's story embodies the three key mechanisms of change that we've seen in this book: how our lives and attitudes shift as we age; how individual events can change everything for whole populations; and how the circumstances we grow up in shape us throughout our lives. George's life, like all of ours, is a blend of these lifecycle, period and cohort effects. His struggles mirror the tension we all face between cutting our own path and falling into line with existing ways of doing things, and the film shows how confronting our mortality sharpens our thinking on what's important and the difference we can make.

We can't all be George, provided with such clear-cut evidence that we matter. But we can hold onto a greater sense of our collective legacy as generations than our legacy as individuals. Indeed, we strive for that. You can see it in how quickly our thoughts are drawn to what our generation 'gave the world' or what it might achieve. We aspire to be the 'generation to end world poverty'[1]. We want future generations to look back on how we've responded to COVID-19 and, as Queen Elizabeth II suggested in her address to the Commonwealth early on in the crisis, recognize that our generation was 'as strong as any'.[2] We also sometimes call on other generations to make a difference, as when Greta Thunberg argues that it is the responsibility of today's adults to save the planet from a climate change disaster that may determine her future.

Why generations matter

Generational perspectives are powerful because they are interwoven with the fundamentals of human existence and societal change; while individuals are born, live and die, society flows on, changed a little or a lot by our cohort's presence and then its absence. We've seen throughout this book how great thinkers have focused on this as *the* mechanism of social progress. Auguste Comte identified the generation as a key factor in 'the basic speed of human development'. He insisted that 'we should not hide the fact that our social progress rests essentially upon death; which is to say that the successive steps of humanity necessarily require a continuous renovation ... from one generation to the next'.[3]

Yet not everything is determined by this process of generational renewal. All the great generational thinkers have recognized the power of events in shaping our future and the role that lifecycles play in creating intergenerational tension. Unlike other generational analysis, my aim in this book has not been to prove that generational difference is *all* that matters in understanding how societies change – the truth usually resists such simple narratives. Societies actually change through the interplay of cohort, lifecycle and period effects: each is powerful, and none is automatically more important than the others. Thinking more carefully about each aids our understanding of how we as individuals are shaped and how societies change. It helps us bust myths about individual generations and separate exaggerated claims and stereotypes from hugely significant shifts. And it suggests what we should do to build the future we want.

A generational perspective is not a substitute for socio-economic measures like class or income – they are all useful in understanding the world and how it's changing. However, studying the interaction between when you were born and the circumstances you were born into highlights new patterns, including some of the most important changes in our societies. It would not be possible to identify the shifting impact of inequality on life chances without a generational perspective, for example. Ultimately, a truly generational perspective – carefully separating cohort, lifecycle and period effects, rather than subscribing to simplistic clichés – provides us with new insights into some of the biggest issues we're facing today, and points to how we should react. Looking back across the book, seven key themes stand out.

Phoney generational stereotypes are feeding a phoney generational war

Our susceptibility to stereotypes is the most common trap we fall into when discussing generational difference. Lurid examples of young people behaving badly during the pandemic may get clicks, but they misrepresent the incredible compliance with which young and old have faced difficult restrictions. Generational thinking helps us understand why we naturally see the young as more likely to behave badly: the latest generation will *always* be an 'invasion of barbarians' in our cultures and practices. Merely recognizing this helps us guard against falling for the clichés of a mini-industry of generational consultants, marketing headlines and sensationalist books. These may seem trivial individually, but together they are destructive.

Similarly, a generational perspective teaches us that we should be wary of moral panics about new technologies: whenever an innovation we didn't grow up with is identified as the cause of an emergent problem, we should be sceptical until we see solid evidence. For example, accepting the simple answer that smartphones and social media are responsible for increased mental disorders among young people would lead us to look in the wrong place for answers and to miss taking more effective – if less straightforward – action.

While the overwhelming tendency is to attach negative stereotypes to young people, it's equally important to resist the overly positive ones too. The way Strauss and Howe lionize a coming wave of super-civic Millennials is an obvious example, but there are a number of other more consequential ones. The myth that our current younger generations are more focused on acting sustainably or with social purpose than previous generations is risky, as it leads to the assumption that there will be an inevitable rise in environmental concern and action as they make up greater proportions of the overall population. This not only gives a false sense of security but also encourages us to dismiss older people's concern about future generations and the planet.

This tendency to stereotype includes the characterization of younger generations as 'woke'. While younger generations are undoubtedly continuing the trend towards more liberal views on key cultural debates, there is nothing in the data to suggest a sudden break into a different cultural tribe: in fact, we've seen much more rapid generational changes in the recent past. Remembering that cohort effects are only one way in which societies change will help us to correctly identify why this rhetoric of 'culture wars' is happening now: it is largely a period effect, where our polarizing politics and social media has created a stronger sense of difference than is justified.

The caricatures of exaggerated difference often exist purely as clickbait commentary, but it is encouraged on both sides of the political divide. It makes sense that parties with an increasingly older voter base would want to take 'campus politics national', and that those on the other side would exaggerate the virtue of the young, but both strategies fuel the overblown sense of generational difference, skirt over the significant minorities who don't hold these views and give a false sense that we can only travel in one direction between generations. Instead, as we've seen, there are ebbs and flows over time, in response to events and how people change over their lifecycle.

A loss of connection is our biggest risk, not conflict

Increased stereotyping and tension are no doubt partly a result of how we have allowed the generations to drift apart, both physically and digitally, to a degree not seen in our history. This not only adds to these negative trends but means we miss out on the significant benefits of interacting with different age groups.

For these reasons, we should have a greater focus on encouraging intergenerational connection than just the piecemeal initiatives of inspired entrepreneurs. We've drifted apart partly by choice, but also through inattention in government and planning. The separation imposed by the necessary response to the COVID-19 pandemic has only emphasized what we're missing, as well as providing endless examples of how the generations have instinctively supported each other. Reflecting on how to re-establish and bolster intergenerational connection should form a key element of our recovery plans.

This may sound like a tall order, given the power of the trends pushing us apart, but some governments have started to engage with the challenge. In 2014 and 2015, Singapore conducted a huge consultation exercise on creating an 'action plan for successful ageing'.[4] This culminated in a $3 billion plan, one of the key strands of which is to create a 'Kampong [village] for all ages', an effort to build 'a cohesive society with intergenerational harmony'. The programme covers much more than just intergenerational contact, including transport, education, employment and much more, but it has a strong focus on bringing the ages together. Singapore's experience to date shows that it won't be easy to get right and will take time to pay off – but also that it is possible to make a difference.

In the meantime, we also need to establish stronger connections between the generations in how we address shared societal challenges. There is increasing interest around the world in deliberative democracy techniques that bring the whole population together, through methods such as Citizens' Assemblies, to debate and decide on key issues. These tools can be highly effective ways to bridge generational divides, and even to encourage us to connect to future generations. For example, Professor Saijo Tatsuyoshi and his colleagues at the Kochi University of Technology have developed a simple but effective approach called 'future design' where citizens are asked to play the role of future generations in deliberative discussions on all sorts of policy challenges, from water supplies to public housing. The impact is clear: simply imagining ourselves as future generations reduces our focus on immediate priorities.[5]

Delayed lifecycles are changing the life course for new generations

The importance of lifecycle effects is easy to miss among the generational narratives we're fed, but they exert an extraordinarily powerful force over our attitudes and behaviour. Time and again, cohorts that start off by moving in a very different direction from previous generations are pulled back towards a well-worn life course. But it's also important to recognize that these lifecycle currents have been changing, with later transitions for recent generations of young people, thanks to a 'delayed adulthood' effect. This is one of the big changes of our time, and it is a result of all sorts of significant shifts in the world facing young people: staying longer in education, wage stagnation, precarious employment, increased debt and soaring housing costs all serve to delay key life stages. It is more the result of difficult circumstances than either a new age of exploration or an active choice of a 'coddled' generation.

Delayed adulthood is also responsible for a lot of the misconceptions about emerging generations on everything from their car ownership to their sex lives and smoking habits in early adulthood. In many of these trends, they come back into line with previous cohorts – just later. This is a result of changed circumstances, rather than innate characteristics within the generation. It does mean that younger generations are coming to adult life with less experience of independence and in need of more support, but that doesn't make them a 'snowflake generation'.

'Mugging grandma' is not the solution

Despite the tough circumstances facing recent generations of young people, they have little desire to improve their lot by taking from the old. There are many reasons for this, but most are deeply personal. We love our parents and grandparents and don't want to see them penalized for that reason, but also in part because it would shift the burden to us. We know that we'll be old one day as well, and how we treat older people now is one of the only indicators we have of how we'll be treated in the future. More generally, we have a strong sense that we should recognize people who have contributed, and older people have contributed the most.

Our main focus, then, should *not* be on a crude redistribution of resources between existing generations. It is right that we look at the balance between generations, but poorer generational outcomes are more a result of wage stagnation and the increasing barriers to building up wealth. Shuffling the burden between the age groups is not what people really want, and it won't do a lot to help. This will be even more the case when the balance of our societies has moved even further towards an older population.

Instead, the public call for better jobs, economic growth that benefits everyone, and a solution to the broken housing market. Of course, such things are hugely difficult to achieve, but that's the nature of the generational problem: rather than a short-term fix, it is about finding a way to restore faith in a better future for all people and their children.

From the evidence we've seen, it's clear that a better solution on housing needs to be a key element of this brighter future. The aspiration to own property is constant across generations, but it is increasingly unmet. Governments need to close this expectation gap, either by supporting homeownership or by shifting aspirations through improvement of the alternatives, by providing more high-quality social housing or better regulation of private renting. We have become incredibly stuck in countries like the UK, but the longer it continues, the more our individual futures will be determined by the resources we can draw on from our family, and the more support private renters will need in retirement. A comprehensive housing plan should be a cornerstone of any plan to 'build back better'.

Inequality is an increasingly intergenerational issue

It is not just housing opportunities that are increasingly linked to our family background – we're seeing new generational patterns in other areas, including health inequality and the stability of families. The likelihood of obesity in children was once unrelated to their social class, but this has become a key factor for recent generations. More generally, the extraordinary growth of wealth and its concentration in a section of older age groups is one of the key economic stories of our time. Future inequalities between generations are being 'baked in', as advantage and disadvantage is increasingly handed down in an incipient caste system.

It used to be that 'today' would always be the right answer if you were asked when you would like to have been born. This was testament to the incredible progress we have seen and how this moved everyone up, even if the better off were progressing more quickly. But we are now seeing actual reversals for those with fewer resources in richer countries, with shocking declines in life expectancies among the left behind and the kept behind. These groups are currently exceptions, but increasing proportions of the population will get pulled into them as the concentration of advantage continues.

Changing this increasingly intergenerational inequality is an almighty task, and one that has had little political focus, partly as a result of the lack of clamour for change from the public. As we've seen, this absence of anger, particularly from young people, is partly due to them being at the end of a trend towards greater individualism. The sense of personal responsibility and belief in meritocracy may be strong, but it has limits. Even if it doesn't lead to revolution, it certainly inspires growing resentment and a dwindling faith in a better future, which will continue to undermine social and political stability.

There is growing recognition of the need for governments to act with greater 'social imagination'[6] to address these challenges, particularly following the COVID-19 crisis. As the economist Mariana Mazzucato suggests, governments have been 'tinkering not leading'.[7] This needs to change, as 'only government has the capacity to steer the transformation necessary', to recast how economic organizations are governed, and how economic actors, civil society and citizens relate to each other. This is a long-term, intergenerational project.

Crises and decline are *not* inevitable

One of the key risks of looking *only* at generational change is that it gives a greater sense of certainty about the future than is justified. This includes the attempt by Strauss and Howe to overlay a rhythm on generational types and the resultant eras they produce. This type of thinking points to unavoidable crises, which, although a politically useful tool for some, is based on a spurious reading of history and is a bad guide to the future.

More than this, it adds a feeling that there is nothing we can do to avert these crises. There is a parallel doom-mongering in every 'new crisis of trust', while the longer-term trends show that trust levels were never that high and they are, at worst, seeing a long, slow decline. These long trends also show that things have often been as bad, or worse. The large fluctuations in satisfaction with democracy that we've seen in past decades should be considered a sign of resilience rather than weakness.

This long view also shows that current outcomes were not nearly as certain as they may now appear to have been. Hindsight bias makes us think that things were always destined to be like this, including the relative good fortune of older generations and the tougher times faced by current younger generations. In fact, both are the result of the interplay between circumstances, decisions and actions.

Together, these facts suggest that we are more in control than we can sometimes appear. We need to remember that we have agency, even when the challenges facing us are huge, complex and interconnected. We have pulled ourselves up from similar lows before; it doesn't happen through a single 'New Deal', but over the long term, through myriad bottom-up and top-down actions.

We need a Ministry for the Future

The Ministry for the Future, a novel by Kim Stanley Robinson, paints a frighteningly realistic picture of a dystopian near-future, where governments are failing to fulfil promises to reduce carbon emissions and climate change is killing millions. In response, the parties to the Paris Agreement create a 'Subsidiary Body for Implementation of the Agreement', which is nicknamed 'The Ministry for the Future'. The Ministry's role is 'to advocate for the world's future generations of citizens, whose rights, as defined in the Universal Declaration of Human Rights, are as valid as our own ... [and] charged with defending all living creatures present and future who cannot speak for themselves, by promoting their legal standing and physical protection'.

The novel raises all sorts of moral dilemmas around what a future-focused, generation-spanning agenda would look like. As one activist tells the head of the Ministry: 'There are about a hundred people walking this Earth, who if you judge from the angle of the future like you're supposed to do, they are mass murderers ... If you really were *from* the future, so that you knew for sure there were people walking the Earth today fighting change, so that they were killing your children and all their children, you'd defend your people. In defence of your home, your life, your people, you would kill an intruder.'

In the novel, which is more hopeful than this sounds, the Ministry helps to rework complex, interconnected social and economic processes and incentives to direct power and money away from the production of fossil fuels and consumption, and towards more sustainable alternatives. Admittedly, it takes some significant interventions to achieve this goal, including a new carbon currency and the type of 'black ops' you'd associate with a terrorist group or intelligence agency.

Somewhere between this imagined extreme and our governments' weak attempts to think and act generationally, there is a middle ground of how we might formalize our responsibility to consider the future.

There are some early signs of a rebalancing towards this longer perspective, both in how we're framing issues and how institutions are reacting. In a papal letter in 2015, Pope Francis affirmed his view that 'intergenerational solidarity is not optional, but rather a basic question of justice, since the world we have received also belongs to those who will follow us'.[8] National governments have also started to act: the United Arab Emirates has a 'Ministry of Cabinet Affairs and the Future' and Hungary has an 'Ombudsman for Future Generations'.[9]

One particularly important example is the Well-being of Future Generations Act 2015 in Wales. As Jane Davidson, the minister who proposed it, says, 'It is revolutionary because it enshrines into law that the well-being of the current and future people of Wales is explicitly the core purpose of the government in Wales.'[10] The Act was the first to do this anywhere in the world, and it required public bodies to 'think about the long-term impact of their decisions ... to prevent persistent problems such as poverty, health inequalities and climate change'. It also established the role of the Future Generations Commissioner to oversee its implementation. The commissioner does not have the power to stop or change policy and can only make recommendations, 'naming and shaming' public bodies that are not acting in line with the objectives of the Act. Even so, this approach has already made an impact, as several decisions to go ahead or block activity have explicitly cited the Act. As Davidson suggests, it is an early step towards the ultimate goal of changing the culture of governance. While it is not the full answer, it is an exciting base to build on.

Of course, such innovations are dwarfed by the scale of the challenge involved in embedding a longer-term perspective, when consumer culture and economic and political systems push us in the other direction. As we respond to COVID-19, it is vital that we test how much further we can take this, partly because it feels like more could be up for grabs, but also to guard against our natural tendency to focus on the here and now when crises hit. It's the right time to institutionalize some longer-term thinking.

... X, Y, Z

I believe that generational thinking tells us something unique and valuable about our future that can help us shape it – but there are many people who would like to see an end to all discussions of generations. I can understand why, given the clichés that we are so often fed as generational analysis. I've written a book that explains why a lot of what you've been told is generational is, in fact, not. This isn't because I don't see any value in generational thinking, but the opposite: it's too important, particularly right now, to be left to these misdirections. Its importance is not because I see an impending, inevitable crisis or all-out generational war, but because we seem to have lost faith in a better life for our current and future generations of young people. That's risky, and in many ways sums up the challenge of our world in the wake of COVID-19. An understanding of generations, including what brings us together as much as what separates us, is vital to our response.

Regardless of my own view, I think it is very unlikely that Gen Z will be the last generational line I'll be plotting on my charts. In the end, the key reason why generational stories will continue to be important is the simplest: they help us figure out who we are. Just like George Bailey, we need to understand how we fit into this overall picture, even if it's not a completely truthful vision. We also clearly find it *irresistible* to ridicule the young, blame the old – and forget about those in the middle.

* *

The rough timespan of family members I currently have memories of will be 200 years. It will stretch from my grandparents, born in the 1910s, to my children who have a good chance of living to the 2110s. People I know and love will have lived in incredibly different times, from grandads who worked in coal mines and steelworks, to jobs my children may do that I cannot even conceive of. On the one hand, it makes my own slice of time seem incredibly small – but on the other, it connects me to a huge range of human experience. The '200-year present' is a term coined by the sociologist Elise Boulding to describe a way of thinking about the present with full awareness of both the effects of past actions on us now, and of our present actions on the future. It encourages a long-term perspective, acknowledging that the past is still with us in its effects and that, in the same way, today's actions will determine the future. We need more 200-year thinking.

Acknowledgements

With many thanks to Louise, Bridget and Martha for their incredible support and patience, to Mike Harpley and Eric Henney for brilliant editing, and to Nick Humphrey, Michele Scotto di Vettimo, Hermione Fricker, Robin Dennis and Sarah Chatwin for their excellent editing and research. Thanks also to the team at Ipsos MORI for their work on the generational studies that started this and their continued support on data, analysis and insight: Ben Page, Hannah Shrimpton, Michael Clemence, Gideon Skinner, Suzanne Hall, Matt Walliams, K. D. Hasler and Fintan O'Connor, and Darrell Bricker and Kelly Beaver for their support on the global studies. I am also very grateful to the past and present teams at the National Centre for Social Research (NatCen) for their generous sharing of data when I first started examining generational change, particularly Alison Park, Nancy Kelley and Peter Dangerfield, who also helped set up the initial analysis. Thanks also go to the team at King's, who've been understanding of my distraction and generous in comments, including Jonathan Grant, Hermione Fricker and George Murkin, and to the many people who've been working to better understand generational dynamics and connections who have helped inform the book. These include: Robert D. Putnam; Jean Twenge; Laura Gardiner and David Willetts at the Resolution Foundation's Intergenerational Centre; Alex Smith at The Cares Family; and Beatrice Pembroke at King's.

Endnotes

Introduction

1   S.L. van Elsland, 'COVID-19 Deaths: Infection fatality ratio is about 1% says new report', Imperial College London, 29 October 2020, https://www.imperial.ac.uk/news/207273/covid-19-deaths-infection-fatality-ratio-about (accessed 1 April 2021).

2   B. Pancevski, S. Meichtry and X. Fontdegloria, 'A Generational War Is Brewing Over Coronavirus', *The Wall Street Journal*, 19 March 2020, https://www.wsj.com/articles/a-generational-war-is-brewing-over-coronavirus-11584437401 (accessed 1 April 2021).

3   H. Sparks, 'Morbid "Boomer Remover" Coronavirus Meme Only Makes Millennials Seem More Awful', *New York Post*, 19 March 2020, https://nypost.com/2020/03/19/morbid-boomer-remover-coronavirus-meme-only-makes-millennials-seem-more-awful/(accessed 1 April 2021).

4   BBC News, 'Coronavirus: Under-25s and women financially worst-hit', 6 April 2020, https://www.bbc.co.uk/news/business-52176666 (accessed 1 April 2021).

5   J. Portes, 'The Lasting Scars of the Covid-19 Crisis: Channels and impacts', VOX EU, 1 June 2020, https://voxeu.org/article/lasting-scars-covid-19-crisis (accessed 1 April 2021).

6   K. Mannheim, *The Problem of Generations. Essays on the Sociology of Knowledge*, 1952, 5, 276–32.

7   D. Comin and M. Mestieri, *Technology Diffusion: Measurement, causes, and consequences*, NBER Working Paper No. 19052, Cambridge, MA, National Bureau of Economic Research, 2013, https://www.nber.org/papers/w19052 (accessed 1 April 2021).

8   H. Rosa, *Social Acceleration: A new theory of modernity*, trans. by J. Treejo-Mathys, New York, Columbia University Press, 2013.

9   Source: Ipsos What Worries the World survey (2010–18); around 1,000 interviews per month.

10 Source: Health Survey for England (1992–2017).

11 Source: US General Social Survey (1974–2018).

12 I have deliberately used a simple graphical approach rather than complicated statistical models to make the analysis as accessible as possible. But there is no way around what statisticians call the 'identification problem' when trying to separate the effects of period, lifecycle and cohort. They are exactly 'colinear' – that is, if we know someone's age and the year we're taking our measurement, we automatically know when they were born. This makes it literally impossible to fully disentangle which of the effects is causing changes. There are statistical techniques that try to get around this, but all of them

rely on assumptions that attempt
to fix or strip out one of the three
effects to measure the others. While
what we've done in this book is much
simpler, the point remains that we
need to be cautious in claiming the
effects are completely separable.

13   K.J. Freeman, *Schools of Hellas: An
essay on the practice and theory of
ancient Greek education from 600 to
300 BC*, Macmillan, p. 74, quoted in:
'Misbehaving Children in Ancient
Times', *Quote Investigator*, 1 May
2010, https://quoteinvestigator.com/
2010/05/01/misbehave/ (accessed 1
April 2021).

14   J. Seder, '15 Historical Complaints
About Young People Ruining
Everything', Mental Floss, 21 March
2016, https://www.mentalfloss.
com/article/77445/15-historical-
complaints-about-young-people-
ruining-everything (accessed 1 April
2021).

15   'Boys are Ruined. Dime Novels Cause
Lads to Murder', *Dawson Daily News*,
1906.

16   C. Thompson, 'Why Chess Will
Destroy Your Mind', Medium.com,
22 May 2014, https://medium.com/
message/why-chess-will-destroy-
your-mind-78ad1034521f (accessed 1
April 2021).

17   K. Taylor, 'Millennials and Their
Spending Habits Are Wreaking Havoc
on These 18 Industries', *Business
Insider*, 1 February 2019, https://www.
businessinsider.com/millennials-hurt-
industries-sales-2018-10?r=US&IR=T
(accessed 1 April 2021).

18   R. Dobson, *Millennial Problems:
Everyday Struggles of a Generation*,
London, Square Peg, 2017, p. 12.

19   M.L. Hummert, 'A Social Cognitive
Perspective on Age Stereotypes', in

Social Cognition and Aging, edited
by T. M. Hess and F. Blanchard-
Fields, Elsevier, 1999, pp. 175–196. L.
Popham and T. Hess, 'Theories of Age
Stereotyping and Views of Aging',
in *Encyclopedia of Geropsychology*,
edited by N.A. Pachana, Singapore,
Springer Science+Business Media,
2015, pp. 1–10. https://www.
researchgate.net/publication/
299478040_Theories_of_Age_
Stereotyping_and_Views_of_Aging
(accessed 7 April 2021).

20   N.R. Gibbs, 'Grays on the Go', *Time*,
131 (8), 22 February 1988, pp. 66–75,
http://content.time.com/time/
subscriber/article/0,33009,966744-
9,00.html (accessed 1 April 2021).

21   E. Kihlstrom, 'Shhh! Ageing Is Good
Business', Innovate UK, 14 May 2018,
https://innovateuk.blog.gov.uk/2018/
05/14/shhh-ageing-is-good-business/
(accessed 1 April 2021).

22   *The Guardian*, '"OK Boomer":
Millennial MP Responds to Heckler
in New Zealand Parliament, YouTube,
6 November 2019, https://www.
youtube.com/watch?v=OxJsPXrEqCI
(accessed 1 April 2021).

23   L. Stone, 'The Boomers Ruined
Everything', *The Atlantic*, 24 June
2019, https://www.theatlantic.com/
ideas/archive/2019/06/boomers-
are-blame-aging-america/592336/
(accessed 1 April 2021).

24   J. Walker [@jonwalker121], 'I am
neither a millennial nor a boomer. I
come from a generation so irrelevant
that people can't even be bothered to
hate us', Twitter, 14 November 2019,
https://twitter.com/jonwalker121/
status/1194919236730343424 (accessed
1 April 2021).

25   P. Fussell, quoted in J. Gordinier,
X Saves the World: How Generation

X Got the Shaft But Can Still Keep Everything From Sucking, London, Penguin, 2008, p. xxi.

26 C. Seemiller and M. Grace, *Generation Z: A Century in the Making*, Abingdon, Routledge, 2018.

27 Gordinier, *X Saves the World*.

28 M. Hennessey, *Zero Hour for Gen X: How the Last Adult Generation Can Save America From Millennials*, New York, Encounter Books, 2018, p. 58.

29 Source: Eurostat (1972–2019).

30 N.N. Taleb, *The Black Swan: The Impact of the Highly Improbable*. London, Penguin, 2010.

31 Worldometer, Countries Where COVID-19 Has Spread, 2020, https://www.worldometers.info/coronavirus/

countries-where-coronavirus-has-spread/ (accessed 1 April 2021).

32 Ipsos Global Trends survey, 2019.

33 H. Shrimpton, G. Skinner and S. Hall, *The Millennial Bug*, London, Resolution Foundation, 2017, https://www.resolutionfoundation.org/app/uploads/2017/09/The-Millennial-Bug.pdf (accessed 1 April 2021). B. Duffy, F. Thomas, H. Shrimpton, H. Whyte-Smith, M. Clemence and T. Abboud, *Beyond Binary: The Lives and Choices of Generation Z*, London, Ipsos MORI, 2018, p. 150, https://www.ipsos.com/ipsos-mori/en-uk/ipsos-thinks-beyond-binary-lives-and-choices-generation-z (accessed 1 April 2021).

Chapter 1

1 'The Baby Boomers – Can They Ever Live as Well as Their Parents?' *Money* magazine, March 1983.

2 D. Willetts, *The Pinch: How the baby boomers took their children's future— and why they should give it back*, London, Atlantic Books, 2010.

3 F. Rahman and D. Tomlinson, *Cross Countries: International Comparisons of Intergenerational Trends*. London, Resolution Foundation and the Intergenerational Commission, 2018, https://www.resolutionfoundation.org/app/uploads/2018/02/IC-international.pdf (accessed 1 April 2021).

4 Ibid.

5 G. Bangham, S. Clarke, L. Gardiner, L. Judge, F. Rahman and D. Tomlinson, *An Intergenerational Audit for the UK: 2019*, June 2019, London, Resolution Foundation, https://www.resolutionfoundation.org/app/uploads/2019/06/Intergenerational-

audit-for-the-UK.pdf (accessed 1 April 2021).

6 Source: British Social Attitudes survey (1983–2017).

7 Office for National Statistics, 'Pensioner Income and Expenditure', in *Pension Trends*, 2012, https://webarchive.nationalarchives.gov.uk/20160107023853/http://www.ons.gov.uk/ons/rel/pensions/pension-trends/chapter-11--pensioner-income-and-expenditure--2012-edition-/sum-ch11-2012.html (accessed 1 April 2021).

8 Willetts, *The Pinch*.

9 M. Belot, S. Choi, E. Tripodi, E. van den Broek-Altenburg, J. C. Jamison and N. W. Papageorge, *Unequal Consequences of COVID-19 across Age and Income: Representative Evidence from Six Countries*, Bonn, Institute of Labor Economics, 2020, http://ftp.iza.org/dp13366.pdf (accessed 1 April 2021).

10 Barclays 'Small "Swaprifices" Could Save Millennials up to £10.5bn a

Year', 20 February 2019, https://home. barclays/news/press-releases/2019/ 02/small--swaprifices--could-save-millennials-up-to-p10-5bn-a-year/ (accessed 1 April 2021).

11 R. Thompson, 'Millennial Spending Habits Are Being Questioned (Again) and the Internet Isn't Here For It', Mashable UK, 20 February 2019, https://mashable.com/article/ millennial-coffee-spending-reaction (accessed 1 April 2021).

12 F. Costello and A. Acland, 'Spending the Kids Inheritance, What It Means for UK Companies', Innovate UK, 19 July 2016, https://innovateuk.blog. gov.uk/2016/07/19/spending-the-kids-inheritance-what-it-means-for-uk-companies/ (accessed 1 April 2021).

13 W. Best, 'Gray Is the New Black: Baby Boomers Still Outspend Millennials', VISA Consulting and Analytics, 17 December 2018, https://usa.visa.com/ partner-with-us/visa-consulting-analytics/baby-boomers-still-outspend-millennials.html (accessed 1 April 2021).

14 A. Scott, 'The "Silver Tsunami" Is the Workforce the World Needs Right Now', Quartz at Work, 1 May 2019, https://qz.com/work/1605206/senior-workers-are-the-key-to-economic-growth/ (accessed 1 April 2021).

15 J.M. Twenge, *Generation Me: Why Today's Young Americans are More Confident, Assertive, Entitled–and More Miserable than Ever Before*, New York, The Free Press, 2006.

16 J.M. Twenge, *Why Today's Super-Connected Kids Are Growing Up Less Rebellious, More Tolerant, Less Happy – and Completely Unprepared for Adulthood*, New York, Atria Books, 2018.

17 Twenge, *Why Today's Super-Connected Kids Are Growing Up Less Rebellious*; Twenge, *Generation Me*.

18 B. Fell and M. Hewstone, *Psychological Perspectives on Poverty: A review of psychological research into the causes and consequences of poverty*, London, Joseph Rowntree Foundation, 2015, https://www.jrf.org.uk/report/ psychological-perspectives-poverty (accessed 1 April 2021).

19 S. Heshmat, 'The Scarcity Mindset: How does being poor change the way we feel and think?', *Psychology Today*, 2 April 2015, https://www. psychologytoday.com/gb/blog/ science-choice/201504/the-scarcity-mindset (accessed 1 April 2021).

20 Source: European Social Survey (2002–18).

21 Bangham et al., *An Intergenerational Audit for the UK: 2019*.

22 Credit Suisse Research Institute, *The Global Wealth Report 2017*, Zurich, Credit Suisse Research Institute, 2017, https://www.credit-suisse.com/ corporate/en/research/research-institute/global-wealth-report.html (accessed 1 April 2021).

23 T. Wiltshire and D. Wood 'Three Charts On: The Great Australian Wealth Gap', *The Conversation*, 1 October 2017, https://theconversation. com/three-charts-on-the-great-australian-wealth-gap-84515 (accessed 1 April 2021).

24 Source: Australian Bureau of Statistics, Survey of Income and Housing (2003–16).

25 A. Josuweit, '5 Money Tips Millennials Can Learn From Their Grandparents', *Forbes*, 15 March 2018, https://www. forbes.com/sites/andrewjosuweit/ 2018/03/15/5-money-tips-millennials-

can-learn-from-their-grandparents (accessed 1 April 2021).

26 Bangham et al., *An Intergenerational Audit for the UK: 2019*.

27 Intergenerational Commission, *A New Generational Contract: The final report of the Intergenerational Commission*, London, Resolution Foundation, 2018, https://www. resolutionfoundation.org/advanced/ a-new-generational-contract/ (accessed 1 April 2021).

28 Willetts, *The Pinch*.

29 Intergenerational Commission, *A New Generational Contract*.

30 Ibid.

31 E. Howker and S. Malik, *Jilted Generation: How Britain Has Bankrupted Its Youth*, London, Icon Books, 2013.

32 K.K. Chan, E.J. Huang and R.A. Lassu, 'Understanding Financially Stressed Millennials' Hesitancy to Seek Help: Implications for Organizations', *Journal of Financial Education* vol. 43, no. 1, 2017, pp. 141–160, https://www. jstor.org/stable/90018423 (accessed 1 April 2021).

33 K. Scanlon, F. Blanc, A. Edge and C. Whitehead, *The Bank of Mum and Dad: How It Really Works*, London, LSE and the Family Building Society, http://www.lse.ac.uk/business- and-consultancy/consulting/assets/ documents/the-bank-of-mum-and- dad.pdf (accessed 1 April 2021).

34 Intergenerational Commission, *A New Generational Contract*.

35 G. Clark and N. Cummins, 'Intergenerational Wealth Mobility in England, 1858–2012: Surnames and Social Mobility', *The Economic Journal*, vol. 125, no. 582, 2015, pp. 61–85. https://doi.org/10.1111/ ecoj.12165.

36 Intergenerational Commission, *A New Generational Contract*.

37 R. Eisenberg, 'The Distressing Growth of Wealth Inequality of Boomers', *Forbes*, 16 October 2019, https://www. forbes.com/sites/nextavenue/2019/10/ 16/the-distressing-growth-of-wealth- inequality-of-boomers/ (accessed 1 April 2021).

38 R.D. Putnam, *Our Kids: The American Dream in Crisis*, New York, Simon and Schuster, 2016.

39 Cited in ibid.

40 Ibid.

41 P. Norris and P. Inglehart, *Cultural Backlash*, Cambridge, UK, Cambridge University Press, 2019.

42 G. Hofstede, *Culture's Consequences: Comparing Values, Behaviors, and Organizations Across Nations*, London and Thousand Oaks, CA, Sage Publications, 2001. S.H. Schwartz, 'A Theory of Cultural Values and Some Implications for Work', *Applied Psychology: An International Review*, vol. 48, no. 1, pp. 23–47, 1999, https:// doi.org/10.1111/j.1464-0597.1999. tb00047.x. S.H. Schwartz, 'Causes of Culture: National Differences in Cultural Embeddedness', in A. Gari and K. Mylonas, *Quod Erat Demonstrandum: From Herodotus' ethnographic journeys to cross- cultural research*, Athens, Pedio Books, 2009, https://scholarworks. gvsu.edu/iaccp_proceedings/5/ (accessed 1 April 2021).

43 M. Thatcher, Speech to Conservative Party Conference, Blackpool, 10 October 1975, https://www. margaretthatcher.org/document/ 102777 (accessed 1 April 2021).

44 R. Reagan, 'A Time for Choosing', televised speech, Los Angeles County, CA, 27 October 1964, https://www.

reaganlibrary.gov/reagans/ronald-reagan/time-choosing-speech-october-27-1964 (accessed 7 April 2021).

45 S. Malik, 'Adults in Developing Nations More Optimistic Than Those in Rich Countries', *The Guardian*, 14 April 2014, https://www.theguardian.com/politics/2014/apr/14/developing-nations-more-optimistic-richer-countries-survey (accessed 1 April 2021).

46 Ibid.

47 D. Thomson, *Selfish Generations?: The Ageing of New Zealand's Welfare State*, Bridget Williams Books, 2015.

48 US General Social Survey, 1984–2016.

49 British Social Attitudes survey, 2016.

50 H. Shrimpton, G. Skinner and S. Hall, *The Millennial Bug: Public attitudes on the living standards of different generations*, London, Resolution Foundation and Intergenerational Commission, 2017, https://www.resolutionfoundation.org/app/uploads/2017/09/The-Millennial-Bug.pdf (accessed 1 April 2021).

51 B. Duffy, S. Hall, D. O'Leary and S. Pope, *Generation Strains: A Demos and Ipsos MORI report on changing attitudes to welfare*, London, Demos, 2013, https://www.demos.co.uk/files/Demos_Ipsos_Generation_Strains_web.pdf?1378677272 (accessed 1 April 2021).

52 J. Hills, in *The Dynamic of Welfare: The Welfare State and The Lifecycle*, edited by J. Falkingham and J. Hills, Prentice-Hall, 1995.

Chapter 2

1 Monty Python, 'Four Yorkshiremen', *At Last the 1948 Show*, ITV (1967), https://www.youtube.com/watch?v=VAdlkunflRs (accessed 1 April 2021).

2 J. Rach, '"The Estate Agent Said I'd Caused Mould by Breathing": "Generation Rent" Share Their Horror Stories – Including a Woman Whose Landlord Had Sex in Her Bed', *Daily Mail*, 23 August 2018, https://www.dailymail.co.uk/femail/article-6090591/Generation-rent-share-horror-stories-including-mould-rip-prices-holes-CEILING.html (accessed 1 April 2021).

3 Ibid, reader comment.

4 *Daily Mail*, 'In the Wealthiest Nation on Earth... But More than 1.6 Million Americans Do Not Have Indoor Plumbing', *Daily Mail*, 23 April 2014, https://www.dailymail.co.uk/news/article-2611602/In-wealthiest-nation-Earth-1-6-million-Americans-dont-indoor-plumbing.html (accessed 1 April 2021). C. Ingraham, '1.6 Million Americans Don't Have Indoor Plumbing', *The Washington Post*, 23 April 2014, https://www.washingtonpost.com/news/wonk/wp/2014/04/23/1-6-million-americans-dont-have-indoor-plumbing-heres-where-they-live/ (accessed 1 April 2021).

5 This is Money, 'Homes Less Affordable Than 50 Years Ago – But At Least More of Them Have Indoor Toilets!', 20 January 2010, https://www.thisismoney.co.uk/money/article-1244777/Homes-affordable-50-years-ago--indoor-toilets.html (accessed 1 April 2021).

6 R. Goodman, *The Domestic Revolution*, London, Michael O'Mara Books, 2020.

7   D. Lavelle, '"Slugs came through the floorboards": What It's Like To Be a Millennial Renting in Britain', *The Guardian*, 5 August 2018, https://www.theguardian.com/society/2018/aug/05/landlord-flat-affordable-rent-millennials-uk-cities-farcical (accessed 1 April 2021).

8   H. Ewens, 'The Real Reason Millennials Complain about Housing', 9 August 2018, *Vice.com*, https://www.vice.com/en_uk/article/bjb5kz/the-real-reason-millennials-complain-about-housing (accessed 1 April 2021).

9   Department for Communities and Local Government, *English Housing Survey: Housing Costs and Affordability, 2015–16*, https://assets.publishing.service.gov.uk/government/uploads/system/uploads/attachment_data/file/627683/Housing_Cost_and_Affordability_Report_2015-16.pdf (accessed 1 April 2021).

10 Ewens, 'The Real Reason Millennials Complain about Housing'.

11 *The Economist*, Global House-Price Index, 27 June 2019, https://www.economist.com/graphic-detail/2019/06/27/global-house-price-index?date=1975-03&index=real_price&places=IRL&places=USA (accessed 1 April 2021).

12 A. Madrigal, 'Why Housing Policy Feels Like Generational Warfare', 13 June 2019, *The Atlantic*, https://www.theatlantic.com/technology/archive/2019/06/why-millennials-cant-afford-buy-house/591532/ (accessed 1 April 2021).

13 Intergenerational Commission, *A New Generational Contract*.

14 Source: British Social Attitudes survey (1983–2017).

15 P. Collinson, 'The Other Generation Rent: Meet the People Flatsharing in Their 40s', *The Guardian*, 25 September 2015, https://www.theguardian.com/money/2015/sep/25/flatsharing-40s-housing-crisis-lack-homes-renting-london (accessed 1 April 2021).

16 J. Kelly, 'Peep Show and the Stigma of Flat-Sharing in Your 40s', BBC News, 11 November 2015, https://www.bbc.co.uk/news/magazine-34775063 (accessed 1 April 2021).

17 A. Corlett and L. Judge, *Home Affront: Housing Across the Generations*, London, Resolution Foundation and Intergenerational Commission, 2017, https://www.resolutionfoundation.org/app/uploads/2017/09/Home-Affront.pdf (accessed 1 April 2021).

18 Source: British Social Attitudes survey (1983–2016).

19 Source: US General Social Survey (1985–2018).

20 M. Phillips, 'Most Germans Don't Buy Their Homes, They Rent. Here's Why', Quartz, 23 January 2014, https://qz.com/167887/germany-has-one-of-the-worlds-lowest-homeownership-rates/ (accessed 1 April 2021).

21 Zeit Online 'Weniger junge Leute wohnen in den eigenen vier Wänden', 9 August 2019, https://www.zeit.de/news/2019-08/09/weniger-junge-leute-wohnen-in-den-eigenen-vier-waenden (accessed 1 April 2021).

22 L.J. Kotlikoff and S. Burns, *The Clash of Generations: Saving Ourselves, Our Kids, and Our Economy*, Cambridge, MA, MIT Press, 2012.

23 J. Sternberg, *The Theft of a Decade: How the Baby Boomers Stole the Millennials' Economic Future*, New York, Public Affairs, 2019.

24 R. Loxton, 'Housing in Germany: Why Are Fewer Young People Buying Their Own Homes?', *The Local*, 9 August 2019, https://www.thelocal.de/20190809/housing-in-germany-why-are-fewer-young-people-buying-their-own-homes (accessed 1 April 2021).

25 J.H. Choi, L. Goodman, B. Ganesh, S. Strochak and J. Zhu, *Millennial Homeownership: Why Is It So Low, and How Can We Increase It?*, Washington, DC, Urban Institute, 2018, https://www.urban.org/research/publication/millennial-homeownership (accessed 1 April 2021).

26 Ibid.

27 Ibid.

28 G.B. White, 'Millennials Who Are Thriving Financially Have One Thing in Common ... Rich Parents', *The Atlantic*, 15 July 2015, https://www.theatlantic.com/business/archive/2015/07/millennials-with-rich-parents/398501/ (accessed 1 April 2021).

29 Ibid.

30 Before the pandemic, the Resolution Foundation attempted to predict whether Millennials in the UK will catch up with the homeownership rates of previous generations, applying the best- and worst-case conditions for homeownership from recent history. In the think tank's most optimistic scenario, Millennials get fairly close, just a few percentage points behind Baby Boomers. But in the most pessimistic scenario, barely half of Millennials will be homeowners by the time they're 45 years old, 20 percentage points lower than the level of Baby Boomers. Corlett and Judge, *Home Affront*.

31 A. Morris, *The Australian Dream: Housing Experiences of Older Australians*, Csiro Publishing, 2016, https://www.publish.csiro.au/book/7269/ (accessed 1 April 2021).

32 S. Baum and M. Wulff, *Housing Aspirations of Australian households*, Australian Housing and Urban Research Institute, Queensland Research Centre, 2003, https://pdfs.semanticscholar.org/eff1/e6c82d6ba380e3611e182741b2ace71b405c.pdf (accessed 1 April 2021).

33 Kotlikoff and Burns, *The Clash of Generations*.

34 J. Kotkin, 'The End of Aspiration', *Quillette*, 10 April 2019, https://quillette.com/2019/04/10/the-end-of-aspiration/ (accessed 1 April 2021).

35 M. Arnold and A. Domitille, 'Surge in European House Prices Stokes Concerns Over Market Resilience', *Financial Times*, 6 November 2020, https://www.ft.com/content/2606dd0d-d009-4fc6-8801-2a089d76bdc5 (accessed 1 April 2021).

36 Corlett and Judge, *Home Affront*.

37 S. Marsh, 'The Boomerang Generation – and the Childhood Bedrooms They Still Inhabit', *The Guardian*, 14 March 2016, https://www.theguardian.com/world/commentisfree/2016/mar/14/the-boomerang-generation-and-the-childhood-bedrooms-they-still-inhabit (accessed 1 April 2021).

38 B. Duffy, *The Perils of Perception: Why We're Wrong About Nearly Everything*, London, Atlantic Books, 2018.

39 Source: US General Social Survey (1975–2017).

40 P. Collinson, 'Record Numbers of Young Adults in UK Living with Parents', *The Guardian*, 15 November 2019, https://www.theguardian.com/uk-news/2019/nov/15/record-numbers-of-young-adults-in-uk-

living-with-parents (accessed 1 April 2021).

41 Office for National Statistics, 'Why Are More Young People Living with Their Parents?', 22 February 2016, https://www.ons.gov.uk/ peoplepopulationandcommunity/ birthsdeathsandmarriages/families/ articles/whyaremoreyoungpeople livingwiththeirparents/2016-02-22 (accessed 1 April 2021).

42 J.J. Arnett, 'Emerging Adulthood: A Theory of Development from the Late Teens through the Twenties', *American Psychologist*, vol. 55, no. 5, 2000, pp. 469–480, http://www. jeffreyarnett.com/articles/ARNETT_ Emerging_Adulthood_theory.pdf (accessed 1 April 2021).

43 J. Côté, *Arrested Adulthood: The Changing Nature of Identity-Maturity in the Late-Modern World*, New York, New York University Press, 2000.

44 J.G. Dey and C.R. Pierret, 'Independence for Young Millennials: Moving Out and Boomeranging Back', *Monthly Labor Review*, vol. 137, no. 1, 2014, https://www.jstor.org/ stable/monthlylaborrev.2014.12.004 (accessed 1 April 2021).

45 J. Stein, 'Millennials: The Me Me Me Generation', *Time*, 20 May 2013, https://time.com/247/millennials-the-me-me-me-generation/ (accessed 1 April 2021).

46 A. Barroso, K. Parker and R. Fry, 'Majority of Americans Say Parents Are Doing Too Much for Their Young Adult Children', Pew Research Center, 23 October 2019, https://www. pewsocialtrends.org/2019/10/23/ majority-of-americans-say-parents-are-doing-too-much-for-their-young-adult-children/ (accessed 1 April 2021).

47 M. Freedman, 'The Perils of Age Segregation', The Aspen Institute, 17 April 2019, https://www.aspenideas. org/articles/the-perils-of-age-segregation (accessed 1 April 2021).

48 M. Freedman and T. Stamp, 'The U.S. Isn't Just Getting Older. It's Getting More Segregated by Age', *Harvard Business Review*, 6 June 2018, https:// hbr.org/2018/06/the-u-s-isnt-just-getting-older-its-getting-more-segregated-by-age (accessed 1 April 2021).

49 L. Neyfakh, 'What "Age Segregation" Does to America', *Boston Globe*, 30 August 2014, https://www. bostonglobe.com/ideas/2014/08/30/ what-age-segregation-does-america/ 0568E8x0AQ7VG6F4grjLxH/story. html (accessed 1 April 2021).

50 M. Freedman, *How to Live Forever: The Enduring Power of Connecting the Generations*, New York, Public Affairs, 2018.

51 Ibid.

52 Freedman and Stamp, 'The U.S. Isn't Just Getting Older'.

53 C. McCurdy, *Ageing, Fast and Slow: When Place and Demography Collide*, London, Resolution Foundation, 2019, https://www.resolutionfoundation. org/publications/ageing-fast-and-slow/ (accessed 1 April 2021).

54 Source: Centre for Towns reanalysis of UK Census data (1981–2011).

55 I. Warren, 'The Unequal Distribution of an Aging Population', Centre for Towns, 20 November 2017, https:// www.centrefortowns.org/blog/16-the-unequal-distribution-of-an-aging-population (accessed 1 April 2021).

56 McCurdy, *Ageing, Fast and Slow*.

57 G.W. Allport, K. Clark and T. Pettigrew, *The Nature of Prejudice*, 1954.

58 Neyfakh, 'What "Age Segregation" Does to America'.

59 Generations United, *All in Together: Creating places where young and old thrive*, 2018, https://www.gu.org/app/uploads/2018/06/SignatureReport-Eisner-All-In-Together.pdf (accessed 1 April 2021).

60 A. Tversky and D. Kahneman, 'Availability: A Heuristic for Judging Frequency and Probability', *Cognitive Psychology*, vol. 5, no. 2, 1973, pp. 207–232, https://doi.org/10.1016/0010-0285(73)90033-9.

61 Wikipedia, 'Hindsight Bias', https://en.wikipedia.org/wiki/Hindsight_bias#Examples (accessed 1 April 2021).

62 B. Milligan, 'Home Ownership: Did Earlier Generations Have It Easier?', BBC News, 29 November 2013, https://www.bbc.co.uk/news/business-24660825 (accessed 1 April 2021).

63 TIC Finance, 'How Many Repossessions in UK Year on Year?', UK Repossession Statistics, 1969–2019, https://www.ticfinance.co.uk/stats/ (accessed 1 April 2021).

Chapter 3

1 L. Gellman, 'Helping Bosses Decode Millennials—for $20,000 an Hour', *The Wall Street Journal*, 18 May 2016, https://www.wsj.com/articles/helping-bosses-decode-millennialsfor-20-000-an-hour-1463505666 (accessed 1 April 2021).

2 H. Nolan, 'Target's Dumb Internal Guide to Millennials (and Other Generations)', Gawker, 9 January 2015, https://gawker.com/targets-dumb-internal-guide-to-millennials-and-other-g-1678496059 (accessed 1 April 2021).

3 H. Shrimpton, G. Skinner and S. Hall, *The Millennial Bug: Public attitudes on the living standards of different generations*, London, Resolution Foundation and Intergenerational Commission, 2017, https://www.resolutionfoundation.org/app/uploads/2017/09/The-Millennial-Bug.pdf (accessed 1 April 2021).

4 OECD, *Education in China: A Snapshot*, Paris, OECD Publishing, 2016, http://www.oecd.org/china/Education-in-China-a-snapshot.pdf (accessed 1 April 2021).

5 K. Stapleton, 'Inside the World's Largest Education Boom', The Conversation, 10 April 2017, https://theconversation.com/inside-the-worlds-largest-higher-education-boom-74789 (accessed 1 April 2021).

6 D. Tomlinson and F. Rahman, *Cross Countries: International Comparisons of Intergenerational Trends*, London, Resolution Foundation, 2018, https://www.resolutionfoundation.org/publications/cross-countries-international-comparisons-of-intergenerational-trends/ (accessed 1 April 2021).

7 Source: Analysis of OECD data, 2000, 2010 and 2019.

8 Source: British Social Attitudes survey (1986–2018).

9 J. Arminio, T.K. Grabosky and J. Lang, *Student Veterans and Service Members in Higher Education*, Routledge, 2014.

10 OECD, *Health at a Glance 2019: OECD Indicators*, Paris, OECD Publishing, 2019, https://www.oecd-ilibrary.org/sites/6303de6b-en/index.html?itemId=/content/component/6303de6b-en (accessed 1 April 2021).

11   L. Rothman, 'Putting the Rising Cost of College in Perspective', *Time*, 31 August 2016, https://time.com/4472261/college-cost-history/ (accessed 1 April 2021).

12   J.H. Choi, L. Goodman, B. Ganesh, S. Strochak and J. Zhu, *Millennial Homeownership: Why Is It So Low, and How Can We Increase It?*, Washington, DC, Urban Institute, 2018, https://www.urban.org/research/publication/millennial-homeownership (accessed 1 April 2021).

13   Z. Friedman, 'Student Loan Debt Statistics In 2019: A $1.5 Trillion Crisis', *Forbes*, 25 February 2019, https://www.forbes.com/sites/zackfriedman/2019/02/25/student-loan-debt-statistics-2019/#6cac7908133f (accessed 1 April 2021).

14   J. Britton, L. Dearden, L. van der Erve and B. Waltmann, 'The Impact of Undergraduate Degrees on Lifetime Earnings', 29 February 2020, Institute for Fiscal Studies, https://www.ifs.org.uk/publications/14729 (accessed 1 April 2021).

15   J.R. Abel and R. Deitz, 'Despite Rising Costs, College Is Still A Good Investment', Federal Reserve Bank of New York, 5 June 2019, https://libertystreeteconomics.newyorkfed.org/2019/06/despite-rising-costs-college-is-still-a-good-investment.html (accessed 1 April 2021).

16   J. Ma, M. Pender and M. Welch, *Education Pays 2019: The Benefits of Higher Education for Individuals and Society*, Trends in Higher Education Series, College Board, 2019, https://research.collegeboard.org/pdf/education-pays-2019-full-report.pdf (accessed 1 April 2021).

17   Universities New Zealand, Key Facts and Stats, https://www.universitiesnz.ac.nz/sites/default/files/uni-nz/NZ-Universities-Key-Facts-and-Stats-Sept-2016_0.pdf (accessed 7 April 2021).

18   C. Belfield, J. Britton, F. Buscha, L. Dearden, M. Dickson, L. van der Erve, L. Sibieta, A. Vignoles, I. Walker and Y. Zhu, *The impact of undergraduate degrees on early-career earnings*, London, Institute for Fiscal Studies and Department for Education, 2018, https://www.ifs.org.uk/uploads/publications/comms/DFE_returnsHE.pdf (accessed 1 April 2021).

19   Britton et al., 'The Impact of Undergraduate Degrees on Lifetime Earnings'.

20   H. Hoffower, Nearly Half of Indebted Millennials Say College Wasn't Worth It, And The Reason Why Is Obvious, *Insider*, 11 April 2019, https://www.businessinsider.com/personal-finance/millennials-college-not-worth-student-loan-debt-2019-4?r=US&IR=T (accessed 7 April 2021).

21   E.T. Pascarella and P.T. Terenzini, *How College Affects Students: A Third Decade of Research*. Volume 2, Hoboken, NJ, John Wiley & Sons, 2005.

22   D. Goodhart, *Head, Hand, Heart: Why Intelligence Is Over-Rewarded, Manual Workers Matter, and Caregivers Deserve More Respect*, Free Press, 2020.

23   E. Ortiz-Ospina, S. Tzvetkova and M. Roser, 'Women's Employment', *OurWorldInData*, 2018, https://ourworldindata.org/female-labor-supply (accessed 1 April 2021).

24   Intergenerational Commission, *A New Generational Contract: The final report of the Intergenerational Commission*, London, Resolution Foundation, 2018, https://www.

resolutionfoundation.org/advanced/
a-new-generational-contract/
(accessed 1 April 2021).

25 A. Scott, 'The "Silver Tsunami" Is the
Workforce the World Needs Right
Now', Quartz at Work, 1 May 2019,
https://qz.com/work/1605206/senior-
workers-are-the-key-to-economic-
growth/ (accessed 1 April 2021).

26 R. Kochhar, 'Hispanic Women,
Immigrants, Young Adults, Those
With Less Education Hit Hardest by
COVID-19 Job Losses', Pew Research
Center, 9 June 2020, https://www.
pewresearch.org/fact-tank/2020/06/
09/hispanic-women-immigrants-
young-adults-those-with-less-
education-hit-hardest-by-covid-19-
job-losses/ (accessed 1 April 2021).

27 Office for National Statistics,
Dataset: EMP17: People in
employment on zero hours contracts,
2021, https://www.ons.gov.uk/
employmentandlabourmarket/
peopleinwork/
employmentandemployeetypes/
datasets/emp17peopleinemployment
onzerohourscontracts (accessed 7
April 2021).

28 Rahman and Tomlinson, Cross
Countries.

29 D. Rounds, 'Millennials and the
Death of Loyalty', Forbes, 4 April
2017, https://www.forbes.com/sites/
forbescoachescouncil/2017/04/04/
millennials-and-the-death-of-loyalty/
#1f0073526745 (accessed 1 April 2021).

30 US Bureau of Labor Statistics, Median
Tenure at Current Employer 1983-
2018, 2018.

31 Ibid.

32 L. Gardiner and P. Gregg, Study,
Work, Progress, Repeat? How and
why pay and progression, London,
Resolution Foundation, 2017, https://

www.resolutionfoundation.org/app/
uploads/2017/02/IC-labour-market.
pdf (accessed 7 April 2021).

33 Ibid.

34 A. Brech, 'Millennials Work Far Fewer
Hours Than Our Parents – So Why
Are We Much More Stressed?', Stylist,
2019, https://www.stylist.co.uk/life/
millennials-less-hours-more-stressed-
parents-study/267863 (accessed 1
April 2021).

35 B. Duffy, H. Shrimpton and M.
Clemence, Millennial Myths and
Realities, London, Ipsos MORI, 2017,
https://www.ipsos.com/ipsos-mori/
en-uk/millennial-myths-and-realities
(accessed 1 April 2021).

36 L. Gratton and A.J. Scott, The 100-Year
Life: Living and Working in an Age
of Longevity, London, Bloomsbury
Publishing, 2016.

37 Source: ALLBUS: German General
Social Survey (1984–2016).

38 Duffy et al., Millennial Myths and
Realities.

39 World Values Survey.

40 J. Twenge, iGen: Why Today's Super-
Connected Kids Are Growing Up Less
Rebellious, More Tolerant, Less Happy-
-and Completely Unprepared for
Adulthood--and What That Means for
the Rest of Us, New York, Atria Books,
2017.

41 Ibid.

42 Source: International Social Survey
Programme (1997–2015).

43 D. Susskind, A World Without Work,
London, Allen Lane, 2020.

44 Ibid.

45 J. Manyika, S. Lund, M. Chui, J.
Bughin, J. Woetzel, P. Batra, R. Ko and
S. Sanghvi, Jobs Lost, Jobs Gained:
Workforce Transitions in a Time
of Automation, McKinsey Global
Institute, 2017, https://www.mckinsey.

com/featured-insights/future-of-work/jobs-lost-jobs-gained-what-the-future-of-work-will-mean-for-jobs-skills-and-wages (accessed 7 April 2021).

46 B.N. Pfau, 'What Do Millennials Really Want at Work? The Same Things the Rest of Us Do', *Harvard Business Review*, 7 April 2016, https://hbr.org/2016/04/what-do-millennials-really-want-at-work (accessed 1 April 2021).

47 C. Seemiller and G. Grace, *Generation Z: A Century in the Making*, London, Routledge, 2018.

48 Ibid.

49 J. Montes, *Millennial Workforce: Cracking the code to Generation Y in your company*, Lulu Publishing Services, 2017.

50 D. Stillman and J. Stillman, *Gen Z Work: How the Next Generation Is Transforming the Workplace*, Harper Collins, 2017.

51 Montes, *Millennial Workforce*.

52 D. Patel, 5 Differences Between Marketing To Millennials Vs. Gen Z, *Forbes*, 27 November 2017, https://www.forbes.com/sites/deeppatel/2017/11/27/5-d%E2%80%8Bifferences-%E2%80%8Bbetween-%E2%80%8Bmarketing-%E2%80%8Bto%E2%80%8B-m%E2%80%8Billennials-v%E2%80%8Bs%E2%80%8B-%E2%80%8Bgen-z/

?sh=306ebfc32c9f (accessed 7 April 2021).

53 Microsoft Canada Consumer Insights team, *Attention Spans*, 2015, https://docs.google.com/viewerng/viewer?url=https://prc.olio.co.za/wp-content/uploads/2016/11/2015-Attention-Spans-Report-Microsoft.pdf&hl=en (accessed 1 April 2021).

54 J.W. MacLeod, M.A. Lawrence, M.M. McConnell, G.A. Eskes, R.M. Klein, and D.I. Shore, 2010. 'Appraising the ANT: Psychometric and theoretical considerations of the Attention Network Test', *Neuropsychology*, vol. 24, no. 5, pp. 637–651, https://www.ncbi.nlm.nih.gov/pubmed/20804252 (accessed 1 April 2021).

55 D.P. Costanza and L.M. Finkelstein, 2015. 'Generationally Based Differences in the Workplace: Is there a there there?' *Industrial and Organizational Psychology*, vol. 8, no. 3, pp. 308–323, https://doi.org/10.1017/iop.2015.15.

56 D.P. Costanza, J.M. Badger, R.L. Fraser, J.B. Severt and P.A. Gade, 'Generational Differences in Work-Related Attitudes: A meta-analysis', *Journal of Business and Psychology*, vol. 27, no. 4, 2012, pp. 375–394, https://www.jstor.org/stable/41682990?seq=1#page_scan_tab_contents (accessed 1 April 2021).

Chapter 4

1 E. Bryce, 'The Flawed Era of GDP Is Finally Coming to an End', *Wired*, 3 August 2019, https://www.wired.co.uk/article/countries-gdp-gross-national-happiness (accessed 1 April 2021).

2 D.M. McMahon, 'For Most of History, People Didn't Assume They Deserved To Be Happy. What Changed?',

Quartz, 18 April 2017, https://qz.com/958677/happiness-a-history-author-darrin-m-mcmahon-explains-when-the-idea-of-happiness-was-invented/ (accessed 1 April 2021).

3 P.N. Stearns, 'The History of Happiness', *Harvard Business Review*, January 2012, https://hbr.org/2012/01/

the-history-of-happiness (accessed 1 April 2021).

4   Ibid.

5   P. Brickman, 'Hedonic Relativism and Planning the Good Society', *Adaptation Level Theory*, 1971, pp. 287–301.

6   D.G. Blanchflower and A.J. Oswald, 'Do Humans Suffer a Psychological Low in Midlife? Two approaches (with and without controls) in seven data sets', NBER Working Paper No. 23724, Cambridge, MA, National Bureau of Economic Research, 2019, https://www.nber.org/papers/w23724.pdf (accessed 1 April 2021).

7   D.G. Blanchflower, Is Happiness U-Shaped Everywhere? Age and subjective well-being in 145 countries', *Journal of Population Economics*, vol. 34, pp. 575–624, https://link.springer.com/article/10.1007/s00148-020-00797-z.

8   J. Jordan, 'Dylan Moran: "Britain is sending itself to its room and not coming down"', *Guardian*, 13 July 2018, https://www.theguardian.com/books/2018/jul/13/dylan-moran-dr-cosmos-britain-brexit (accessed 1 April 2021).

9   J. Rauch, 'The Real Roots of Midlife Crisis', *The Atlantic*, December 2014, https://www.theatlantic.com/magazine/archive/2014/12/the-real-roots-of-midlife-crisis/382235/ (accessed 1 April 2021).

10   C. Wunder, A. Wiencierz, J. Schwarze and H. Küchenhoff, 'Well-Being Over the Life Span: Semiparametric evidence from British and German longitudinal data', *Review of Economics and Statistics*, vol. 95, no. 1, 2013, pp. 154–167, https://papers.ssrn.com/sol3/papers.cfm?abstract_id=1403203 (accessed 1 April 2021).

11   B.F. López Ulloa, V. Møller and A. Sousa-Poza, 'How Does Subjective Well-Being Evolve with Age? A Literature Review', *Population Ageing*, vol. 6, 2013, pp. 227–246. https://doi.org/10.1007/s12062-013-9085-0.

12   R.A. Easterlin, 'Lifecycle Happiness and Its Sources: Intersections of Psychology, Economics, and Demography', *Journal of Economic Psychology*, vol. 27, no. 4, 2006, pp. 463–482.

13   B. Judd, '"Middle age misery" peaks at 47.2 years of age – but do the statistics ring true?', ABC News, 14 January 2020, https://www.abc.net.au/news/2020-01-15/middle-age-misery-peaks-at-47.2-midlife-crisis/11866110 (accessed 1 April 2021).

14   Source: Blanchflower reanalysis of Eurobarometer data (2009–19) in Blanchflower, 'Is Happiness U-Shaped Everywhere?'.

15   D.G. Blanchflower and A.J. Oswald, 'Is Well-Being U-Shaped Over the Life Cycle?', *Social Science & Medicine*, vol. 66, no. 8, 2008, pp. 1733–1749, https://www.sciencedirect.com/science/article/abs/pii/S0277953608000245 (accessed 1 April 2021).

16   A.E. Clark, 'Born To Be Mild? Cohort Effects Don't (Fully) Explain Why Well-Being Is U-Shaped in Age', IZA Discussion Paper No. 3170, Bonn, Institute for the Study of Labor, 2007, https://www.econstor.eu/bitstream/10419/34422/1/551074736.pdf (accessed 1 April 2021).

17   D.G. Blanchflower and A.J. Oswald, 'Do Humans Suffer a Psychological Low in Midlife? Two Approaches (With and Without Controls) in Seven Data Sets', IZA Discussion Paper No. 10958, Bonn, Institute for the Study of Labor, 2017, https://papers.ssrn.com/

sol3/papers.cfm?abstract_id=3029829 (accessed 7 April 2021).

18 G. Vassilev and M. Hamilton, *Personal and economic well-being in Great Britain: May 2020*, Office for National Statistics, 2020, https://www.ons.gov.uk/peoplepopulationandcommunity/wellbeing/bulletins/personalandeconomicwellbeingintheuk/may2020 (accessed 1 April 2021).

19 J. De Neve and M. Norton, 'Busts Hurt More Than Booms Help: New lessons for growth policy from global wellbeing surveys', VOX EU, 8 October 2014, https://voxeu.org/article/wellbeing-research-recessions-hurt-more-booms-help (accessed 1 April 2021).

20 D. Kahneman and A. Tversky, 'Prospect Theory: An Analysis of Decision Under Risk', *Econometrica*, vol. 47, no. 2, 1979, pp. 263–292, https://www.jstor.org/stable/1914185?origin=crossref&seq=1 (accessed 1 April 2021).

21 E. Yechiam, 'The Psychology of Gains and Losses: More complicated than previously thought', *Psychological Science Agenda*, January 2015, https://www.apa.org/science/about/psa/2015/01/gains-losses (accessed 1 April 2021).

22 Source: Eurobarometer (1986–2018).

23 L. Greene, 'Are Millennials Really the Most Mentally Ill Generation?', *Moods Magazine*, 1 June 2016, www.moodsmag.com/blog/millennials-really-mentally-ill-generation/ (accessed 1 April 2021).

24 L. Soeiro, 'Why Are Millennials So Anxious And Unhappy?', *Psychology Today*, 24 July 2019, https://www.psychologytoday.com/gb/blog/i-hear-you/201907/why-are-millennials-so-anxious-and-unhappy (accessed 1 April 2021).

25 C. Thorley, *Not By Degrees: Improving student mental health in the UK's universities*, London, London, Institute for Public Policy Research, 2017, https://www.ippr.org/files/2017-09/1504645674_not-by-degrees-170905.pdf (accessed 1 April 2021).

26 J.M. Twenge, A.B. Cooper, T.E. Joiner, M.E. Duffy and S.G. Binau, 'Age, Period, and Cohort Trends in Mood Disorder Indicators and Suicide-Related Outcomes in a Nationally Representative Dataset, 2005–2017', *Journal of Abnormal Psychology*, vol. 128, no. 3, 2019, 185–199, https://www.apa.org/pubs/journals/releases/abn-abn0000410.pdf (accessed 1 April 2021).

27 J. Twenge, *iGen: Why Today's Super-Connected Kids Are Growing Up Less Rebellious, More Tolerant, Less Happy--and Completely Unprepared for Adulthood--and What That Means for the Rest of Us*, New York, Atria Books, 2017.

28 D. James, J. Yates and E. Ferguson, 'Can the 12-item General Health Questionnaire Be Used To Identify Medical Students Who Might "Struggle" on the Medical Course? A prospective study on two cohorts', *BMC Medical Education*, vol. 13, no. 1, 2013, 48, https://www.ncbi.nlm.nih.gov/pmc/articles/PMC3616988 (accessed 1 April 2021).

29 Source: Health Survey for England (1991–2016).

30 Mental Health of Children and Young People Surveys, 'Mental health of children and young people in England, 2017', November 2018, https://digital.nhs.uk/data-and-

information/publications/statistical/
mental-health-of-children-and-
young-people-in-england/2017/2017
(accessed 1 April 2021).

31 Source: Adult Psychiatric Morbidity
Survey (1993–2014). S. McManus,
P. Bebbington, R. Jenkins, T. Brugha
(eds), *Mental Health and Wellbeing in
England: Adult Psychiatric Morbidity
Survey 2014*, Leeds, NHS Digital,
https://webarchive.nationalarchives.
gov.uk/20180328140249/http://digital.
nhs.uk/catalogue/PUB21748 (accessed
7 April 2021)

32 Ibid.

33 Twenge, *iGen: Why Today's Super-
Connected Kids Are Growing Up Less
Rebellious*.

34 World Health Organization,
'Adolescent Mental Health in
the European Region', factsheet,
Copenhagen, WHO Europe,
2018, http://www.euro.who.int/
__data/assets/pdf_file/0005/383891/
adolescent-mh-fs-eng.pdf?ua=1
(accessed 1 April 2021).

35 L.Z. Li and S. Wang, 'Prevalence and
Predictors of General Psychiatric
Disorders and Loneliness during
COVID-19 in the United Kingdom:
Results from the Understanding
Society UKHLS', medRxiv,
12 June 2020, https://www.
medrxiv.org/content/10.1101/
2020.06.09.20120139v1 (accessed 1
April 2021).

36 I. Sample, 'Covid poses "greatest
threat to mental health since
second world war"', *The Guardian*,
27 December 2020, https://www.
theguardian.com/society/2020/dec/
27/covid-poses-greatest-threat-to-
mental-health-since-second-world-
war (accessed 1 April 2021).

37 C. Gayer, R.L. Anderson, C. El Zerbi,
L. Strang, V.M. Hall, G. Knowles, S.
Marlow, M. Avendano, N. Manning
and J. Das-Munshi, 'Impacts of social
isolation among disadvantaged and
vulnerable groups during public
health crises', ESRC Centre for Society
& Mental Health, King's College
London, 2020, https://esrc.ukri.org/
files/news-events-and-publications/
evidence-briefings/impacts-of-social-
isolation-among-disadvantaged-and-
vulnerable-groups-during-public-
health-crises/ (accessed 1 April 2021).

38 Mental Health Foundation,
'Coronavirus: The divergence of
mental health experiences during
the pandemic', n.d., https://www.
mentalhealth.org.uk/coronavirus/
divergence-mental-health-
experiences-during-pandemic
(accessed 1 April 2021).

39 K. Rawlinson, 'Social Media Firms
Must Share Child Mental Health
Costs', *The Guardian*, 14 June 2018,
https://www.theguardian.com/society/
2018/jun/14/nhs-child-mental-health-
costs-social-media-firms-must-share
(accessed 1 April 2021).

40 B. Duffy, H. Shrimpton and M.
Clemence, *Millennial Myths and
Realities*, London, Ipsos MORI, 2017,
https://www.ipsos.com/ipsos-mori/
en-uk/millennial-myths-and-realities
(accessed 1 April 2021).

41 Y. Kelly, A. Zilanawala, C. Booker
and A. Sacker, 'Social Media Use
and Adolescent Mental Health:
Findings from the UK Millennium
Cohort Study', *EClinical Medicine*,
vol. 6, 2018, pp. 59–68, https://www.
thelancet.com/journals/eclinm/
article/PIIS2589-5370(18)30060-9/
fulltext (accessed 7 April 2021).

42   A. Orben and A.K. Przybylski, 'The
     Association Between Adolescent
     Well-Being and Digital Technology
     Use', *Nature Human Behaviour*, vol. 3,
     no. 2, 2019, pp. 173–182, https://www.
     gwern.net/docs/psychology/2019-
     orben.pdf (accessed 1 April 2021).
43   A. Orben, T. Dienlinand A.K.
     Przybylski, 'Social Media's Enduring
     Effect on Adolescent Life Satisfaction',
     *Proceedings of the National Academy
     of Sciences*, vol. 116, no. 21, 2019,
     10226–10228, https://www.pnas.
     org/content/116/21/10226 (accessed
     1 April 2021). While this paper looks
     at technology use in general, similar
     papers by the same authors find the
     same lack of relationship with social
     media use specifically.
44   R.M. Viner, A. Gireesh, N. Stiglic,
     L.D. Hudson, A.-L. Goddings, J.L.
     Ward and D.E. Nicholls, 'Roles of
     Cyberbullying, Sleep, and Physical
     Activity in Mediating the Effects of
     Social Media Use on Mental Health
     and Wellbeing Among Young People
     in England: A secondary analysis of
     longitudinal data', *The Lancet Child &
     Adolescent Health*, vol. 3, no. 10, 2019,
     pp. 685–696, https://www.thelancet.
     com/journals/lanchi/article/PIIS2352-
     4642(19)30186-5/fulltext (accessed 1
     April 2021).
45   Department for Education, *State of
     the Nation 2019: Children and Young
     People's Wellbeing*, 2019, https://
     assets.publishing.service.gov.uk/
     government/uploads/system/uploads/
     attachment_data/file/838022/State_
     of_the_Nation_2019_young_people_
     children_wellbeing.pdf (accessed 1
     April 2021).
46   P.M. Markey and C.J. Ferguson,
     'Teaching Us To Fear: The Violent
     Video Game Moral Panic and The

     Politics of Game Research', *American
     Journal of Play*, vol. 10, no. 1, 2017,
     pp. 99–115, https://files.eric.ed.gov/
     fulltext/EJ1166785.pdf (accessed 1
     April 2021).
47   Burdick. A., 'How to Fight Crime With
     Your Television', *The New Yorker*, 5
     July 2018, https://www.newyorker.
     com/science/elements/how-to-fight-
     crime-with-your-television (accessed
     7 April 2021).
48   Markey and Ferguson, 'Teaching Us
     To Fear'.
49   N. Howe, 'Millennials and the
     Loneliness Epidemic', *Forbes*, 3 May
     2019, https://www.forbes.com/sites/
     neilhowe/2019/05/03/millennials-
     and-the-loneliness-epidemic/
     #e5951b57676a (accessed 1 April
     2021).
50   CBC Radio, 'Loneliness in
     Canadian Seniors an Epidemic,
     Says Psychologist', 20 September
     2016, https://www.cbc.ca/radio/
     thecurrent/the-current-for-
     september-20-2016-1.3770103/
     loneliness-in-canadian-seniors-an-
     epidemic-says-psychologist-1.3770208
     (accessed 1 April 2021).
51   L.C. Hawkley, K. Wroblewski,
     T. Kaiser, M. Luhmann and L.P.
     Schumm, 'Are US Older Adults Getting
     Lonelier? Age, period, and cohort
     differences', *Psychology and Aging*,
     vol. 34, no. 8, 2019, 1144–1157, https:/
     /www.ncbi.nlm.nih.gov/pubmed/
     31804118 (accessed 1 April 2021).
52   F. Nyqvist, M. Cattan, M. Conradsson,
     M. Näsman and Y. Gustafsson,
     'Prevalence of Loneliness Over
     Ten Years Among the Oldest Old',
     *Scandinavian Journal of Public
     Health*, vol. 45, no. 4, 2017, pp.
     411–418.

53 Both studies cited in Hawkley et al., 'Are US Older Adults Getting Lonelier?'.

54 D.M.T. Clark, N.J. Loxton and S.J. Tobin, 'Declining Loneliness Over Time: Evidence from American colleges and high schools', *Personality and Social Psychology Bulletin*, vol. 41, no. 1, 2015, pp. 78–89, https://journals.sagepub.com/doi/abs/10.1177/0146167214557007?journalCode=pspc (accessed 1 April 2021).

55 B. DiJulio, L. Hamel, C. Muñana and M. Brodie, *Loneliness and Social Isolation in the United States, the United Kingdom, and Japan: An International Survey*, San Francisco, Kaiser Family Foundation, http://files.kff.org/attachment/Report-Loneliness-and-Social-Isolation-in-the-United-States-the-United-Kingdom-and-Japan-An-International-Survey (accessed 1 April 2021).

56 Source: Community Life Study (2014–2018).

57 E. Klinenberg, *Going Solo: The extraordinary rise and surprising appeal of living alone*, London, Penguin, 2013.

58 US Census Bureau, 'U.S. Census Bureau Releases 2018 Families and Living Arrangements Tables', 14 November 2018, https://www.census.gov/newsroom/press-releases/2018/families.html (accessed 7 April 2021).

59 S.J. Dubner, 'Is There Really a "Loneliness Epidemic"?' (Ep. 407), *Freakonomics* podcast, 26 February 2020, https://freakonomics.com/podcast/loneliness/ (accessed 1 April 2021).

60 J. Lepore, 'The History of Loneliness', *The New Yorker*, 6 April 2020, https://www.newyorker.com/magazine/2020/04/06/the-history-of-loneliness (accessed 1 April 2021).

61 D. Scheimer and M. Chakrabarti, 'Former Surgeon General Vivek Murthy: Loneliness Is A Public Health Crisis', WBUR, 23 March 2020, https://www.wbur.org/onpoint/2020/03/23/vivek-murthy-loneliness (accessed 1 April 2021).

62 J. Holt-Lunstad, T.B. Smith, and J.B. Layton, 'Social Relationships and Mortality Risk: A meta-analytic review', *PLoS medicine*, vol. 7, no. 7, 2010, e1000316, https://doi.org/10.1371/journal.pmed.1000316 (accessed 1 April 2021).

63 T. Chivers, 'Is the "epidemic of loneliness" fake news?', UnHerd, 8 May 2019, from https://unherd.com/2019/05/is-the-epidemic-of-loneliness-fake-news/ (accessed 1 April 2021).

64 T. Chivers, 'Do we really have a "suicidal generation"?', UnHerd, 4 February 2019, https://unherd.com/2019/02/do-we-really-have-a-suicidal-generation/ (accessed 1 April 2021).

65 Office for National Statistics, Suicides in the UK: 2018 registrations. Registered deaths in the UK from suicide analysed by sex, age, area of usual residence of the deceased and suicide method, 2018, https://www.ons.gov.uk/peoplepopulationandcommunity/birthsdeathsandmarriages/deaths/bulletins/suicidesintheunitedkingdom/2018registrations (accessed 1 April 2021). When the ONS looks at trends, they group the data together in wider age ranges, because of the volatility of such rare events, to avoid precisely

the over-interpretation you so often see in the media.

66 Office for National Statistics, Middle-aged generation most likely to die by suicide and drug poisoning, 2019, https://www.ons.gov.uk/peoplepopulation andcommunity/healthandsocialcare/healthandwellbeing/articles/middleagedgenerationmost likelytodiebysuicideand drugpoisoning/2019-08-13 (accessed 1 April 2021).

67 Source: Office for National Statistics, National Records of Scotland and Northern Ireland Statistics and Research Agency (1981–2018).

68 Ibid.

69 N. Dougall, C. Stark, T. Agnew, R. Henderson, M. Maxwell and P. Lambert, 'An Analysis of Suicide Trends in Scotland 1950–2014: Comparison with England & Wales', *BMC Public Health*, vol. 17, no. 1, 2017, 970, https://www.ncbi.nlm.nih.gov/pmc/articles/PMC5738808/ (accessed 1 April 2021).

70 BBC News, 'Deaths by Suicide and Drugs Highest Among Generation X', 13 August 2019, https://www.bbc.co.uk/news/health-49329595 (accessed 1 April 2021).

71 J. Emyr and A. Butt, Deaths related to drug poisoning by selected substances, dataset, 2020, https://www.ons.gov.uk/peoplepopulationandcommunity/birthsdeathsandmarriages/deaths/datasets/deaths relatedtodrugpoisoning byselectedsubstances (accessed 1 April 2021).

72 A. Case and A. Deaton, *Deaths of Despair and the Future of Capitalism*, Princeton University Press, 2020.

73 Psychology Wiki, 'Clustering illusion', n.d., https://psychology.wikia.org/wiki/Clustering_illusion (accessed 1 April 2021).

74 Wikipedia, 'Correlation does not imply causation', n.d., https://en.wikipedia.org/wiki/Correlation_does_not_imply_causation (accessed 1 April 2021).

75 C.G. O'Boyle, *History of Psychology: A Cultural Perspective*, Psychology Press, 2014.

Chapter 5

1   A. Case and A. Deaton, *Deaths of Despair and the Future of Capitalism*, Princeton University Press, 2020.

2   Ibid.

3   M. Roser, 'The Spanish Flu (1918-20): The global impact of the largest influenza pandemic in history', *OurWorldInData*, 2020, https://ourworldindata.org/spanish-flu-largest-influenza-pandemic-in-history (accessed 1 April 2021).

4   D.M. Morens, J.K. Taubenberger and A.S. Fauci, 'Predominant Role of Bacterial Pneumonia as a Cause of Death in Pandemic Influenza: Implications for pandemic influenza preparedness', *Journal of Infectious Diseases*, vol. 198, no. 7, 2008, 962Y970, https://www.ncbi.nlm.nih.gov/pmc/articles/PMC2599911/ (accessed 1 April 2021).

5   Roser, 'The Spanish Flu (1918-20)'.

6   P. Jha, 'Avoidable Global Cancer Deaths and Total Deaths From Smoking', *Nature Reviews Cancer*, vol. 9, no. 9, 2009, pp. 655–664, https://www.nature.com/articles/nrc2703 (accessed 1 April 2021).

7 Centers for Disease Control Prevention, Current cigarette smoking among adults in the United States, 2016, https://www.cdc.gov/tobacco/data_statistics/fact_sheets/adult_data/cig_smoking/ (accessed 1 April 2021).

8 NHS, 'Around 1.8m Fewer Adult Smokers in England in 2018 Compared With Seven Years Ago', 2 July 2019, https://digital.nhs.uk/news-and-events/around-1.8m-fewer-adult-smokers-in-england-in-2018-compared-with-seven-years-ago (accessed 1 April 2021).

9 NHS, Statistics on Smoking, England, 27 May 2016, https://digital.nhs.uk/data-and-information/publications/statistical/statistics-on-smoking/statistics-on-smoking-england-2016 (accessed 1 April 2021).

10 Centers for Disease Control Prevention, Current cigarette smoking among adults in the United States.

11 The Tobacco Atlas, Consumption, 2020, https://tobaccoatlas.org/topic/consumption/ (accessed 1 April 2021).

12 L. Saad, 'U.S. Smoking Rate Still Coming Down', Gallup, 24 July 2008, https://news.gallup.com/poll/109048/us-smoking-rate-still-coming-down.aspx (accessed 1 April 2021).

13 Source: Health Survey for England (1999–2017).

14 Public Health England, 'E-cigarettes Around 95% Less Harmful Than Tobacco Estimates Landmark Review', 19 August 2015, https://www.gov.uk/government/news/e-cigarettes-around-95-less-harmful-than-tobacco-estimates-landmark-review (accessed 1 April 2021).

15 R. Harris and C. Wroth, 'FDA To Banish Flavored E-Cigarettes To Combat Youth Vaping', NPR, 11 September 2019, https://www.npr.org/sections/health-shots/2019/09/11/759851853/fda-to-banish-flavored-e-cigarettes-to-combat-youth-vaping?t=1588112377545&t=1588799163720 (accessed 1 April 2021).

16 E. Nilsen, 'The FDA Has Officially Raised the Age to Buy Tobacco Products to 21', VOX, 27 December 2019, https://www.vox.com/2019/12/27/21039149/fda-officially-raised-age-to-buy-tobacco-from-18-to-21 (accessed 1 April 2021).

17 J. Belluz, 'Cigarette Packs Are Being Stripped of Advertising Around The World. But Not in the US', VOX, 2 June 2016, https://www.vox.com/2016/6/2/11818692/plain-packaging-policy-us-australia (accessed 1 April 2021).

18 Source: Health Survey for England (1997–2017).

19 B. Duffy, H. Shrimpton and M. Clemence, *Millennial Myths and Realities*, London, Ipsos MORI, 2017, https://www.ipsos.com/ipsos-mori/en-uk/millennial-myths-and-realities (accessed 1 April 2021).

20 G. Borrud, 'German Teenagers Are Drinking Less Alcohol, But More Irresponsibly', DW, 4 February 2011, https://www.dw.com/en/german-teenagers-are-drinking-less-alcohol-but-more-irresponsibly/a-14818251 (accessed 1 April 2021); M. Livingston, J. Raninen, T. Slade, W. Swift, B. Lloyd and P. Dietze, 'Understanding Trends in Australian Alcohol Consumption—An Age–Period–Cohort Model', *Addiction*, vol. 111, no. 9, 2016, 1590–1598, https://onlinelibrary.wiley.com/doi/epdf/10.1111/add.13396 (accessed 1 April 2021).

21 A. Bhattacharya, *Youthful Abandon: Why are young people drinking less?*,

Institute of Alcohol Studies, 2016, https://www.ias.org.uk/uploads/pdf/IAS%20reports/rp22072016.pdf (accessed 7 April 2021).

22   World Health Organization, *Global Status Report on Alcohol And Health 2018*, Geneva, WHO, 2018, https://www.who.int/publications/i/item/9789241565639 (accessed 1 April 2021).

23   M. Daly, 'Gen Z Is Too Busy to Drink or Do Drugs', *Vice*, 2 February 2017, https://www.vice.com/en/article/wnzg3y/this-is-why-gen-z-takes-fewer-drugs-than-you (accessed 7 April 2021).

24   L.D. Johnston, R.A. Miech, P.M. O'Malley, J.E. Bachman and M.E. Patrick, *Monitoring the Future National Survey Results on Drug Use, 1975-2019: Overview, Key Findings on Adolescent Drug Use*, Institute for Social Research, 2020, http://www.monitoringthefuture.org/pubs/monographs/mtf-overview2019.pdf (accessed 1 April 2021).

25   Source: US General Social Survey (1975–2017).

26   R.A. Smith, 'The Effects of Medical Marijuana Dispensaries on Adverse Opioid Outcomes', *Economic Inquiry*, vol. 58, no. 2, 2020, 569–588, https://onlinelibrary.wiley.com/doi/pdf/10.1111/ecin.12825 (accessed 1 April 2021). P. Grinspoon, 'Access to Medical Marijuana Reduces Opioid Prescriptions', Harvard Health Blog, 25 June 2019, https://www.health.harvard.edu/blog/access-to-medical-marijuana-reduces-opioid-prescriptions-2018050914509 (accessed 1 April 2021).

27   B. Duffy, *How Britain Became Socially Liberal*, The Policy Institute, King's College London, https://www.kcl.ac.uk/policy-institute/research-analysis/moral-attitudes (accessed 1 April 2021).

28   Johnston et al., *Monitoring the Future National Survey Results on Drug Use.*

29   J. Ball, 'Teen Use of Cannabis Has Dropped in New Zealand, But Legalisation Could Make Access Easier', The Conversation, 20 February 2020, https://theconversation.com/teen-use-of-cannabis-has-dropped-in-new-zealand-but-legalisation-could-make-access-easier-132165 (accessed 1 April 2021).

30   Source: Health Survey for England (1992–2017).

31   A. Menayang, 'Millennials Are "The Most Health-Conscious Generation Ever," Says Report by The Halo Group', Food Navigator, 26 March 2017, from https://www.foodnavigator-usa.com/Article/2017/03/27/Millennials-scrutinize-health-claims-more-than-other-generations (accessed 1 April 2021).

32   Goldman Sachs, 'Millennials Coming of Age', 2020, www.goldmansachs.com/our-thinking/pages/millennials/ (accessed 1 April 2021).

33   World Health Organization, 'Obesity and Overweight', factsheet, Geneva, WHO, 2020, https://www.who.int/news-room/fact-sheets/detail/obesity-and-overweight (accessed 1 April 2021).

34   World Health Organization, 'Commission on Ending Childhood Obesity', 2018, https://www.who.int/end-childhood-obesity/en/ (accessed 1 April 2021).

35   D. Bann, W. Johnson, L. Li, D. Kuh and R. Hardy, 'Socioeconomic Inequalities in Body Mass Index Across Adulthood: Coordinated

analyses of individual participant data from three British birth cohort studies initiated in 1946, 1958 and 1970', *PLoS medicine*, vol. 14, no. 1, 2017, e1002214, doi:10.1371/journal.pmed.1002214.

36   F.J. Elgar, T.-K. Pförtner, I. Moor, B. De Clercq, G.W. Stevens and C. Currie, 'Socioeconomic Inequalities in Adolescent Health 2002–2010: A time-series analysis of 34 countries participating in the Health Behaviour in School-aged Children study', *The Lancet*, vol. 385, no. 9982, 2015, pp. 2088–2095, https://www.researchgate.net/publication/271207089_Socioeconomic_inequalities_in_adolescent_health_2002-2010_A_time-series_analysis_of_34_countries_participating_in_the_Health_Behaviour_in_School-aged_Children_study (accessed 1 April 2021).

37   W. Johnson, L. Li, D. Kuhand R. Hardy, 'How Has the Age-Related Process of Overweight or Obesity Development Changed Over Time? Co-ordinated analyses of individual participant data from five United Kingdom birth cohorts', *PLoS Medicine*, vol. 12, no. 5, 2015, e1001828, https://www.ncbi.nlm.nih.gov/pmc/articles/PMC4437909/ (accessed 1 April 2021).

38   Centers for Disease Prevention and Control, Mortality in the United States, 2017, November 2018, https://www.cdc.gov/nchs/products/databriefs/db328.htm (accessed 1 April 2021).

39   Office for National Statistics, Life expectancy at birth and selected older ages, 2020, https://www.ons.gov.uk/peoplepopulationandcommunity/birthsdeathsandmarriages/deaths/datasets/lifeexpectancy atbirthandselectedolderages (accessed 1 April 2021).

40   M. Marmot, J. Allen, T. Boyce, P. Goldblatt and J. Morrison, *Health Equity in England: The Marmot Review 10 years on*, Institute of Health Equity, 2020, http://www.instituteofhealthequity.org/resources-reports/marmot-review-10-years-on/the-marmot-review-10-years-on-full-report.pdf (accessed 1 April 2021).

41   *Wired*, 'Barack Obama: Now Is the Greatest Time to Be Alive', 12 October 2016, https://www.wired.com/2016/10/president-obama-guest-edits-wired-essay/ (accessed 1 April 2021).

42   B. Obama, Remarks by President Obama at Stavros Niarchos Foundation Cultural Center in Athens, Greece, 16 November 2016, https://obamawhitehouse.archives.gov/the-press-office/2016/11/16/remarks-president-obama-stavros-niarchos-foundation-cultural-center (accessed 1 April 2021).

43   Office for National Statistics, 'Deaths involving COVID-19 by local area and socioeconomic deprivation: deaths occurring between 1 March and 17 April 2020', 1 May 2020, https://www.ons.gov.uk/peoplepopulationandcommunity/birthsdeathsandmarriages/deaths/bulletins/deathsinvolvingcovid19bylocalareasanddeprivation/deathsoccurringbetween1marchand17april (accessed 1 April 2021).

Chapter 6

1   S. Stephens-Davidowitz, *Everybody lies*, Harper Collins, 2017.

2   E. Cara, 'The Kids Are Boning Less', Gizmodo, 15 January 2018, https://gizmodo.com/the-kids-are-boning-less-1821823267 (accessed 1 April 2021).

3   A. Hirschlag, 'Millennials Are Killing Relationships and We Should Be Concerned', SheKnows, 6 August 2015, https://www.sheknows.com/health-and-wellness/articles/1091871/millennial-daters-too-casual/ (accessed 1 April 2021).

4   S. Ramachandran, 'Let's Watch Netflix: Three Words Guaranteed to Kill a Romantic Mood', *Wall Street Journal*, 21 April 2019, from https://www.wsj.com/articles/three-words-guaranteed-to-kill-a-romantic-mood-lets-watch-netflix-11555863428 (accessed 1 April 2021).

5   The Original Boggart Blog, 'Silver Shaggers Risk STDs', 5 October 2010, https://originalboggartblog.wordpress.com/2010/10/05/silver-shaggers-risk-stds-9527525 (accessed 1 April 2021). A. Pereto, 'Patients over 60? Screen for STIs', *Athena Health*, 16 May 2018, https://www.athenahealth.com/insight/over-60-stis-may-not-be-done-you (accessed 1 April 2021). UK version: K. Forster, 'More Elderly People Being Diagnosed With STIs such as Chlamydia and Genital Warts', *Independent*, 8 December 2016, from https://www.independent.co.uk/life-style/health-and-families/health-news/older-people-stis-sexually-transmitted-infections-50-to-70-chief-medical-officer-report-dame-sally-a7463861.html (accessed 1 April 2021).

6   A. Abgarian, 'What's the Sexual Taboo That Will Define the Next Generation?', *Metro,* 29 May 2019, https://metro.co.uk/2019/05/29/sexual-taboo-will-define-next-generation-9689501/ (accessed 1 April 2021).

7   S. Coontz, *The Way We Never Were: American Families and the Nostalgia Trap*, Basic Books, 1992.

8   Ibid.

9   K. Paul, 'Millennials Are Killing Marriage—Here's Why That's A Good Thing', Market Watch, 16 February 2018, https://www.marketwatch.com/story/millennials-are-killing-marriage-heres-why-thats-a-good-thing-2018-02-08 (accessed 7 April 2021).

10 My analysis from survey data: Centers for Disease Control and Prevention, *Youth Risk Behavior Survey Data Summary & Trends Report 2009–2019*, 2019, https://www.cdc.gov/healthyyouth/data/yrbs/yrbs_data_summary_and_trends.htm (accessed 7 April 2021).

11 B. Fearnow, 'Study: Millennials Waiting Much Longer to Have Sex, 1-in-8 Virgins at 26', *Newsweek,* 6 May 2018, https://www.newsweek.com/millennial-virginity-sex-intimacy-university-college-london-next-steps-project-912283 (accessed 1 April 2021).

12 B. Zaba, E. Pisani, E. Slaymaker and J.T. Boerma, 'Age at First Sex: Understanding recent trends in African demographic surveys', *Sexually Transmitted Infections*, 80 (suppl 2), ii28-ii35, 2004, https://sti.bmj.com/content/80/suppl_2/ii28.full (accessed 1 April 2021).

13 Source: US General Social Survey (1988–2018).

14 S. Knapton, 'Couples Who Have Sex Just Once a Week Are Happiest', *The Telegraph*, 3 December 2016, https://www.telegraph.co.uk/science/2016/03/12/couples-who-have-sex-just-once-a-week-are-happiest/ (accessed 1 April 2021).

15 Source: US General Social Survey (1988–2018).

16 K. Julian, 'Why Are Young People Having So Little Sex?', *The Atlantic*, December 2018, https://www.theatlantic.com/magazine/archive/2018/12/the-sex-recession/573949/ (accessed 1 April 2021).

17 J.M. Twenge, R.A. Sherman and B.E. Wells, 'Declines in Sexual Frequency Among American Adults, 1989–2014', *Archives of Sexual Behavior*, vol. 46, no. 8, 2017, pp. 2389–2401, https://www.researchgate.net/publication/314273096_Declines_in_Sexual_Frequency_among_American_Adults_1989-2014 (accessed 1 April 2021).

18 K.R. Mitchell, C.H. Mercer, G.B. Ploubidis, K.G. Jones, J. Datta, N. Field, A.J. Copas, C. Tanton, C. Erens and P. Sonnenberg, 'Sexual Function in Britain: Findings from the third National Survey of Sexual Attitudes and Lifestyles (Natsal-3)', *The Lancet*, vol. 382, no. 9907, 2013, pp. 1817–1829, https://www.thelancet.com/journals/lancet/article/PIIS0140-6736(13)62366-1/fulltext (accessed 7 April 2021).

19 The Local, '"Tired" Swedes Have Less Sex Than Ever: Study', 24 May 2013, https://www.thelocal.se/20130524/48104 (accessed 1 April 2021).

20 F. Jackson-Webb, 'Australians Are Having Sex Less Often Than a Decade Ago', The Conversation, 7 November 2014, https://theconversation.com/australians-are-having-sex-less-often-than-a-decade-ago-33935 (accessed 1 April 2021).

21 J. Schifter, 'The End of Sex: The frequency of sexual activity has decreased significantly in the West of the world, *Wall Street International Magazine*, 13 January 2018, https://wsimag.com/culture/35096-the-end-of-sex (accessed 1 April 2021).

22 Cited in Introduction to: K. Wellings, M.J. Palmer, K. Machiyama and E. Slaymaker, 'Changes in, and factors associated with, frequency of sex in Britain: evidence from three National Surveys of Sexual Attitudes and Lifestyles (Natsal)', *BMJ*, 365, 2019, https://www.bmj.com/content/365/bmj.l1525 (accessed 1 April 2021).

23 Ibid.

24 University of Tokyo, 'First National Estimates of Virginity Rates in Japan: One in ten adults in their 30s remains a virgin, heterosexual inexperience increasing', https://www.u-tokyo.ac.jp/focus/en/press/z0508_00035.html (accessed 1 April 2021).

25 OECD, SF2.3: Age of mothers at childbirth and age-specific fertility, Paris, OECD Publishing, May 2019, https://www.oecd.org/els/soc/SF_2_3_Age_mothers_childbirth.pdf (accessed 3 April 2021).

26 Office for National Statistics, 'Marriage and divorce on the rise at 65 and over', 18 July 2017, https://www.ons.gov.uk/peoplepopulationandcommunity/birthsdeathsandmarriages/marriagecohabitationandcivilpartnerships/articles/marriageanddivorceontheriseat65andover/2017-07-18 (accessed 7 April 2021).

27 M. Campbell, 'Forget Teen Pregnancies. Older Moms Are the New Normal', Maclean's, 20 August 2016, https://www.macleans. ca/society/health/forget-teen-pregnancies-older-moms-new-normal/ (accessed 1 April 2021).

28 A. Picchi, 'Will Childless Millennials Turn America into Japan?', CBS News, 2015, https://www.cbsnews.com/news/will-childless-millennials-turn-america-into-japan/ (accessed 1 April 2021).

29 M. Roser, 'Fertility Rate', *OurWorldInData*, 2 December 2017, https://ourworldindata.org/fertility-rate (accessed 1 April 2021).

30 BBC News, 'Birth Rate in England and Wales Hits Record Low', 1 August 2019, https://www.bbc.co.uk/news/health-49192445 (accessed 1 April 2021).

31 BBC News, 'US Birth Rates Drop to Lowest Since 1987', 17 May 2018, https://www.bbc.co.uk/news/world-us-canada-44151642 (accessed 1 April 2021).

32 Office for National Statistics, National population projections, fertility assumptions: 2018-based, 2019, https://www.ons.gov.uk/peoplepopulationandcommunity/populationandmigration/populationprojections/methodologies/national populationprojections fertilityassumptions2018based (accessed 1 April 2021).

33 D. Mangan, 'Baby Bust! Millennials' Birth Rate Drop May Signal Historic Shift', CNBC, 27 April 2015, https://www.cnbc.com/2015/04/27/baby-bust-millenials-birth-rate-drop-may-signal-historic-shift.html (accessed 1 April 2021).

34 Pew Research Center, *Attitudes About Aging: A Global Perspective*, 2014, https://www.pewresearch.org/global/2014/01/30/chapter-4-population-change-in-the-u-s-and-the-world-from-1950-to-2050/#:~:text=The%20 old%2Dage%20dependency%20 ratio,drop%2Doff%20in%20 population%20growth (accessed 1 April 2021)..

35 F. Bakar, 'Are We Going to See a Coronavirus Baby Boom?', *Metro*, 31 March 2020, https://metro.co.uk/2020/03/31/going-see-coronavirus-baby-boom-12484432/ (accessed 1 April 2021).

36 J.R. Udry, 'The Effect of the Great Blackout of 1965 on Births in New York City', *Demography*, vol. 7, no. 3, pp. 325–327, https://www.jstor.org/stable/2060151?seq=2#metadata_info_tab_contents (accessed 1 April 2021).

37 M.S. Kearney and P.B. Levine, 'Half a Million Fewer Children? The coming COVID baby bust', Brookings, 15 June 2020, from https://www.brookings.edu/research/half-a-million-fewer-children-the-coming-covid-baby-bust/ (accessed 1 April 2021).

38 Ibid.

39 Source: US General Social Survey (1974–2018).

40 Source: British Social Attitudes survey (1984–2018).

41 D. Vilibert, 'Jessica Valenti Debunks the Purity Myth', *Marie Claire*, 22 April 2009, https://www.marieclaire.com/sex-love/a2975/jessica-valenti-purity-myth/ (accessed 1 April 2021).

42 L.B. Finer, 'Trends in Premarital Sex in the United States, 1954–2003', *Public Health Reports*, vol. 122, no. 1, 2007, pp. 73–78, https://www.ncbi.nlm.

nih.gov/pmc/articles/PMC1802108/ (accessed 1 April 2021).

43 B. Duffy, *How Britain Became Socially Liberal*, The Policy Institute, King's College London, https://www.kcl. ac.uk/policy-institute/research-analysis/moral-attitudes (accessed 1 April 2021).

44 United Nations Department of Economic and Social Affairs, Singulate Mean Age at Marriage, 2008, https:// www.un.org/en/development/desa/ population/publications/dataset/ marriage/age-marriage.asp (accessed 1 April 2021).

45 Source: UN World Marriage data, Singulate Mean Age at Marriage (2017).

46 J. Twenge, *iGen: Why Today's Super-Connected Kids Are Growing Up Less Rebellious, More Tolerant, Less Happy--and Completely Unprepared for Adulthood--and What That Means for the Rest of Us*, New York, Atria Books, 2017.

47 A. Cherlin, 'Marriage Has Become a Trophy', *The Atlantic*, March 2018, https://www.theatlantic.com/ family/archive/2018/03/incredible-everlasting-institution-marriage/ 555320/ (accessed 1 April 2021).

48 Source: British Social Attitudes survey (1983–2017).

49 K.S. Hymowitz, 'Alone – The decline of the family has unleashed an epidemic of loneliness', *City Journal*, Spring 2019, https://www.city-journal. org/decline-of-family-loneliness-epidemic (accessed 1 April 2021).

50 Wikipedia, 'Rights and responsibilities of marriages in the United States', n.d., https://en.wikipedia.org/wiki/ Rights_and_responsibilities_of_ marriages_in_the_United_States (accessed 1 April 2021).

51 J. Cloud, '1,138 Reasons Marriage Is Cool', *Time*, 1 March 2004, http:// content.time.com/time/magazine/ article/0,9171,596123,00.html (accessed 1 April 2021).

52 R.D. Putnam, *Our Kids: The American Dream in Crisis*, New York, Simon and Schuster, 2016.

53 Source: US General Social Survey (1988–2018).

54 D. Brooks, 'Was the Nuclear Family a Mistake?', Medium.com, 10 February 2020, https://medium.com/the-atlantic/was-the-nuclear-family-a-mistake-f9fdddf8bde (accessed 1 April 2021).

55 K. Musick and A. Meier, 'Are Both Parents Always Better Than One? Parental conflict and young adult well-being', *Social Science Research*, vol. 39, no. 5, 2010, pp. 814–830, https://www.ncbi.nlm.nih.gov/pmc/ articles/PMC2930824/ (accessed 1 April 2021).

56 B. Jeffreys, 'Do Children in Two-Parent Families Do Better?', BBC News, 5 February 2019, https://www. bbc.co.uk/news/education-47057787 (accessed 1 April 2021).

57 R.V. Reeves and E. Krause, 'Cohabiting Parents Differ From Married Ones in Three Big Ways', Brookings, 5 April 2017, https://www.brookings.edu/ research/cohabiting-parents-differ-from-married-ones-in-three-big-ways/ (accessed 1 April 2021).

58 S. Harkness, P. Gregg and M. Salgado, 'The Rise in Lone Mother Families and Children's Cognitive Development: Evidence from the 1958, 1970 and 2000 British Birth Cohorts', Centre for Analysis of Social Policy, University of Bath, 2016, https://editorialexpress. com/cgi-bin/conference/download.

cgi?db_name=SAEe2018&paper_
id=127 (accessed 1 April 2021).

59 A.J. Cherlin, *The Marriage-Go-Round:
    The State of Marriage and the Family
    in America Today*, Vintage, 2010.

60 W.B. Wilcox and L. DeRose, 'Ties
    That Bind Childrearing in the Age
    of Cohabitation', *Foreign Affairs*,
    14 February 2017, https://www.
    foreignaffairs.com/articles/2017-02-
    14/ties-bind (accessed 1 April 2021).

61 Office of National Statistics,
    Divorces in England and Wales:
    2015, 2017, https://www.ons.gov.uk/
    peoplepopulationandcommunity/
    birthsdeathsandmarriages/divorce/
    bulletins/divorcesinenglandandwales/
    2015 (accessed 7 April 2021).

62 A. McCathie, 'Marriages Prove
    Enduring in Germany as Divorce
    Rate Falls', 2017 https://www.dpa-
    international.com/topic/marriages-
    prove-enduring-germany-divorce-
    rate-falls-urn%3Anewsml%3Adpa.
    com%3A20090101%
    3A170711-99-199835 (accessed 7 April
    2021).

63 F. Olito, 'How the Divorce Rate Has
    Changed Over the Last 150 Years',
    Insider, 30 January 2019, https://www.
    insider.com/divorce-rate-changes-
    over-time-2019-1 (accessed 1 April
    2021).

64 J. Wood, 'The United States
    Divorce Rate Is Dropping, Thanks
    to Millennials', World Economic
    Forum, 5 October 2018, https://www.
    weforum.org/agenda/2018/10/divorce-
    united-states-dropping-because-
    millennials/ (accessed 1 April 2021).

65 J. Pinsker, 'The Not-So-Great Reason
    Divorce Rates Are Declining', *The
    Atlantic,* September 2018, https://
    www.theatlantic.com/family/archive/
    2018/09/millennials-divorce-baby-

boomers/571282/ (accessed 1 April
2021).

66 H. Boyd, 'Silver Splicers Make Sixty
    the New Sexy', *The Times*, 15 June
    2014, https://www.thetimes.co.uk/
    article/silver-splicers-make-sixty-the-
    new-sexy-lh87snwhtxp (accessed 1
    April 2021).

67 Office for National Statistics, Marriage
    and divorce on the rise at 65 and over,
    2017, from https://www.ons.gov.uk/
    peoplepopulationandcommunity/
    birthsdeathsandmarriages/
    marriagecohabitation
    andcivilpartnerships/articles/
    marriageanddivorceon
    theriseat65andover/2017-07-18
    (accessed 1 April 2021).

68 Ibid.

69 C. Allred, 'Age Variation in the Divorce
    Rate, 1990 & 2017', Bowling Green
    State University, 2019, https://www.
    bgsu.edu/ncfmr/resources/data/
    family-profiles/allred-age-variation-
    div-rate-fp-19-13.html (accessed 1
    April 2021).

70 Guardian Pass Notes, 'Meet the
    Silver Separators: Why Over-50s Top
    the Divorce Charts', *The Guardian*,
    24 November 2015, https://www.
    theguardian.com/lifeandstyle/
    shortcuts/2015/nov/24/silver-
    separators-over-50s-divorce-splitting-
    up-children (accessed 1 April 2021).

71 M. Race, '"Divorce boom" forecast
    as lockdown sees advice queries
    rise', BBC News, 13 September 2020,
    https://www.bbc.co.uk/news/uk-
    england-54117821 (accessed 1 April
    2021).

72 E. Eckholm, 'Saying No to "I Do," With
    the Economy in Mind', *The New York
    Times*, 28 September 2010, https://
    www.nytimes.com/2010/09/29/us/

29marriage.html?_r=2 (accessed 1 April 2021).

73 J. Wolfers, 'How Marriage Survives', *The New York Times*, 13 October 2010, https://www.nytimes.com/2010/10/13/opinion/13wolfers.html (accessed 1 April 2021).

74 Source: US General Social Survey (1975–2018).

75 Mr Skin, 'Game of Nudes: 7 Seasons of nudity from the HBO series "Game of Thrones"', 2019, https://www.mrskin.com/infographic/game-of-thrones-nudity-statistics (accessed 1 April 2021).

76 G.M. Hald, L. Kuyper, P.C. Adam and J.B. de Wit, 'Does Viewing Explain Doing? Assessing the Association Between Sexually Explicit Materials Use and Sexual Behaviors in a Large Sample of Dutch Adolescents and Young Adults', *Journal of Sexual Medicine*, vol. 10, no. 12, 2013, pp. 2986–2995, https://www.jsm.jsexmed.org/article/S1743-6095(15)30225-3/fulltext (accessed 1 April 2021).

77 University of Montreal, 'Are the Effects of Pornography Negligible?', *Science Daily*, 1 December 2009, https://www.sciencedaily.com/releases/2009/12/091201111202.htm (accessed 1 April 2021).

78 Alexa (Producer), Top Sites in GB, 2020, https://www.alexa.com/topsites/countries/GB (accessed 1 April 2021).

79 B. Duffy, H. Shrimpton and M. Clemence, *Millennial Myths and Realities*, London, Ipsos MORI, 2017, https://www.ipsos.com/ipsos-mori/en-uk/millennial-myths-and-realities (accessed 1 April 2021).

80 Stephens-Davidowitz, *Everybody Lies*.

81 S. Dubner, 'How to Think About Sex?' A Freakonomics Quorum, 12 September 2008, https://freakonomics.com/2008/09/12/how-to-think-about-sex-a-freakonomics-quorum/ (accessed 1 April 2021).

82 D. Kushner, 'A Brief History of Porn on the Internet', *Wired*, 9 April 2019, https://www.wired.com/story/brief-history-porn-internet/ (accessed 1 April 2021).

83 William A. Fisher and Taylor Kohut, 'Pornography Viewing: Keep Calm and Carry On', *Journal of Sexual Medicine*, vol. 14, no. 3, pp. 320–322, https://pubmed.ncbi.nlm.nih.gov/28262103/ (accessed 7 April 2021).

84 Department for Digital Culture, Media and Sport, Age Verification for pornographic material online: Impact Assessment, 13 June 2018, https://assets.publishing.service.gov.uk/government/uploads/system/uploads/attachment_data/file/747187/Impact_Assessment_Age_Verification_FINAL_20181009.pdf (accessed 1 April 2021).

85 D. Bricker and J. Ibbitson, *Empty Planet: The Shock of Global Population Decline*, Robinson, 2019.

86 S. Coontz, 'The Way We Never Were: For much of the century, traditional "family values" have been more myth than reality', *The New Republic*, 29 March 2016, https://newrepublic.com/article/132001/way-never (accessed 1 April 2021).

87 Putnam, *Our Kids*.

Chapter 7

1 J. Bush [@JebBush] 'Not Cool, University of Manchester. Not Cool.' Twitter, 2 October 2018, https://twitter.com/JebBush/status/

1047234246916677633 (accessed 1 April 2021).

2   CNN, 'Jeb Bush to Audience: "Please Clap"', 4 February 2016, https://www.youtube.com/watch?v=OUXvrWeQUog (accessed 1 April 2021).

3   F. Furedi, 'Ban Applause? What Utter Claptrap!', *Daily Mail*, 27 October 2019, https://www.dailymail.co.uk/debate/article-7619941/Professor-lashes-Oxford-latest-university-insist-jazz-hands-student-events.html (accessed 1 April 2021).

4   J. Bacharach, 'Sometimes inclusion is going to be a bit embarrassing, But disability — invisible or otherwise — is a working-class issue that the left and right must take seriously', The Outline, 12 August 2019, https://theoutline.com/post/7800/dsa-conference-2019-invisible-disability?zd=1&zi=dw23p6wl (accessed 1 April 2021).

5   Newshub, 'Sydney School Disputes "Clapping Ban"', July 2016, https://www.newshub.co.nz/home/world/2016/07/sydney-school-disputes-clapping-ban.html (accessed 1 April 2021).

6   S. Weale and F. Perraudin, 'Jazz Hands at Manchester University: The Calm behind the Storm', *The Guardian*, 5 October 2018, https://www.theguardian.com/society/2018/oct/05/jazz-hands-at-manchester-university-the-calm-behind-the-storm#maincontent (accessed 1 April 2021).

7   J. Haidt [@JonHaidt], 'If Oxford Students Replace Clapping With "Jazz Hands" to Protect Some From Anxiety, Then Those Students Will Find Clapping Even More Traumatizing After They Leave Oxford. Safetyism Backfires in the Long Run', Twitter, 26 October 2019, https://twitter.com/jonhaidt/status/1188090469164765184?s=11 (accessed 1 April 2021).

8   N.B. Ryder, 'The Cohort as a Concept in the Study of Social Change', in: *Cohort Analysis in Social Research*, Springer, pp. 9–44, https://link.springer.com/chapter/10.1007/978-1-4613-8536-3_2 (accessed 1 April 2021).

9   Ibid.

10 Cision PR Newswire, 'New Report Reveals Demographics of Black Lives Matter Protesters Shows Vast Majority Are White, Marched Within Their Own Cities', 18 June 2020, https://www.prnewswire.com/news-releases/new-report-reveals-demographics-of-black-lives-matter-protesters-shows-vast-majority-are-white-marched-within-their-own-cities-301079234.html (accessed 1 April 2021).

11 G.E. Pauley, '"Speech at the March on Washington" by John Lewis (28 August 1963)', *Voices of Democracy*, vol. 5, 2010, pp. 18–36, https://voicesofdemocracy.umd.edu/lewis-speech-at-the-march-on-washington-speech-text/ (accessed 1 April 2021).

12 J. Lewis, 'Together, You Can Redeem the Soul', *The New York Times*, 30 July 2020, https://www.nytimes.com/2020/07/30/opinion/john-lewis-civil-rights-america.html (accessed 1 April 2021).

13 T. Chivers, 'How Racist Is Britain?' UnHerd, 14 December 2018, https://unherd.com/2018/12/how-racist-is-britain/ (accessed 1 April 2021).

14 J. Singal, 'Psychology's Favorite Tool for Measuring Racism Isn't Up to the Job', The Cut, January 2017, https://www.thecut.com/2017/01/psychologys-racism-measuring-tool-

isnt-up-to-the-job.html (accessed 1
April 2021).

15   N. Kelley, O. Khan and S. Sharrock,
Racial Prejudice in Britain Today,
London, NatCen Social Research and
Runnymede Trust, http://natcen.
ac.uk/media/1488132/racial-prejudice-
report_v4.pdf (accessed 1 April 2021).

16   Source: British Social Attitudes survey
(1983–2013).

17   Source: US General Social Survey
(1990–2018).

18   G. Livingston and A. Brown, 'Trends
and Patterns in Intermarriage', Pew
Research Center, 18 May 2017, https:/
/www.pewsocialtrends.org/2017/
05/18/1-trends-and-patterns-in-
intermarriage/ (accessed 1 April 2021).

19   L. Quillian, D. Pager, O. Hexel and A.H.
Midtbøen, 'Meta-Analysis of Field
Experiments Shows No Change in
Racial Discrimination in Hiring Over
Time', *Proceedings of the National
Academy of Sciences*, vol. 114, no. 41,
2017, pp. 10870–10875, https://www.
pnas.org/content/early/2017/09/11/
1706255114 (accessed 1 April 2021).

20   R.D. Putnam, *The Upswing: How
America Came Together a Century
Ago and How We Can Do It Again*,
Simon & Schuster, 2020.

21   C. Young, K. Ziemer and C. Jackson,
'Explaining Trump's Popular Support:
Validation of a Nativism Index',
Social Science Quarterly, vol. 100,
no. 2, 2019, pp. 412–418, https://
onlinelibrary.wiley.com/doi/abs/
10.1111/ssqu.12593 (accessed 1 April
2021).

22   M. Goodwin and C. Milazzo, 'Taking
Back Control? Investigating the Role
of Immigration in the 2016 Vote for
Brexit', *The British Journal of Politics
and International Relations*, vol.
19, no. 3, 2017, pp. 450–464, https:/

/nottingham-repository.worktribe.
com/preview/865063/Taking%20
Back%20Control%20FINAL%20
SUBMISSION%2028%20April%20
2017.pdf (accessed 1 April 2021).

23   L. Davis and S.S. Deole, 'Immigration
and the Rise of Far-Right Parties in
Europe', *ifo DICE Report*, vol. 15, no.
4, 2017, pp. 10–15, https://www.ifo.
de/DocDL/dice-report-2017-4-davis-
deole-december.pdf (accessed 1 April
2021).

24   Source: Ipsos MORI Issues Index
(1997–2018).

25   J. Cliffe, *Britain's Cosmopolitan Future.
How the Country is Changing and
Why its Politicians Must Respond*,
London, Policy Network, 2015,
http://policynetwork.org/wp-
content/uploads/2017/08/Britains-
cosmopolitan-future.pdf (accessed 1
April 2021).

26   D. Sosnik, 'America's Hinge Moment:
Presidential Politics in 2016 Will
Reflect the Shifting Reality of
America', Politico, 29 March 2015,
https://www.politico.com/magazine/
story/2015/03/2016-predictions-
americas-sosnik-clinton-116480
(accessed 1 April 2021).

27   Ipsos MORI, *Shifting Ground: 8 Key
Findings from a Longitudinal Study on
Attitudes Towards Immigration and
Brexit*, 2017, https://www.ipsos.com/
ipsos-mori/en-uk/shifting-ground-
attitudes-towards-immigration-and-
brexit (accessed 1 April 2021).

28   Source: Ipsos MORI Issues Index
(1997–2018).

29   B. Chiripanhura and N. Wolf, 'Long-
Term Trends in UK Employment:
1861 to 2018', Office for National
Statistics, 2019, https://www.ons.
gov.uk/economy/nationalaccounts/
uksectoraccounts/compendium/

economicreview/april2019/longterm
trendsinukemployment1861to2018#
womens-labour-market-participation
(accessed 1 April 2021).

30 C. Goldin, 'A Grand Gender
Convergence: Its Last Chapter',
American Economic Review, vol. 104,
no. 4, 2014, pp. 1091–1119, https://
scholar.harvard.edu/files/goldin/files/
goldin_aeapress_2014_1.pdf (accessed
1 April 2021).

31 S. Faludi, 'American Electra:
Feminism's Ritual Matricide', *Harpers*,
October 2010, https://harpers.org/
archive/2010/10/american-electra/
(accessed 1 April 2021).

32 Source: US General Social Survey
(1977–2018).

33 K.L. Eaves, *Moms in the Middle:
Parenting Magazines, Motherhood
Texts and the 'Mommy Wars'*, MA
thesis, Wichita State University.
https://pdfs.semanticscholar.org/
03df/007b8788ce337609
6234e1e55f8d9a8e3317.pdf (accessed 1
April 2021).

34 Source: US General Social Survey
(1974–2018).

35 B. Duffy, K. Hewlett, J. McCrae and
J. Hall, *Divided Britain? Polarisation
and Fragmentation Trends in the
UK*, Policy Institute, King's College
London, 2019, https://www.kcl.ac.uk/
policy-institute/assets/divided-
britain.pdf (accessed 1 April 2021).

36 S. Kliff, 'What Americans Think of
Abortion', VOX, 8 April 2018, https:/
/www.vox.com/2018/2/2/16965240/
abortion-decision-statistics-opinions
(accessed 1 April 2021).

37 Source: British Social Attitudes survey
(1983–2018).

38 Source: US General Social Survey
(1974–2018).

39 Pew Research Center, 'The Global
Divide on Homosexuality. Greater
Acceptance in More Secular and
Affluent Countries', 4 June 2013,
https://www.pewresearch.org/global/
2013/06/04/the-global-divide-on-
homosexuality/ (accessed 1 April
2021).

40 GSS Data Explorer, Sexual
Orientation, NORC at University
of Chicago, 2020, https://
gssdataexplorer.norc.org/
trends/Gender%20&%20
Marriage?measure=sexornt (accessed
1 April 2021).

41 W. Dahlgreen and A.-E. Shakespeare,
'1 in 2 Young People Say They Are
Not 100% Heterosexual', YouGov, 16
August 2015, https://yougov.co.uk/
topics/lifestyle/articles-reports/2015/
08/16/half-young-not-heterosexual
(accessed 1 April 2021).

42 B. Spencer, 'Only Half of Young
Attracted Exclusively to Opposite Sex'
The Times, 28 February 2021, https://
www.thetimes.co.uk/article/only-half-
of-young-attracted-exclusively-to-
opposite-sex-zbt9ckxwt (accessed 1
April 2021).

43 Z. Tsjeng, 'Teens These Days Are
Queer AF, New Study Says', Vice, 10
March 2016, https://www.vice.com/
en_us/article/kb4dvz/teens-these-
days-are-queer-af-new-study-says
(accessed 1 April 2021).

44 A.C. Kinsey, W.B. Pomeroy, C.E. Martin
and P.H. Gebhard, *Sexual Behavior in
the Human Male*, W. B. Saunders &
Co, 1948.

45 K.R. Mitchell, C.H. Mercer, G.B.
Ploubidis, K.G. Jones, J. Datta, N.
Field, A.J. Copas, C. Tanton, C.
Erens and P. Sonnenberg, 'Sexual
Function in Britain: Findings from
the third National Survey of Sexual

Attitudes and Lifestyles (Natsal-3)',
The Lancet, vol. 382, no. 9907, 2013,
pp. 1817–1829, https://www.thelancet.
com/journals/lancet/article/PIIS0140-
6736(13)62366-1/fulltext (accessed 7
April 2021).

46 G. Hinsliff, 'The Pansexual
Revolution: How Sexual Fluidity
Became Mainstream', *Guardian*,
14 Febuary 2019, https://www.
theguardian.com/society/2019/feb/
14/the-pansexual-revolution-how-
sexual-fluidity-became-mainstream
(accessed 1 April 2021).

47 K. Steinmetz, 'The Transgender
Tipping Point', *Time*, 29 May 2014,
https://time.com/135480/transgender-
tipping-point/ (accessed 1 April 2021).

48 S. Marsh, 'The Gender-Fluid
Generation: Young People on Being
Male, Female or Non-Binary',
The Guardian, 23 March 2016,
https://www.theguardian.com/
commentisfree/2016/mar/23/gender-
fluid-generation-young-people-male-
female-trans (accessed 1 April 2021).

49 Pew Research Center, *Generation Z
Looks a Lot Like Millennials on Key
Social and Political Issues*, 2019,
https://www.pewsocialtrends.org/
wp-content/uploads/sites/3/2019/01/
Generations-full-report_FINAL_1.18.
pdf (accessed 7 April 2021).

50 H. Shrimpton [@h_shrimpton], 'Could
in part be driven by differences in
familiarity: 7 in 10 Baby Boomers have
never met or encountered someone
who uses gender neutral terms but
3 in 10 Gen Z has someone in their
social circle who uses gender neutral
terms', Twitter, 15 July 2020, https:/
/twitter.com/h_shrimpton/status/
1283394380850696192 (accessed 1
April 2021).

51 YouGov, YouGov/PinkNews Survey
Results: Do you think a person should
or should not be able to self-identify
as a gender different to the one
they were born in? 2020, https://
docs.cdn.yougov.com/ogu5gtx9us/
PinkNewsResults_200629_
Education_Selfidentity.pdf (accessed 1
April 2021).

52 Ipsos, 'The Future of Gender is
Increasingly Nonbinary: New
Report Explores Public Opinion,
Marketing and Business in the Gender
Spectrum', press release, 7 January
2020, https://www.ipsos.com/sites/
default/files/ct/news/documents/
2020-01/final_what_the_future_
gender_pr.pdf (accessed 1 April 2021).

53 A. Brown, 'Republicans, Democrats
Have Starkly Different Views on
Transgender Issues', Pew Research
Center, 8 November 2017, https://
www.pewresearch.org/fact-tank/2017/
11/08/transgender-issues-divide-
republicans-and-democrats/ (accessed
1 April 2021).

54 T. Stanley, 'The Gender Fad Will Pass,
What's Important Is Getting Through
it Without Permanent Damage', *The
Telegraph*, 13 November 2017, https://
www.telegraph.co.uk/news/2017/11/
13/gender-fad-will-pass-important-
getting-without-permanent-damage/
(accessed 1 April 2021).

55 R. Neale, 'Working-Class Women and
Women's Suffrage', *Labour History*,
vol. 12, 1967, pp. 16–34, https://www.
jstor.org/stable/27507859?seq=1
(accessed 1 April 2021).

56 S. Allen, 'Over a Third of Generation
Z Knows a Non-Binary Person', Daily
Beast, 24 January 2019, https://www.
thedailybeast.com/over-a-third-of-
generation-z-knows-a-non-binary-
person (accessed 1 April 2021).

57 Source: British Social Attitudes survey (1984–2017).

58 Grace Davie, 'What Are the Main Trends in Religion and Values in Britain?', Westminster Debates, 2 May 2012, https://www.reonline.org.uk/resources/westminster-faith-debate-what-are-the-main-trends-in-religion-and-values-in-britain/ (accessed 7 April 2021).

59 Source: US General Social Survey (1974–2018).

60 Justin Welby, 'Good News for Everyone? Evangelism and Other Faiths', lecture 13 March 2019, https://www.archbishopofcanterbury.org/speaking-and-writing/speeches/archbishop-justin-welbys-deo-gloria-trust-lecture-evangelism-and (accessed 7 April 2021).

61 Pew Research Center, 'The Future of World Religions: Population Growth Projections 2010–2050', 2015, https://www.pewforum.org/2015/04/02/religious-projections-2010-2050/ (accessed 7 April 2021).

62 W. Lippmann, *Drift and Mastery: An Attempt to Diagnose the Current Unrest*, University of Wisconsin Press, 2015.

63 D. Murray, *The Madness of Crowds: Gender, Race and Identity*, London, Bloomsbury Publishing, 2019.

64 B. Obama, *A Promised Land*, Penguin Books, 2020.

Chapter 8

1 The reality is that Macmillan didn't say those words, and his actual, clunkier response was that he most feared 'the opposition of events'. The re-working didn't just make the saying more elegant, the quaint Edwardian phrasing has no doubt added to its popularity, giving a sense that the impact of the unforeseen is an historical constant of politics. 'Book Reveals the Famous One-Liners They Never Said', *Evening Standard*, 25 October 2006, https://www.standard.co.uk/showbiz/book-reveals-the-famous-one-liners-they-never-said-7086553.html (accessed 7 April 2021).

2 N. Bochenski, 'Lying is Easy: Turnbull Calls for Less Spin', *Sydney Morning Herald*, 28 December 2012, https://www.smh.com.au/politics/federal/lying-is-easy-turnbull-calls-for-less-spin-20121228-2bybw.html (accessed 7 April 2021).

3 M.T. Grasso, S. Farrall, E. Gray, C. Hay and W. Jennings, 'Thatcher's Children, Blair's Babies, Political Socialisation And Trickle-Down Value-Change: An age, period and cohort analysis', *British Journal of Political Science*, vol. 49, no. 1, 2019, pp. 17–36, https://eprints.soton.ac.uk/390558/ (accessed 7 April 2021).

4 D. Desilver, 'The Politics of American Generations: How age affects attitudes and voting behaviour', Pew Research Center, 9 July 2014, https://www.pewresearch.org/fact-tank/2014/07/09/the-politics-of-american-generations-how-age-affects-attitudes-and-voting-behavior/ (accessed 7 April 2021).

5 D. Thompson, 'The Millennials-Versus-Boomers Fight Divides the Democratic Party', *The Atlantic*, 10 December 2019, https://www.theatlantic.com/ideas/archive/2019/12/young-left-third-party/603232/ (accessed 7 April 2021).

6 OECD, *Youth Stocktaking Report*, Paris, OECD Publishing, n.d., http://www.oecd.org/gov/youth-stocktaking-report.pdf (accessed 7 April 2021).

7 I.P. Philbrick, 'Why Does America Have Old Leaders?' *New York Times*, 16 July 2020, https://www.nytimes.com/2020/07/16/opinion/america-presidents-old-age.html (accessed 7 April 2021).

8 A. Matheson, 'There Are Almost Five Times as Many Millennials in the House Than Last Session', 5 January 2019, *Boston Globe*, https://www.bostonglobe.com/news/politics/2019/01/05/there-are-almost-five-times-many-millennials-house-than-last-session/un75ohNKZSQHEQGCHHw7dI/story.html (accessed 7 April 2021).

9 J. Filipovic, 'Why Is Congress So Old?' Medium.com, 11 December 2020, https://gen.medium.com/why-is-congress-so-old-64f014a9d819 (accessed 7 April 2021).

10 Joe Biden, in a speech given in Miami, 6 October 2020.

11 J. Van Bavel and D.S. Reher, 'The Baby Boom and Its Causes: What We Know and What We Need to Know', *Population and Development Review*, vol. 39, no. 2, 2013, pp. 257–288, https://onlinelibrary.wiley.com/doi/epdf/10.1111/j.1728-4457.2013.00591.x?saml_referrer# (accessed 7 April 2021).

12 C. Berry, *The Rise of Gerontocracy? Addressing the Intergenerational Democratic Deficit*, Intergenerational Foundation, 2012, http://www.if.org.uk/wp-content/uploads/2012/04/IF_Democratic_Deficit_final.pdf (accessed 7 April 2021).

13 Source: European Social Survey and US General Social Survey, 2018.

14 L. Gardiner, *Votey McVoteface: Understanding the Growing Turnout Gap Between the Generations*, London, Resolution Foundation, 2016, https://www.resolutionfoundation.org/publications/votey-mcvoteface-understanding-the-growing-turnout-gap-between-the-generations/ (accessed 7 April 2021).

15 Note that this is based on reported turnout, where people self-report whether they voted or not. We know that this overstates actual turnout, either because the people responding to these sort of surveys are more interested in politics than the general population, or people misremember whether they voted, whether deliberately to present themselves in a better light or not. There is no official record of the proportions of each age group who actually vote, but some survey studies do inspect the electoral register to check whether people who claimed they voted actually did, and these show that young people tend to overclaim *more* than older people. So, for our purposes, this confirms that generational gaps in turnout are real, and, if anything, probably bigger than shown here.

16 London School of Economics, 'Why 2017 May Have Witnessed a Youthquake After All', LSE British Politics and Policy blog, 6 December 2018, https://blogs.lse.ac.uk/politicsandpolicy/was-there-a-youthquake-after-all/ (accessed 7 April 2021).

17 'Millennials Across the Rich World Are Failing to Vote', *The Economist*, 4 February 2017, https://www.economist.com/international/2017/02/04/millennials-across-the-rich-

world-are-failing-to-vote (accessed 7 April 2021).

18 K. Burns, 'Democrats Are Coalescing around Biden – Except for Young Voters', Vox, 18 March 2020, https://www.vox.com/policy-and-politics/2020/3/18/21184884/democrats-biden-young-voters-turnout-sanders (accessed 7 April 2021).

19 C. Vinopal, 'Sanders Banked on Young Voters. Here's How the Numbers Have Played Out', PBS, 11 March 2020, https://www.pbs.org/newshour/politics/sanders-banked-on-young-voters-heres-how-the-numbers-have-played-out (accessed 7 April 2021).

20 D. Broockman and J. Kalla, 'Bernie Sanders Looks Electable in Surveys — But It Could Be a Mirage', Vox, 25 February 2020, https://www.vox.com/policy-and-politics/2020/2/25/21152538/bernie-sanders-electability-president-moderates-data (accessed 7 April 2021).

21 Source: US General Social Survey (1974–2018).

22 Source: US General Social Survey (1974–2018).

23 A. Walczak, W. Van der Brug and C.E. De Vries, 'Long- and Short-Term Determinants of Party Preferences: Inter-generational differences in Western and East Central Europe', Electoral Studies, vol. 31, no. 2, June 2012, pp. 273–284, https://www.sciencedirect.com/science/article/abs/pii/S0261379411001399?via%3Dihub (accessed 7 April 2021).

24 Source: British Social Attitudes survey (1984–2017).

25 'Millennials across the Rich World Are Failing to Vote', The Economist.

26 Source: British Social Attitudes survey (1983–2017).

27 Source: Ipsos MORI Political Monitor (1996–2017).

28 J. Tilley and G. Evans, 'Ageing and Generational Effects on Vote Choice: Combining Cross-Sectional and Panel Data to Estimate APC Effects', Electoral Studies, vol. 33, March 2014, pp. 19–27, https://www.sciencedirect.com/science/article/abs/pii/S0261379413000875 (accessed 7 April 2021).

29 M. Ambinder, 'The GOP Generational Time Bomb', The Atlantic, 28 April 2008, https://www.theatlantic.com/politics/archive/2008/04/the-gop-generational-time-bomb/52869/ (accessed 7 April 2021).

30 E. Siegfried, 'Hey, GOP, Here's Why Millennials Hate Us', Daily Beast, 26 June 2017, https://www.thedailybeast.com/hey-gop-heres-why-millennials-hate-us (accessed 7 April 2021).

31 R. Larimore, 'Darwin Is Coming for the GOP', The Bulwark, 25 January 2019, https://thebulwark.com/darwin-is-coming-for-the-gop/ (accessed 7 April 2021).

32 N. Ferguson and E. Freymann, 'The Coming Generation War', The Atlantic, 6 May 2019, https://www.theatlantic.com/ideas/archive/2019/05/coming-generation-war/588670/ (accessed 7 April 2021).

33 Exit poll results and analysis for the 2020 presidential election, Washington Post, 14 December 2020, https://www.washingtonpost.com/elections/interactive/2020/exit-polls/presidential-election-exit-polls/ (accessed 7 April 2021).

34 'How the 2020 Presidential Election Divided Voters', Wall Street Journal, 4 November 2020, https://www.wsj.com/articles/how-the-2020-presidential-election-divided-

voters-11604521705 (accessed 7 April 2021).

35   Source: US General Social Survey (1974–2018).

36   D. Muller, *The 2019 Australian Election Study*, 2019, https://www.aph.gov.au/About_Parliament/Parliamentary_Departments/Parliamentary_Library/FlagPost/2019/December/The_2019_Australian_Election_Study (accessed 7 April 2021).

37   G. Chan, 'From Tax to Climate: Five Factors that Could Swing 2019 Federal Election', *The Guardian*, 11 April 2019, https://www.theguardian.com/australia-news/2019/apr/11/from-tax-to-climate-five-factors-that-could-swing-2019-federal-election (accessed 7 April 2021).

38   Edelman, 'Trust in Government Plunges to Historic Low', 19 January 2014, https://www.edelman.com/news-awards/trust-government-plunges-historic-low (accessed 7 April 2021).

39   Edelman, '2017 Edelman Trust Barometer Reveals Global Implosion of Trust', 2017, https://www.edelman.com/news-awards/2017-edelman-trust-barometer-reveals-global-implosion (accessed 7 April 2021).

40   Edelman, '2018 Edelman Trust Barometer Reveals Record-Breaking Drop in Trust in the U.S.', 22 January 2018, https://www.edelman.com/news-awards/2018-edelman-trust-barometer-reveals-record-breaking-drop-trust-in-the-us (accessed 7 April 2021).

41   A. Prokop, 'Millennials Have Stopped Trusting the Government', Vox, 5 May 2014, https://www.vox.com/2014/5/5/5683176/millennials-have-stopped-trusting-the-government (accessed 7 April 2021).

42   O. O'Neill, 'How to Trust Intelligently', TED Blog, 25 September 2013, https://blog.ted.com/how-to-trust-intelligently/#:~:text=Onora%20O'Neill%3A%20What%20we,sensible%20simply%20wants%20more%20trust.&text=They%20want%20well%2Ddirected%20trust,and%20honest%20%E2%8-0%94%20so%2C%20trustworthy (accessed 7 April 2021).

43   N. Clarke, W. Jennings, J. Moss and G. Stoker, *The Good Politician: Folk Theories, Political Interaction, and the Rise of Anti-Politics*, Cambridge, Cambridge University Press, 2018.

44   Source: US General Social Survey (1974–2018).

45   A. Taub, 'How Stable Are Democracies? Warning Signs Are Flashing Red', *The New York Times*, 29 November 2016, https://www.nytimes.com/2016/11/29/world/americas/western-liberal-democracy.html (accessed 7 April 2021).

46   'Global Democracy Has Another Bad Year', *The Economist*, 22 January 2020, https://www.economist.com/graphic-detail/2020/01/22/global-democracy-has-another-bad-year?gclsrc=aw.ds&gclid=EAIaIQobChMIy6erlvux6wIVFO3tCh1e6Q_XEAAYASAAEgJoRPD_BwE&gclsrc=aw.ds (accessed 7 April 2021).

47   S. Saul, 'Watch Obama's Full Speech at the Democratic National Convention', *The New York Times*, 19 August 2020, https://www.nytimes.com/2020/08/19/us/politics/obama-speech.html (accessed 7 April 2021).

48   Y. Mounk and R.S. Foa, 'This Is How Democracy Dies', *The Atlantic*,

29 January 2020, https://www.
theatlantic.com/ideas/archive/2020/
01/confidence-democracy-lowest-
point-record/605686/ (accessed 7
April 2021).

49   Source: Eurobarometer (1975–2018).

50   M. Crozier, S.P. Huntington and J.
Watanuki, *The Crisis of Democracy:
Report on the Governability of
Democracies to the Trilateral
Commission*, New York University
Press, 1975.

51   W. Strauss and N. Howe, *The
Fourth Turning: What the Cycles of*

*History Tell Us About America's Next
Rendezvous with Destiny*, Bantam
Press, 1997.

52   Ferguson and Freymann, 'The Coming
Generation War'.

53   L. Gardiner and T. Bell, *My
Generation, Baby: The Politics of Age
in Brexit Britain*, London, Resolution
Foundation, 2019, https://www.
resolutionfoundation.org/comment/
my-generation-baby-the-politics-of-
age-in-brexit-britain/ (accessed 7 April
2021).

Chapter 9

1   Z. Rahim, 'Davos 2019: David
Attenborough issues stark warning
about future of civilisation as he
demands "practical solutions"
to combat climate change', *The
Independent*, 22 January 2019,
https://www.independent.co.uk/
environment/david-attenborough-
davos-2019-climate-change-
switzerland-world-economic-
forum-a8739656.html (accessed 7
April 2021).

2   R. Krznaric, *The Good Ancestor: How
to Think Long-Term in a Short-Term
World*, London, Random House, 2020.

3   D. Gilbert, *Stumbling on Happiness*,
Vintage Canada, 2009.

4   R. Krznaric, *The Good Ancestor*.

5   R. Skidelsky, *John Maynard Keynes:
The Economist as Saviour 1920-1937*,
Macmillan, 1992.

6   Quoted in D. Willetts, *The Pinch: How
the baby boomers took their children's
future–and why they should give it
back*, London, Atlantic Books, 2010.

7   'Extinction Rebellion: Climate
protesters "making a difference"',
BBC News, 21 April 2019, https://
www.bbc.co.uk/news/uk-england-

london-48003955 (accessed 7 April
2021).

8   NASA, 'Global Temperature', 2019,
https://climate.nasa.gov/vital-signs/
global-temperature/ (accessed 7 April
2021).

9   'Consensus on Consensus: A
Synthesis of Consensus Estimates
on Human-Caused Global Warming',
Environmental Science Letters, vol.
11, no. 4, 2016, https://iopscience.iop.
org/article/10.1088/1748-9326/11/4/
048002/meta (accessed 7 April 2021).

10   Source: US General Social Survey
(1993–2018).

11   Source: Ipsos MORI Issues Index
(1997–2018).

12   B. Kennedy and C. Johnson, 'More
Americans See Climate Change as
a Priority, But Democrats Are Much
More Concerned Than Republicans',
28 February 2020, https://www.
pewresearch.org/fact-tank/2020/
02/28/more-americans-see-climate-
change-as-a-priority-but-democrats-
are-much-more-concerned-than-
republicans/ (accessed 7 April 2021).

13   Source: US General Social Survey
(1974–2018).

14 S. Cohen, 'The Age Gap in Environmental Politics', State of the Planet blog, 4 February 2019, https://blogs.ei.columbia.edu/2019/02/04/age-gap-environmental-politics/ (accessed 7 April 2021).

15 D. Becker and J. Gerstenzang, 'Millennials Reject Car Culture', USA Today, 19 June 2013, https://eu.usatoday.com/story/opinion/2013/06/19/millenials-car-culture-column/2435173/ (accessed 7 April 2021).

16 S. Wynes and K. Nicholas, 'The Climate Mitigation Gap: Education and Government Recommendations Miss the Most Effective Individual Actions', Environmental Research Letters, vol. 12, no. 7, 2017, https://iopscience.iop.org/article/10.1088/1748-9326/aa7541 (accessed 7 April 2021).

17 D. Thompson and J. Weissmann, 'The Cheapest Generation', The Atlantic, September 2012, https://www.theatlantic.com/magazine/archive/2012/09/the-cheapest-generation/309060/ (accessed 7 April 2021).

18 'The End of Car Culture', The New York Times, 29 June 2013, https://www.nytimes.com/2013/06/30/sunday-review/the-end-of-car-culture.html (accessed 7 April 2021).

19 A. Delbosc and K. Ralph, 'A Tale of Two Millennials', Journal of Transport and Land Use, vol. 10, no. 1, 2017, pp. 903–910.

20 Thompson and Weissmann, 'The Cheapest Generation'; D. Thompson, 'Cars? Not For Us: The Cheapest Generation Explains "The Freedom of Not Owning"', The Atlantic, 24 August 2012, https://www.theatlantic.com/business/archive/2012/08/cars-not-for-us-the-cheapest-generation-explains-the-freedom-of-not-owning/261516/ (accessed 7 April 2021).

21 C.R. Knittel and E. Murphy, Generational Trends in Vehicle Ownership and Use: Are Millennials Any Different?, National Bureau of Economic Research Working Paper No. 25674, 2019, https://www.nber.org/papers/w25674 (accessed 7 April 2021).

22 A.T.M. Oakil, D. Manting and H. Nijland, 'Determinants of Car Ownership among Young Households in the Netherlands: The Role of Urbanization and Demographic and Economic Characteristics', Journal of Transport Geography, vol. 51, 2016, pp. 229–335, https://pure.uva.nl/ws/files/2734560/177530_JTRG_Manuscript.pdf (accessed 7 April 2021).

23 J. Vitale, K. Bowman and R. Robinson, 'How the Pandemic Is Changing the Future of Automotive', Deloitte, 13 July 2020, https://www2.deloitte.com/us/en/insights/industry/retail-distribution/consumer-behavior-trends-state-of-the-consumer-tracker/future-of-automotive-industry-pandemic.html?id=us:2el:3pr:4di6831:5awa:6di:071420:&pkid=1007226 (accessed 7 April 2021).

24 Source: Eurobarometer (2005–2018).

25 P. Campbell, J. Miller, C. Bushey and K. Inagaki, 'Time to Buy a Car? Industry Hopes for Coronavirus Silver Lining', Financial Times, 20 May 2020, https://www.ft.com/content/488d5886-c6af-4e80-a479-36aca26edd1d (accessed 7 April 2021).

26 'Why Ethical Brands Must Engage More: Millennials', Fortune, 6 October 2015.

27 'Green Generation: Millennials Say Sustainability Is A Shopping Priority', Nielsen, 2015.

28 B. Duffy, F. Thomas, H. Shrimpton, H. Whyte-Smith, M. Clemence and T. Abboud, *Beyond Binary: The Lives and Choices of Generation Z*, London, Ipsos MORI, 2018, https://www.ipsos.com/ipsos-mori/en-uk/ipsos-thinks-beyond-binary-lives-and-choices-generation-z (accessed 7 April 2021).

29 Ipsos MORI, Key Influencer Tracking, n.d., www.ipsos-mori.com/researchspecialisms/reputationresearch/whatwedo/kit/sustainablebusinessmonitor.aspx (accessed 7 April 2021).

30 Source: European Social Survey (2002–2018).

31 K. Kusek, 'The Death Of Brand Loyalty: Cultural Shifts Mean It's Gone Forever', *Forbes*, 2016, https://www.forbes.com/sites/kathleenkusek/2016/07/25/the-death-of-brand-loyalty-cultural-shifts-mean-its-gone-forever/?sh=667137234dde (accessed 7 April 2021).

32 Retail Customer Experience, 'Study: Brand Loyalty Not Such a Biggie for Millennials', 2016, www.retailcustomerexperience.com/news/study-brand-loyalty-not-such-a-biggie-for-millennials/ (accessed 7 April 2021).

33 Workplace Intelligence, The Millennial Consumer Study, 2015, http://workplaceintelligence.com/millennial-consumer-study/ (accessed 7 April 2021).

34 Bazaar Voice, *Talking to Strangers: Millennials Trust People over Brands*, 2012, media2.bazaarvoice.com/documents/Bazaarvoice_WP_Talking-to-Strangers.pdf (accessed 7 April 2021).

35 Yahoo Small Business, n.d., https://smallbusiness.yahoo.com/advisor/resource-center/millennials-changing-face-retail-shopping-025220847/ (accessed 7 April 2021).

36 N.G. Barnes, 'Millennials Adept at Filtering Out Ads', eMarketer, 10 April 2015, www.emarketer.com/Article/Millennials-Adept-Filtering-Ads/1012335 (accessed 7 April 2021).

37 J.-F. Damais and R. Sant, *Healing the Pain: Responding to Bad Experiences to Boost Customer Loyalty*, Ipsos, 2016, https://www.ipsos.com/sites/default/files/publication/1970-01/Ipsos-Loyalty-Healing-the-Pain.pdf (accessed 7 April 2021).

38 A. Gore, *The Future*, WH Allen, 2013.

39 G. Monbiot, 'My Generation Trashed the Planet. So I Salute the Children Striking Back', *The Guardian*, 15 February 2019, https://www.theguardian.com/commentisfree/2019/feb/15/planet-children-protest-climate-change-speech (accessed 7 April 2021).

40 A. Karpf, 'Don't Let Prejudice Against Older People Contaminate the Climate Movement', *The Guardian*, 18 January 2020, https://www.theguardian.com/commentisfree/2020/jan/18/ageism-climate-movement-generation-stereotypes (accessed 7 April 2021).

41 E.G. Hunter and G.D. Rowles, 'Leaving a Legacy: Toward a Typology', *Journal of Aging Studies*, vol. 19, no. 3, 2005, pp. 327–347.

42 M. McGrath, 'UN Report: Covid Crisis Does Little to Slow Climate Change', BBC News, 9 September 2020, https://www.bbc.co.uk/news/science-environment-54074733 (accessed 7 April 2021).

43 B. Gates, 'COVID-19 Is Awful. Climate Change Could Be Worse', Gates Notes, 4 August 2020, https://www.gatesnotes.com/Energy/Climate-and-COVID-19 (accessed 7 April 2021).

44 P. Davies and M. Green, 'The EU Recovery Fund: "Building Back Better" in a Post-COVID-19 World', Environment, Land and Resources, 29 May 2020, https://www.globalelr.com/2020/05/the-eu-recovery-fund-building-back-better-in-a-post-covid-19-world/ (accessed 7 April 2021).

45 'Covid-19 and the Generational Divide', *Financial Times*, 2020, https://www.ft.com/content/6a880416-66fa-11ea-800d-da70cff6e4d3 (accessed 7 April 2021).

Chapter 10

1   Massis quoted in M. Hentea, 'The Problem of Literary Generations: Origins and Limitations', *Comparative Literature Studies*, vol. 50, no. 4, 2013, 567–588.

2   Dylan Thomas, quote taken from biography of Wilfred Owen, The Wilfred Owen Association, http://www.wilfredowen.org.uk/wilfred-owen/biography#:~:text=Wilfred%20Owen's%20Draft%20Preface&text=Nor%20is%20it%20about%20deeds,Poetry%20is%20in%20the%20pity (accessed 7 April 2021).

3   Ibid

4   Hentea, 'The Problem of Literary Generations'.

5   B.S. Turner, 'Ageing and Generational Conflicts: A Reply to Sarah Irwin', *British Journal of Sociology*, 1998, pp. 299-304.

6   Quoted in: J. Bristow, *Stop Mugging Grandma: The 'Generation Wars' and Why Boomer Blaming Won't Solve Anything*, Yale University Press, 2019.

7   Pew Research Center, 'Most Millennials Resist the "Millennial" Label', 3 September 2015, https://www.pewresearch.org/politics/2015/09/03/most-millennials-resist-the-millennial-label/ (accessed 7 April 2021).

8   Ipsos MORI, BBC Identity Polling, 2014, https://www.ipsos.com/sites/default/files/migrations/en-uk/files/Assets/Docs/Polls/ipsos-mori-bbc-identity-poll-2014-tables.pdf (accessed 7 April 2021).

9   Source: Ipsos Global Trends survey (2019).

10 Ipsos, 'Ok, Boomer! Baby Boomers and the Consumption of the Future', 2019, https://www.ipsos.com/en-us/knowledge/overview/ok-boomer (accessed 7 April 2021).

11 Source: Ipsos Global Trends survey (2017 and 2019).

12 J. Lloyd Jones, 'The Worst-Raised Generation in History', *Muscatine Journal* (IA), 7 May 1969.

13 C. Martin, 'One In 10 Millennials Would Rather Lose A Finger Than Give Up Their Smartphone: Survey', AI&IOT Daily, 25 July 2018, https://www.mediapost.com/publications/article/322677/one-in-10-millennials-would-rather-lose-a-finger-t.html (accessed 7 April 2021).

14 G.F. Cooper, 'Fur Real: 40 Percent of People Would Give Up Dog to Keep Smartphone', 23 September 2020, https://www.cnet.com/news/survey-says-40-percent-of-people-would-give-up-dog-to-keep-smartphone/ (accessed 7 April 2021).

15 A. Chansanchai, 'Survey: One-third would rather give up sex than phone', NBC News, 4 August 2011, https://www.nbcnews.com/news/world/survey-one-third-would-rather-give-sex-phone-flna121757 (accessed 7 April 2021).

16 'Survey Finds One-Third of Americans More Willing to Give Up Sex Than Their Mobile Phones', Telenav, 3 August 2011, http://investor.telenav.com/news-releases/news-release-details/survey-finds-one-third-americans-more-willing-give-sex-their (accessed 7 April 2021); D. Bates, 'Truth About Women's Relationship With Technology: Half would rather go without sex than give up a smart phone', MailOnline, 19 December 2013, https://www.dailymail.co.uk/news/article-2521626/Half-women-sex-smart-phone.html (accessed 7 April 2021).

17 J. Ballard, 'Over Half of Millennials Say They Waste Too Much Time on Smartphones', 25 June 2018, https://today.yougov.com/topics/technology/articles-reports/2018/06/25/smartphone-habits-millennials-boomers-gen-x (accessed 7 April 2021).

18 Source: Ipsos MORI Tech Tracker (2010–19).

19 Source: Eurobarometer (2010–17).

20 Digital Day Research, 2016, http://www.digitaldayresearch.co.uk/ (accessed 7 April 2021).

21 F. Comunello, M. Fernández Ardevol, S. Mulargia and F. Belotti, 'Women, Youth, and Everything Else. Age-Based and Gendered Stereotypes in Relation to Digital Technology Among Elderly Italian Mobile Phone Users', *Media, Culture & Society*, vol. 39, no. 6 (2016), pp. 798–815, https://doi.org/10.1177/0163443716674363 (accessed 7 April 2021).

22 M. Sweney, 'Is Facebook for Old People? Over-55s Flock in as the Young Leave', *The Guardian*, 12 February 2018, https://www.theguardian.com/technology/2018/feb/12/is-facebook-for-old-people-over-55s-flock-in-as-the-young-leave (accessed 7 April 2021).

23 A. Cuthbertson, 'Facebook Is Officially for Old People', *Newsweek*, 12 February 2018, https://www.newsweek.com/facebook-officially-old-people-803196 (accessed 7 April 2021).

24 Source: Ipsos MORI Tech Tracker (2019).

25 'A Group Where we all Pretend to be Boomers', Facebook, https://www.facebook.com/groups/1288197298014311/?ref=group_header (accessed 7 April 2021).

26 A. Whalen, 'What Is "Boomer Remover" and Why Is It Making People So Angry?' *Newsweek*, 13 March 2020, https://www.newsweek.com/boomer-remover-meme-trends-virus-coronavirus-social-media-covid-19-baby-boomers-1492190 (accessed 7 April 2021).

27 The Irish Times [@IrishTimes], 'More than half of young people who worked before pandemic now claiming support' [Twitter], 4 May 2020, https://twitter.com/irishtimes/status/1257320516144074752?s=21 (accessed 7 April 2021).

28 '"Generation Covid" Hit Hard by the Pandemic, Research Reveals', BBC News, 26 October 2020, https://www.bbc.co.uk/news/uk-54662485 (accessed 7 April 2021).

29 H. Robertson, 'Young People Face Economic "Scarring" from Covid,

Says Top Think Tank', City AM, 3 July 2020, https://www.cityam.com/young-people-face-economic-scarring-from-covid-says-top-think-tank (accessed 7 April 2021).

30 J. Ball [@jamesrbuk], 'Millennials and Gen Z are supportive of lockdown largely to protect others' [Twitter], 18 May 2020, https://twitter.com/jamesrbuk/status/1262325042525941762?s=12 (accessed 7 April 2021).

31 D. Byrne, 'As an Isolated Older Person, I've Been Deeply Moved by the Sacrifices of Others', *The Guardian*, 31 March 2020, https://www.theguardian.com/commentisfree/2020/mar/31/isolated-older-person-underlying-conditions-coronavirus-crisis (accessed 7 April 2021).

32 A. Evans, 'COVID-19 and the Intergenerational Covenant', Global Dashboard, 31 March 2020, https://www.globaldashboard.org/2020/03/31/covid19-and-the-intergenerational-covenant/ (accessed 7 April 2021).

33 C.W. Rudolph and H. Zacher, '"The COVID-19 Generation": A Cautionary Note. Work, Aging and Retirement', 2020, https://www.ncbi.nlm.nih.gov/pmc/articles/PMC7184414/ (accessed 7 April 2021).

34 N. Goff [@nickgoff79], 'I would open pubs for 35-45 year olds exclusively first' [Twitter], 28 April 2020, https://twitter.com/nickgoff79/status/1255103061841842177?s=21 (accessed 7 April 2021).

35 P. Gray, 'The Special Value of Children's Age-Mixed Play', *American Journal of Play*, vol. 3, no. 4, 2011, pp. 500–522, https://www.psychologytoday.com/files/attachments/1195/ajp-age-mixing-published.pdf (accessed 7 April 2021).

36 S. McLeod, 'Erik Erikson's Stages of Psychosocial Development', *Simply Psychology*, 2018, https://www.simplypsychology.org/Erik-Erikson.html (accessed 7 April 2021).

37 D. Brooks, 'The Moral Bucket List', *The New York Times*, 11 April 2015, https://www.nytimes.com/2015/04/12/opinion/sunday/david-brooks-the-moral-bucket-list.html (accessed 7 April 2021).

38 Nesterly, https://www.nesterly.io/ (accessed 7 April 2021).

39 Hentea, 'The Problem of Literary Generations'.

40 J. Bristow, *The Sociology of Generations: New Directions and Challenges*, Palgrave Macmillan, 2016.

41 N. Annan, 'Grand Disillusions', *The New York Review*, 3 April 1980, https://www.nybooks.com/articles/1980/04/03/grand-disillusions/?lp_txn_id=991894 (accessed 7 April 2021).

42 T.A. Lambert, 'Generations and Change: Toward a Theory of Generations as a Force in Historical Process', *Youth & Society*, vol. 4, no. 1, 1972, pp.21–45, https://journals.sagepub.com/doi/pdf/10.1177/0044118X7200400103 (accessed 7 April 2021).

43 George E. Vaillant, 'Happiness is Love: Full Stop', Harvard Medical School and Brigham and Women's Hospital, n.d., https://www.duodecim.fi/xmedia/duo/pilli/duo99210x.pdf (accessed 7 April 2021).

44 K. Delaney, 'The Robot that Takes Your Job Should Pay Taxes, says Bill Gates', *Quartz*, 2017, https://qz.com/911968/bill-gates-the-robot-that-takes-your-job-should-pay-taxes/ (accessed 7 April 2021).

Chapter 11

1   United Nations, Ending Poverty, n.d., https://www.un.org/en/global-issues/ending-poverty (accessed 7 April 2021).

2   Queen's broadcast to the UK and the Commonwealth, 5 April 2020, https://www.royal.uk/queens-broadcast-uk-and-commonwealth (accessed 7 April 2021).

3   A. Comte, *Cours de philosophie positive*, 3rd ed., 6 vols., Paris, J.B. Baillière, 1869, 4:450–51.

4   'I Feel Young in My Singapore: Action Plan for Successful Ageing', The Singapore Ministerial Committee on Ageing, 2016, https://sustainabledevelopment.un.org/content/documents/1525Action_Plan_for_Successful_Aging.pdf (accessed 7 April 2021).

5   'Discussion between Professor Sakura Osamu and Professor Saijo Tatsuyoshi', Discuss Japan, 9 January 2019, https://www.japanpolicyforum.jp/society/pt20190109210522.html (accessed 7 April 2021).

6   G. Mulgan, 'Social Sciences and Social Imagination', *Campaign for Social Science*, 12 May 2020.

7   M. Mazzucato, *Mission Economy: A Moonshot Guide to Changing Capitalism*, Allen Lane, 2021.

8   Encyclical Letter, 'Laudato Si Of The Holy Father Francis On Care For Our Common Home, the Vatican…', 24 May 2015, http://www.vatican.va/content/francesco/en/encyclicals/documents/papa-francesco_20150524_enciclica-laudato-si.html (accessed 7 April 2021).

9   R. Fisher, 'The Perils of Short-Termism: Civilisation's Greatest Threat', BBC News, 10 January 2019, https://www.bbc.com/future/article/20190109-the-perils-of-short-termism-civilisations-greatest-threat (accessed 7 April 2021).

10 J. Davidson, *#Futuregen: Lessons from a Small Country*, London, Chelsea Green Publishing Co, 2020.

Index